MAKING MUSIC WITH SOUNDS

Leigh Landy

DE MONTFORT UNIVERSITY, UK

with Illustrations by Manuella Blackburn

LIVERPOOL HOPE UNIVERSITY, UK

 Routledge
Taylor & Francis Group

NEW YORK AND LONDON

First published 2012
by Routledge
711 Third Avenue, New York, NY 10017

Simultaneously published in the UK
by Routledge
2 Park Square, Milton Park, Abingdon, Oxon OX14 4RN

Routledge is an imprint of the Taylor & Francis Group, an informa business

© 2012 Taylor & Francis

The right of Leigh Landy to be identified as author of this work has been
asserted by him in accordance with sections 77 and 78 of the
Copyright, Designs and Patents Act 1988.

Illustrations by Manuella Blackburn.

All rights reserved. No part of this book may be reprinted or reproduced
or utilised in any form or by any electronic, mechanical, or other means,
now known or hereafter invented, including photocopying and recording,
or in any information storage or retrieval system, without permission in
writing from the publishers.

Trademark Notice: Product or corporate names may be trademarks or
registered trademarks, and are used only for identification and
explanation without intent to infringe.

Library of Congress Cataloging-in-Publication Data
Landy, Leigh, 1951- author.
　Making music with sounds / Leigh Landy.
　pages cm
　Includes bibliographical references.
　1. Composition (Music)　2. Computer music—Instruction and study.
　3. Soundscapes (Music)—Instruction and study.　I. Title.
　MT40.L26 2012
　781.2'3—dc23
　2011044494

ISBN13: 978–0–415–80678–7 (hbk)
ISBN13: 978–0–415–89846–1 (pbk)
ISBN13: 978–0–203–12064–4 (ebk)

Typeset in Bembo
by Swales & Willis Ltd, Exeter, Devon

UNIVERSITY
LIBRARY

1 2 JUN 2013

HUDDERSFIELD

5910725148

SFI° Certified Sourcing
www.sfiprogram.org
SFI-00453

Printed and bound in the United States of America
by Edwards Brothers, Inc.

CONTENTS

LIST OF ILLUSTRATIONS

PREFACE

As a young child of nursery school age, I can remember the joy of the discovery that I felt during a demonstration where it was shown that identical glasses with different levels of liquid in them could produce numerous sounds when rubbed or struck, as did rocks of various shapes and contours. Little did I know at the time that this introduction was going to be highly relevant to the focus of my future career.

In fact I had to postpone the continued discovery of the delights and the challenges of experimenting with music until my final year as a secondary school student as I, and so many others, had no opportunity to find out about such experimental sonic creativity in the interim. Early in my career I found the challenges posed by organising sounds—and most of these sounds would not qualify to be called notes (think of the five-lined staff)—to be extremely gratifying, a similar experience to the discovery made all those years ago with the glasses and the stones, and it subsequently became the focus of my music and my writings about music. It is the joy of composing music with this type of sonic content that *Making Music with Sounds* is intended to share.

Why I Wrote this Book

Making Music with Sounds has been written due to my deeply rooted belief that the music of sounds is potentially of interest to people of all ages and backgrounds. Ironically, many people are not consciously aware of the fact that we can make music with any sounds despite the fact that such forms of music can be heard around the globe in a number of wide-ranging audio and audio-visual contexts, including some computer games. This is indeed a shame for, as will be demonstrated in the coming chapters, making music with sounds can be simultaneously

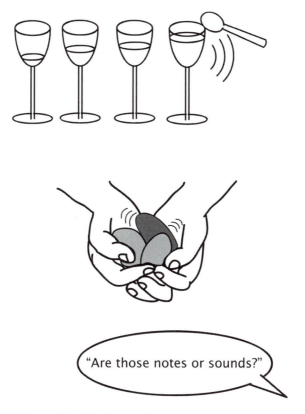

FIGURE P.1 Making music with glasses and stones

innovative and highly accessible. When people make music with sounds, at least with sounds with which they are acquainted, they can be creatively involved with music while experimenting with materials related to their shared aural experiences. This allows them to make relationships between their daily lives and the adventure of creativity, in our case sonic creativity. *Making Music with Sounds* attempts to raise this consciousness through facilitating aural awareness and applying this awareness creatively using relevant tools and approaches.

Sound-Based Music

The term that we shall use for the type of music that I shall be focusing upon is sound-based music★.[1] There are other terms in use, such as sonic art★, electronic and electroacoustic music★, that cover music of the same ground. These are introduced in Chapter 1. I have defined sound-based music as follows: "the art form

---

1   All entries followed by an asterisk in this book can be found in the book's glossary. The asterisk only appears at the first usage of a term.

in which the sound, that is, not the musical note, is its basic unit" (Landy 2007a, 17). In a sense sound-based music can be found at the end of a continuum that has note-based music at its other end. Many pieces of music move along this continuum or can be found to focus on a point somewhere in the middle.

Therefore, to speak of sound-based music without acknowledging its much older partner, the music of notes, would be ridiculous. Similarly, although much sound-based music uses technology, acoustic (that is non-amplified or technologically treated) creativity is equally possible. Those stones and glasses could make either note-based or sound-based music depending on the approach of those playing them and no further technology is needed. Nonetheless, the majority of this type of music making today involves the use of one or many forms of technology as creative tools.

Readership

Making Music with Sounds is intended for music educators to facilitate creative activity in sound-based music. Although I became aware of this phenomenon when I was only three, and believe that many children could start working in this area in primary education, the approach and examples have been pitched for more mature children in the age group of 11–14. I am certain that many examples, called "activities" in this book, can easily be amended for younger pupils. Similarly, the activities in this book can be adapted to older secondary students. The book could also be used with people of all ages becoming acquainted with this music for the first time, thus including university-level students.

I am of the belief that more music educators would provide the time for this type of music if they were offered appropriate background information, as most forms of music education training today do not include any or, at best, few of its key components. *Making Music with Sounds* has been designed to present music educators with both the background information as well as practical experience.

Focus on Composition

Making Music with Sounds focuses on the act of composition, whether this refers to something made on one's computer and performed from its hard disk or on an MP3 or CD player or by way of real-time★ performance, on stage, perhaps improvised, perhaps involving remixes. This book focuses primarily on the act of creation prior to performance as there is more than enough ground to cover to keep us busy and, hopefully, excited for quite some time. What one does with the approaches that are introduced in the following chapters is as diverse as the musicians' imaginations. Those completing the book's curriculum can move on to intermediate or even advanced software programs for sound-based composition and performance.

How to Use this Book

Learning situations will differ enormously:

- This book offers a complete curriculum, more than many teachers will be able to deliver.
- Choose, sequence, time and tailor your teaching material to suit your own learning situation based on the models. The amount of time a teacher needs will vary from a few hours to perhaps several weeks or even longer. Therefore, the amount of concepts and activities that you want to introduce will vary in similar measure.
- Go through the entire book first. In this way, you will learn to be able to create sound-based music yourself if you have never had the chance to do so as well as to become acquainted with its concepts and its related genres.
- Choose or eventually adapt (some of) the activities into a form that is most useful to your students.
- Combine verbal, still image, online sonic and multimedia content. Different learning groups and certainly different individuals will react best to a certain emphasis.
- There is a Glossary for terms and phrases that are of particular relevance to this book. These are marked with an asterisk (*) when they first appear.
- Though created with the 11–14-year-old age group as its target audience, people of all ages can find something useful in this book. Some of the more sophisticated concepts, such as multiple and composite gestures at the end of Chapter 4 or some of the activities focused on parameters, might be less challenging for older students at secondary level than the younger secondary audience.

The ElectroAcoustic Resource Site (EARS) Pedagogical Project

The EARS site (www.ears.dmu.ac.uk) provides a multi-lingual online reference including glossary, index and bibliography of resources related to the field as well as a number of publications that have been presented by way of this site. The next phase, which is taking place in parallel with the writing of this book, called the EARS II Pedagogical Project, offers an eLearning environment that complements all aspects of this volume's content where sound and other multimedia examples can be found. Here particular skills can be acquired and creative challenges undertaken utilising a user-friendly software program called *Sound Organiser*. There is also an appreciation section in EARS II that can serve all involved in terms of gaining understandings related to the repertoire upon which this book is focused. The URL is: www.ears2.dmu.ac.uk.

Leigh Landy
October 2011

ACKNOWLEDGEMENTS

The following book is in many ways the sum of experiences that I have had making, writing about and teaching the music of sounds. Nonetheless, being someone of a collaborative spirit, I have called upon the support and also been supported by a number of colleagues, friends and family.

I would like to thank Manuella Blackburn for creating the illustrations for the volume as well as allowing me to look at her research on teaching gestures to novice composers before some of it had been published. I am grateful to Simon Emmerson, colleague and friend of old, for reading through yet another text and keeping me focused in every way as well as to Jeff Martin in Beijing, whose talk at the Electroacoustic Music Studies Network conference in 2010 was an eye opener to me, as he was asking all of the right questions from the point of view of having worked in his career with the age group addressed in this text. His comments on the first draft based on his teaching experiences at secondary level have proven invaluable.

A word of thanks is needed to my colleagues who formed the former DigiArts team at Unesco in Paris. Without their suggestion that I compile something for younger users, this book would never have been written.

Closer to home, my colleagues on the original ElectroAcoustic Resource Site team, Simon Atkinson, Rob Weale and Pierre Couprie, and all of the EARS translators deserve an acknowledgement as issues related to terminology have been discussed with them for years. I cannot imagine a better group of collaborators. The original EARS II team consisting of some EARS members as well as Motje Wolf, Pete Batchelor and Hongji Yang have helped me consider how best we can deliver the online content that supports this book, content that will continue to be updated after publication. The extended EARS II team with Richard Hall and Mike Unwins and Sound Organiser development group with the GRM, ZKM and NOTAM centres that were developing the site and its creative software platform in parallel with this book being written and prepared for publication have played an invaluable role. All colleagues working at the Music, Technology and Innovation Research Centre deserve thanks for supporting our common goal of widening interest and participation in the field and acting as discussion partners for numerous items in this book as well as ambassadors of the music of sounds around the globe.

I would naturally like to acknowledge the input from the Music Books Editor at Routledge, Constance Ditzel, who met with me a couple of years ago to talk through a number of book ideas and became most excited by this one. As she picked up where the Unesco team left off, this book has become a reality.

Finally, I would like to thank the two women in my life: Evelyn, my wife, and Marissa, my daughter, who not only enjoy sound-based musical works—Evelyn has also made new choreographic work to sound-based compositions—but have supported me throughout all those days when I sat in front of the computer screen preparing this book. Their feedback and warmth have made its writing possible.

1

CROSSING THE THRESHOLD

Although a significant number of music educators internationally have had a fairly difficult run in the late stages of the twentieth century and the early years of this new one due to decreasing support for music in schools, many have bravely attempted to find ways to offer music programmes in which music's wonderful diversity can be introduced. This may involve musical traditions around the globe, various forms of popular and art music as well as more recent forms of musical experimentalism. This volume is intended to help those interested in sharing the excitement and joy of making music with sounds as part of this broad curriculum. Although one might consider sound-based music to be of fairly marginal importance, the fact is that it is rather ubiquitous in today's world. It can be found in a variety of audio only and audio-visual forms including films, advertisements, computer games and a wide variety of compositional approaches.

This book's point of departure is to allow teachers and students to maximise their own creativity, as was the case in my 1994 book, *Experimental Music Notebooks* (Landy 1994a). In *Making Music with Sounds*, given its emphasis on technology, the idea is that teachers are invited to adapt activities to local circumstances. In other words, without a great deal of equipment and software, it is still possible to reach a high level of creativity in the book's areas of focus. Some educators might prefer a list, similar to a manual, of carefully worked-out examples. This formula has been rejected for a number of reasons, the most important of which is that this kind of music is rarely produced in this manner. Furthermore, many formulaic educational publications are written for a particular group with particular skills in a particular place or, alternatively, expecting only some of their examples to be useful to any given group. In contrast, this book's underlying philosophy is that it is more important to facilitate creativity than to prescribe it.

In this manner, the book can be seen to act as a source of inspiration as well as a basis for teaching, allowing the EARS II online resource to pick up where the book leaves off, as it were. It is worthy to note that virtually no specific hardware or software is mentioned throughout, as these things seem to get dated, thus placing a time stamp on the book. Instead, more generic terms will be used, e.g., sampling★ instead of naming a hardware or software sampler. After this introduction, which will include a survey of types of music related to the book's focus, the structure of the following chapters is one moving forward progressively commencing with an awareness of our aural environments, whether rural or urban or anything in between. In so doing, the notion of different types of listening, also known as listening strategies, will be introduced. The soundscape★, the aural equivalent of a landscape, will act as the second chapter's focus in terms of sound organisation. Chapter 3 takes us to the level of the sound unit. It will be proposed that any sound can be made musical. The chapter will discuss how to "grab" a sound for artistic use, how to generate one from scratch and how to manipulate sounds. The content of Chapters 4 and 5 takes us beyond that of the sound level. Their focus increases to the sequence or gestural level and then to that of an entire piece. The chapters include sections on vertical and horizontal relationships regarding sound organisation (in traditional terms, think of harmony and counterpoint) and both include important sections concerning evaluating one's work. It is never easy to say what is good or bad, what is powerful or weak, but avoiding this kind of discussion is not very helpful. The volume does not have the pretension to suggest that it is presenting a new vision regarding the aesthetics for sound-based music; what it does do is allow groups of people to discuss what individuals or groups have come up with and then to see whether the results are representing the maker's intention. Special subjects include the notion of "breathing" in sound-based music and how rhythm fits into music in which pitch and harmony are not necessarily important. The final chapter summarises the key aspects that have been presented and suggests further challenges for those who have developed an interest in sound organisation, such as (online) group performance. The book concludes with a glossary and a bibliography that includes an annotated section for further reading.

Before commencing this incremental presentation, the rest of this introductory chapter will focus on the delineation of the two areas that we will be involved with: sound-based music and making music with technology. A brief description of the approach including the role of the book's flexible activities follows before the introduction's concluding survey is presented.

A Delineation of the Two Key Areas

This text will focus on two key areas, although not exclusively. To speak of sound-based music without acknowledging its much older partner, the music of notes, would be ridiculous. Similarly, to discuss music that uses technology without allowing acoustic creativity to take place is equally absurd. Nonetheless, the two key areas are the reason for this book's existence. Let's briefly attempt to draw a virtual fence around these foci.

Sound-Based Music

A few years ago while preparing another book, *Understanding the Art of Sound Organization* (Landy 2007a), a problem was highlighted to specialists, namely the less-than-satisfactory state of the field's terminology. I was particularly aware of this, as one of my main projects in the years preceding the writing of that book was the creation of the glossary section of the EARS site. I was faced with the dilemma of attempting to make a choice among a number of existent ambiguous terms for the music that I make and wanted to discuss. After a great deal of consideration I decided to create a new, unambiguous term, sound-based music defined in the preface, and this is the one that will be used here. Let's start with this term and a few of the other ones as readers may confront them in other literature that they may consult.

Admittedly all notes are indeed sounds, so some people in the field have claimed that sound-based music taken literally is a synonym for music. However, the purpose of *Understanding the Art of Sound Organization* was to introduce the co-existence of a note-based as well as a sound-based musical paradigm and demonstrate that, although these two clearly overlapped with one another, they were highly distinct as well, both in terms of aspects related to musical construction and reception.

Terms that were also in contention included:

- *Sonic art*★, which could be defined in the same manner. The issue with this term is that it allows people to consider its works not to be music, something that I find problematic. There are even universities today that have departments that are named Music and Sonic Art. People cannot even agree whether the term takes on the singular or plural form, sonic arts.
- *Electroacoustic music*★, which many specialists would assume to be synonymous with sound-based music; however, there exist electroacoustic works that are in fact focused on notes; furthermore, electroacoustic music cannot be solely acoustic.
- Similarly *electronic music*★ might be seen to be synonymous by some people, particularly in the United States; however, most people view this term to refer to music in which sounds are generated synthetically.
- Two other rejected terms were *sound art*★ (too specific) and
- *Computer music*★ (too broad).
- Even the older term, *organised sound*★ (also the title of a journal that I edit), did not seem appropriate for the same reason that sonic art(s) was rejected. Furthermore, the composer who originally coined the term, Edgard Varèse,

as visionary as he was, was thinking of all sounds including notes; the term also does not really sound like a musical category.

- Another historical term, *musique concrète*★ (literally concrete music, but the French term is normally used) is worthy of mention. In the early days of sound-based music, some musicians focused on synthetically generated sounds, thus making electronic music. Others, following the lead of Pierre Schaeffer, made musique concrète. This music was largely based on recordable sounds, although synthetically generated ones were not explicitly forbidden. The term is now dated, but its works fully belong within sound-based music.

Having chosen among those terms, there remains one controversial point to be shared: one person might reject what another person hears as music. Suffice to say that there are many who do not consider most pop music to be music, something most readers might find lamentable. I have known of individuals who do not consider African drumming to be music, as it possesses no audible melody.

Whatever one calls this creative work that we shall be discussing, many perceive it to be music, and it is due to this conviction that sonic art had to be rejected. Still, people who encounter a subset of sonic art known as *sound art*, that is works often displayed in art venues or public spaces sometimes in the form of installations, may have difficulty with this view. My reaction to this is that there are art works that fit into more than one medium and sound installations★

FIGURE 1.1   A sound installation

represent a typical case in point: they fit within three-dimensional art as does sculpture and they also fit within music. To conclude this part of the discussion, I propose that organised sounds are music in the ears of the beholder and hope that readers and their students will join me in beholding such works as sound-based works of music too.

Making Music with Technology

How often have you read about the impact of new technologies in our daily life? Of course, music forms no exception. All one needs to do is consider how music was heard just over one hundred years ago—you had to be there. Now compare that with the current situation—music is heard mainly by way of technology.

We have to be careful, for without technology, the violin bow, just to name something at random, could never have been made. We are of course referring to technologies here that are driven by electricity or similar form of power, and mainly new forms of digital technology.

Such technologies have allowed us to record and re-record sounds by way of multi-tracking, also known as overdubbing. Of course, re-recording is relevant to traditional forms of music as well as to what we are to discuss. They have also allowed for sounds to be manipulated, sometimes to the point where their source can no longer be recognised. Furthermore, using these technologies, we can make or generate new sounds from scratch. It is the art of applying such technologies to make music using sounds that is at the heart of our journey.

Still, such technology is not necessary to make music with sounds. Those stones and glasses could make either note-based or sound-based music depending on the approach by those playing them. Therefore we need not be obsessive about technology for technology's sake, but instead look to use it for specific purposes. Today's technology serves all of the above purposes and many more. Of these, several will be introduced in the remaining chapters.

Before moving on, some readers may be unaware of the fact that a number of practices today have been responsible for the redefinition of aspects related to composition and performance. In a sense some traditional practices are being recycled or renewed. For example, as in traditional societies, a significant number of sound-based pieces are composed collectively, that is, without the need to name a composer as one does traditionally. The performance is the work of all involved. Improvisation is also something commonly practised within sound-based music. This raises interesting questions related to the act of composition.

For example, in today's remix culture, the re-use of sound material does not necessarily mean that the musicians involved are interpreting those materials. They are re-composing them. But who is the author of a piece of "appropriated" sounds? In short, some may still practise the trade of composer, performer or improviser. In sound-based music all of these are possible, but increasingly for many musicians, composing, improvising and remixing are three forms of creating. As much of this can be done in real time, that is, on stage, composition, improvisation and performance can be one and the same in such cases. With this in mind, what one does with the approaches that are introduced below is as diverse as the musicians' imaginations. As stated in the Preface, this book will focus on composition prior to performance given the number of concepts that will be introduced.

The Book's Approach

As suggested above a non-time-stamped approach has been chosen where one will speak of sampling instead of any particular sampler and so on. Furthermore, as stated, the amount of resources is not being imposed; therefore people with modest resources will be able to achieve a great deal of what is proposed in this volume. Just to offer one example, there are two ways to "hunt" for specific sounds: find them and record them or, if that option is not available, attempt to download them from sites that offer sounds such as the well-known Freesound Project (www.freesound.org). There are no ivory tower approaches here nor am I seeking to reach the lowest common denominator, as it were. It is with this in mind that the only assumption is that people taking part in activities in the following chapters have access to a computer, speakers attached to that computer and an Internet connection. For those users who possess more than this, options, for example the use of a microphone and something on which to make recordings as just mentioned, will be presented alongside the basic way of doing things.

Every group in schools has a different level, a different dynamic and different means to achieve things. It is for this reason that the book's activities seek to enhance creative thinking and creativity in terms of skills acquisition as opposed to learning specific skills in specific ways, as this is simply impossible to generalise. I have done a great deal of work in what is known as the community arts. It is awful to work with people with top-of-the-line equipment and to leave with that equipment. People are offered a great ride in a Bentley and are left afterwards with whatever they had previously. It is much better to provide exciting experiences with what people possess already. We all know there's bigger and better out there if we are offered the means to improve our situations.

In *Experimental Music Notebooks* I included the remark (paraphrasing the artist Josef Albers): "Our approach calls for the creation of musical problems and trying things out. Experimentation is based on trial and error—a healthy phenomenon and a wonderful way of discovering creative processes. [Music appreciation and active music making] are essential for a more complete musical experience, especially when combined with the individual's imagination" (Landy 1994a, 12). That point of view worked then and remains the basis for the current, more focused book.

To conclude this part of the introduction related to the book's approach I have to admit that I find that those who make computer games have come up with an excellent formula for most users that can be applied in this book's educational context. Set new challenges at every level of a given game, as the player will be keen to learn (read: overcome the challenge), gain the new skill and climb to the higher level. Most of the challenges proposed in the following chapters can be stepped up, just like a computer game, depending on the time, abilities and facilities available. The activities are flexible and thus dynamic in this way. Another thing implicit in computer games is that they are to be enjoyed (although many players work very hard to achieve that enjoyment); similarly, art making is about enjoyment. If we turn this enjoyment into just work, our students or we may lose interest. Therefore applying such aspects related to computer games can lead to a valuable educational approach. The chapters and challenges posed are based on this very combination of learning and enjoyment. I hope that this works for you and, where relevant, your students.

An Overview of Selected Genres and Categories Related to Sound-Based Music

This chapter concludes with an overview of types of music that are associated with sound-based music; one might call it a supergenre or genre of genres. This overview will commence with the difference between music using real-world sounds and generating material by way of sound synthesis★. Furthermore, some key historical points will be touched on briefly as they should also be of interest to many readers. Sound examples of all of the following types of sound-based music can be found on EARS II. It is by no means necessary to include all of the following in a given curriculum; this final section of Chapter 1 is intended simply to provide readers with basic contextual information related to sound-based music.

Both words, genres and categories, are used in the section header as many terms utilised regarding sound-based music tend to be categories, terms that group pieces together based on an approach, a medium or the like, not the sound of the works themselves. The term electronic music exemplifies this well. Ironically few genre names have evolved; of these, a selection is included in the survey. This lack of genre names is probably due to sound-based music's broad spectrum and its relatively young age. As the music evolves its communities of participants and listeners further, a more developed vocabulary of genre descriptions is to be expected. A wide selection of genre and category names can be found on the original EARS site at: www.ears.dmu.ac.uk/spip.php?/rubrique3.

Real-World Music★

We shall start this survey with the type of sound-based music that normally allows us to make clear links between art and life. Real-world music refers to those sound-based works in which at least some of the sources used are recognisable to the listener. In today's jargon, real-world music involves sampling sounds from a very short snippet to very lengthy recordings and reusing them in an artistic context.

The most extreme case is perhaps soundscape composition★ (see Chapter 2) in which it is a conscious goal for listeners to have a sense of the context in which the sounds have been recorded. Things become slightly less real when sounds are combined that were not necessarily found together in an original environment. In this case we may speak of "imaginary soundscapes". Furthermore, sounds used can be manipulated (see Chapter 3) to such an extent that one can no longer perceive the source. This forms another extreme.

Historical note: Non-real time vs. real time Traditionally, many works focusing on real-world sounds were made in a non-real-time environment. This refers to a place where one works to prepare a sound-based piece completely beforehand. Today one might do that on a laptop. In earlier days this was done in a specialist studio or on a huge computer. Most such works, when completed, became what is known as fixed medium works.

Our current computers and other digital processors are so fast that we are able to retrieve bits of audio data instantly, allowing for real-time performance. With this in mind, real-world music is no longer restricted to non-real-time environments. Some sounds to be used in performance can be prepared beforehand and subsequently retrieved and treated in performance in real time.

Historical note: Non-real-time music in performance One of the most radical aspects of early sound-based music concert performance was the fact that this involved the performance of music by way of pushing the "play" button on a tape recorder or equivalent recording medium. Such events have existed since the late 1940s. Now, more than six decades later, there is still some discomfort related to going to a concert where there is nothing to see. Counterarguments have often been based on the fact that we listen to most music aurally, by way of radio, CD or MP3, without visuals, and that such concerts retained two key ingredients of traditional concert performance: a) as high a standard as possible in terms of the fidelity of sound, and b) the communal function of sharing art works socially.

Musique Concrète/Acousmatic Music*

Some music has very clearly been made for audio–only fixed medium performance. Within the world of real-world music, the pioneering musique concrète, later rebranded acousmatic music, is an excellent case in point.

Historical note: Musique concrète Musique concrète, as well as *elektronische Musik** (electronic music, see under synthesised sound below), was originally made in studios that formed part of a broadcast organisation. In this case, Pierre Schaeffer, who already worked at the ORTF (French radio–television organisation), was investigating whether the technology used for radio plays could be further developed towards a musical artistic goal. He established the Groupe de Recherches de Musique Concrète (Musique Concrète Research Group) in 1948 which in 1958 became the Groupe de Recherches Musicales or GRM that still operates today in the building of Radio France and offered concerts of what Michel Chion, a one-time GRM member and theorist, called "cinema for the ears." Schaeffer suggested the creation of pieces using real-world sounds. Some of these sounds became abstract through various forms of sound manipulation (see Chapter 3). Years later, composers, though still focusing on the use of real-world sounds, felt that hybrid works including synthesised sounds could also be effective. They chose the term acousmatic music, which was associated with Pythagoras, who, according to tale, gave lectures behind a curtain in order to provide his listeners with a more profound aural experience without the accompanying visual information.

Where soundscape composition is associated with contextual association, Schaeffer, at one point, believed that musique concrète worked best when the source of the sounds used was not the focus of listening. Instead, he spoke of listeners' "reduced listening"★ whereby the sounds' innate musical qualities became the focus. In this way, soundscape music and musique concrète based on reduced listening became opposites of a sort within real-world music. In fact, the ultimate aim of reduced listening was to take the real-world aspect out of the sounds. We shall refer to these two means of listening as contextual★ and musical★ from Chapter 2 onwards.

Historical note: Analogue to digital technology 1 One might wonder where to begin when writing a mini-history of technology related to sound-based music: old mechanical and early electric (note-based) instruments, the telegraph, electricity, the gramophone, the amplifier? Other than some of those musical instruments that are not terribly relevant to this tale, most of that history is likely to be common knowledge to readers. Composers of musique concrète needed a recording medium (phonograph, tape recorder), one or more microphones and means of manipulating sounds. This translates to one piece of apparatus for each sonic operation, many of which could not be interconnected until the 1960s, when the concept of voltage-control became a reality. Working in such a studio was a highly laborious task with every generation of a recording losing some of its quality due to the restrictions associated with the recording technologies such as tape hiss. Once these pieces of apparatus became interconnected, things remained laborious, but were highly efficient in comparison with what existed beforehand. With the appearance of synthesisers* in the 1960s (see under synthesised sound below), another step was taken and subsequently even individuals would be able to afford personal equipment.

Just before 1960 computers started to be used for the composition of music as well as the synthesis and manipulation of sound. Our digital age commenced. In the early years, mainframe computers, owned by universities or large organisations, were the only means of making digital music. As the decades progressed mini-computers and microcomputers, also known as PCs, came into being and, today, the notion of an individual having access to a computer is no longer a dream—it is reality, and many of these machines are infinitely more efficient than the mainframes of decades past. Today, an individual can possess a multichannel recording studio and performance device on a single laptop, often with little to no other equipment needed. Older musicians will have seen a huge amount of labour disappear and an equally huge amount of potential added with each new generation of digital systems.

Historical note: Sampling technologies Some of the techniques used in musique concrète and other types of sound-based music that followed will be introduced in Chapter 3. It is useful to single out the idea of capturing a sound or a number of sounds for further musical use here to see how radically our technology has evolved.

In terms of analogue technology, the words "do it yourself" come to mind. There was no specific equipment for maintaining samples beyond the recording medium itself. This has, of course, come back to us in the form of hip hop scratching, a modern analogue form of sampling and sample-based performance. In olden days, the tape loop*—select the segment; stick the end of the segment to the beginning and you can reuse it when needed—was one form of playing with a sample (although the word "sample" was not used in this context at the time). Cut and paste—literally—and manipulate until you end up with the sound you seek was the only way to work.

With digital technologies everything changed. Of course, how people work is highly dependent on the technologies involved. For example, early hardware-based samplers had fairly restricted memories and therefore sounds could never last more than, say, a few seconds. For most musical purposes, this was sufficient, but for others it meant becoming dependent on the technology.

These restrictions remain true today, although higher processing speeds and much larger memories lead to far fewer problems for most people. Samplers have also become software-based so the only investment involved is the software if it is a commercial as opposed to a freeware product.

This evolution from laborious DIY work to expensive, restricted modular systems to today's efficient software-based opportunities is extraordinary and typifies how our supporting technology has evolved and will continue to evolve in support of our ability to organise sounds artistically.

Plunderphonics*

Plunderphonics, intrinsically related to sampling culture, is a special case raising interesting questions for today's sound-based musicians regarding where the border might lie between note-based and sound-based music. The word is most often linked with its creator, John Oswald, but many people take existent materials, mainly or solely recordings of music, and transform/remix this into a new work as part of today's sampling culture. In Oswald's case, he tends to cut the recordings into very short durations, thus creating what I have called "music-based music" which indeed has one foot in the note-based traditions of the original works and the other in the world of sound organisation.

Plunderphonics or any music recycling existent sound materials allows people to confront their own lived experience within an artistic context, similar to soundscape composition and other forms of real-world music mentioned already. Its name suggests something counter-cultural as plundering has something to do with stealing something valuable, doesn't it?

Synthesised Sound

As suggested earlier in this chapter, many people call any form of sound-based music, and even some forms of synthesised note-based music, electronic music. What we shall be discussing here is sound-based music in which the material has been generated synthetically.

Historical note: Electronic music The tale commences at the NWDR radio-television studies in Cologne where, instead of focusing on developments directly related to the world of radio plays and the like, as was the case in Paris, the idea was to create music using electronic sources of sound, such as the tone generator or oscillator. Thus *elektronische Musik* was born only a couple of years after the first musique concrète experiments. Much of the early experimentation was influenced by the works of earlier twentieth-century composers who were interested in formalised aspects of composition. As new sound qualities* were created, an increasing number of musicians considered the challenge to organise sounds as opposed to creating new types of notes similar to those in instrumental music. "Electronic music" is a category, not a genre; it refers to both note-based and sound-based composition, so the term will be used carefully from now on.

Historical note: Adding or subtracting Two key early forms of sound generation are known today as additive* and subtractive synthesis*, both of which will be introduced in Chapter 3. In the former case, sounds are created on the basis of the sum of their components. A sine wave* is the purest form of sound and consists of one single frequency*. Most pitched sounds that we hear, such as that of an instrument or a voice, are actually very complex sounds in which the fundamental frequency is its defining melodic characteristic. It often involves harmonics or overtones and, sometimes, extra sounds as well, such as the sound of the bow touching a violin string. To create such complex sounds synthetically, the relationship or balance of all of the sound's frequency components is generated in time as the sound evolves. This bottom-up means of synthesising sound is called additive synthesis. In the old analogue studios, several oscillators were needed to achieve this. Their amplitudes were modified individually in time in general.

Subtractive synthesis begins from another extreme: any complex sound including noise. Complex sounds contain many pitches, in fact in the case of noise an infinite number of them. Here one starts with a complex sound and erases part of it as it were until the sound quality is created that is being sought. In Chapter 3 we shall learn that this is done mainly using filters*.

Historical Note: Analogue to digital technology 2 As described above, originally sounds were generated by individual pieces of equipment. In these early studios, many instruments were called upon that could be found in physics and acoustic laboratories. This was quite costly and making an electronic work was at least as laborious as making an early musique concrète piece. During the first decade of electronic music composition the first synthesiser, the RCA synthesiser, was constructed and placed in the Columbia University Electronic Music Center in New York City. It was about two metres high and ran the width of a wall in a large studio space. Its advantage was that its components could influence one another without having to be recorded or sent to a mixing desk. Readers will know that, as time progressed, synthesisers became smaller. Many analogue synthesisers were built, many of which became well known through their use in popular music contexts as well as in more innovative types of art music. Digital synthesisers were not available until two decades after digital or computer music was born. These use digital signal processing, like the computers, to produce sounds. In both cases, at one point digital information is transformed into audio. (When computers digitise sound, the reverse process takes place.) Today synthesis is available on individuals' computers. The main role for electronic instruments including synthesisers is in performance. As was the case with real-world sounds, much work that used to be done in non-real-time environments is now available in real time.

Many will be acquainted with the MIDI protocol first associated with digital synthesisers. This is an awkward subject as far as this book is concerned. The Musical Instrument Digital Interface was specifically created based on the chromatic scale. Where synthesis allowed artists to create any sound at any pitch and at any volume, MIDI, on the other hand, is based on the five-line staff and thus is best used in a note-based context. Although it can be used towards sound-based musical goals, this is not what MIDI was created for, and therefore it will not be returned to in this book.

The use of synthesised sound in sound-based music is quite common. It permeates many genres associated with sound organisation with the exception of those focused on real-world sounds only. Only in the very early period were the two types of materials separated. Today it is quite common for musicians simply to seek the sounds they desire and use them wherever they want, whether synthetic or from the real world. In both cases many musicians' focus is *sound quality*, for example the colour of a sound, as opposed to rhythm and pitch. Some of the schools of thought that focus on sound quality now follow.

Within the world of synthesised sounds, many artists have actively sought to create *new sounds* as part of their innovative spirit. The composer Iannis Xenakis was known to have said that he was not interested in works that did not include new sounds, a fairly ambitious desire.

Our ability to create sounds from scratch or, alternatively, to record sounds and then manipulate them, thus creating new sounds, forms part of the world of sound-based music. In a sense this is a bit of a dangerous way of going about things, as most listeners like to make connections with their own lived experience. This is rather difficult when using new sound material. Some sounds, such as different noises (see below), are also generally known as unwanted sounds. This is the perception of many listeners at least. Therefore listeners' desire or lack thereof in terms of listening to alienating sounds must be taken into account as part of the experimentation related to the creation of new sounds, as many such sounds can fall into this category.

The fact that we are able to create sounds so short that they are barely audible on their own has led to an entire world of new sounds: microsound* and granular synthesis* are important terms related to this approach (see Chapter 3). As we shall discover, in the world of microsound one uses a huge number of microscopic interrelated sounds to create a (dynamic) sound quality similar to the relationship between single grains of sand and the entirety of sand found on a particular beach. Many types of sounds created in this manner generate new, often attractive, sonic qualities. As with all approaches named in this section, listening to an excerpt of microsound-based composition can open new doors musically.

It was the Italian Futurists at the beginning of the last century who were responsible for the concept of a "noise orchestra." Their Russian counterparts desired to make (note-based) music inspired by the sounds of factories. Therefore today's music involving *noise* is not entirely new.

There exists quite a bit of interest in noise music*. This interest is most likely the product of two things: the high levels of loudness found in many types of today's music and artists' desire to find a creative outlet related to today's sound pollution. Noise need not be synthesised, of course. It can also be captured in our natural world, so this subject is not solely but is primarily rooted in synthesised forms of music.

Electronica*

This is both an important yet ambiguous term in sound-based music. Many people are acquainted with the term as related to: "innovative forms of popular electroacoustic music created in the studio, on one's personal computer, or in live performance. Typically, although influenced by current forms of dance music, the music is often designed for a non-dance-oriented listening situation" (EARS). In terms of sound-based music, electronica actually means something else. It consists of a number of genres of music that do not easily fit in either popular or art music traditions. In fact, like much sound-based music, this type of music belongs to a space all of its own although it might also be linked with more traditional forms of music as it does with the other new media arts. Noise and other audio oddities are used in novel ways.

The former definition can lead to sound-based and note-based work. In fact they are often combined, although not necessarily simultaneously, in experimental pop music settings.

The latter, which is more important to us, includes genres such as minimal electronica and lowercase sound* in which few materials are used and little is heard at any given moment; lowercase sound is quiet as well. One of the other current forms of this type of electronica is glitch*, which uses audio defects such as CD clicks as a basis.

Artists may have a background in pop music, for example, club culture, but may have been traditionally trained as well or even come from the world of the fine arts. Although many electronica works are pre-recorded, a good deal of today's electronica scene is focused on live performance, something that is relevant to this and the next two entries. Material used in electronica includes both synthesised and sampled sounds.

Pop Music Roots

Innovative music with pop music roots is rarely solely sound-based, but may lean on its materials and means of production. In some cases, sound-based works are also made. Electronica, and all of the popular music associated with it, has already been mentioned. Turntable-based performance from hip hop to turntablist* teams' work is often at the cusp between sounds and notes. IDM (Intelligent Dance Music) often borrows sound-based music techniques and includes sound-based passages in what normally evolves into note-based music. Ambient music is a very interesting example for a number of reasons, not least of which is that it often does not contain an audible beat, as is the case in some other forms of innovative sound-based pieces based on pop roots. We shall return to the question of whether music with a beat is compatible with sound-based music in Chapter 5.

There is also some crosstalk between some genres and categories previously mentioned and music with pop music roots, such as rock concrète, that borrowed some musique concrète techniques but clearly did not become disassociated from its rock roots.

To be honest, with few exceptions (think of the *White Album* track "Revolution 9" by The Beatles), most music with pop roots is note-based. It is only on the experimental fringes where sound-based works are made. With this in mind it is fascinating to note how interesting such pop-inspired sound-based works can be for the public normally associated with the other types of sound-based music. The reverse is also true. It is for this reason that the pop vs. art music split is much less rigid (if existent at all) in terms of many sound-based works.

Many sound-based initiatives with pop music roots involve performance. Still, there exist pieces that end up on a fixed medium, such as the above-mentioned Beatles example. There are pieces that exist in both studio and live mix forms. What types of sounds do they use? The answer is anything from samples of instruments to sounds from our daily lives to synthesised sound. Their choice is the same infinite horizon as ours will be in the coming chapters.

Focus on Performance

Having presented some historical markers above, it will probably come as no surprise that live sound-based music was an exception, not the rule, until digital music became both efficient and affordable.

Historical Note: Live performance In the 1960s very inventive individuals such as David Tudor and the members of the Sonic Arts Union were involved in live electronic* performance, creating new, often homemade electronic instruments for concert performance. Similarly, acoustic and electronic sound installations were installed in galleries and museums at the time.

As technology developed, the word "interactive" entered our vocabulary. New instruments, digital and analogue, devices and interfaces were developed for live use, thus involving some form of human–machine (or machine–machine) interaction. More recently, the notion of using a portable computer on stage became a reality and new forms of music including laptronica, the synthesis of laptop and electronica, were born.

One of the key reasons for the slow progression on to the stage was the somewhat primitive quality of some of the early electronic instruments. Therefore, live electronic music remained marginal over a fairly lengthy period of time.

Furthermore, when using analogue equipment normally one was only able to access information from fixed media, such as a tape, consecutively. That infers that "grabbing" a sound anywhere on a tape took too much time and likely included the clunking sound of the tape recorder's search for that sound in the process. This made the reuse of samples in a live context inefficient at best. This can now be done at the click of a mouse, thus largely opening up new means of real-time performance.

Today, we can gain rapid access to a large number of sounds on our laptops or other digital music instruments and can also manipulate and spatialise the sounds in real time. This, plus the fact that new musical interfaces, devices and instruments are being constantly developed, has led to an extremely lively performance scene related to sound-based forms of music. Similarly the presence of sound installations in art venues and public places has increased with time as well as becoming a) more dependable and b) more cost efficient with time.

Sound Art

Sound art, according to most of its artists, refers to sound-based creative art that is not destined for concert performance. Clearly this includes the above-mentioned sound installations, including sound sculptures where the object itself creates the sounds, whether interactive or simply installations that do not involve public involvement in terms of triggering or influencing the sounds it produces. Some of these works are placed in public locations and are therefore public artworks. Most are located at arts venues. Some consider radiophonic* sound-based works, that is, creative works made specifically for radio broadcast, as sound art, too.

Many sound art pieces do not have a start or an end, thus no fixed duration. Sound art works are often audio-visual; they are normally a form of multimedia in the sense that they are intended to be presented as art works as well as works of organised sound. In my view, sound art works are also a form of sound-based music.

Audio-Visual Sound-Based Music

We live in an image culture so it comes as no surprise that there are varieties of sound-based music used in a wide variety of audio-visual contexts. Our sound installations fall into that category. So do works in which sound-based music is wed with image. This case is rooted in the tradition of video, now known as new media art. If the sound is taking the lead, the product is often known as visual music, especially when there is some sort of relationship between sound and image. Some VJs' work in clubs is based on sound-based music being visualised. There are also new immersive environments that use sound-based musical elements, as do many computer games. Taking an even broader view, sound-based music has become ubiquitous thanks to the media; sound-based music can be heard as part of sound design for movies, videos, advertisements (including audio-only ones for radio) and so on.

Sound-based music can create a cinema for the ears, but equally create innovative art for both the eyes and ears, and it is here where a great deal of development is taking place due to the fact that our societies are indeed dictated by image.

Internet Sound-Based Music

In this overview we have discovered that sound-based music can be heard in a huge number of venues. In Chapter 2 we shall speak of soundwalks★ that can take place anywhere, just like we can listen to music anywhere on our portable devices. The concert hall is but one venue for this art form.

In recent years, one place that many people tend to frequent is cyberspace by way of the Internet. Therefore it comes as no surprise that Internet music is one of the most dynamic areas of development both in note-based and sound-based forms of music, as communities are easily formed online. There is no basic "sound" for Internet music, just as there isn't one for sound art either. Internet music can be made by the user independently or can be made in multiple user environments. New forms of social networking have acted as a catalyst in terms of community forming and it is for this reason that it might be said that part of the future of what is known as folk music, that is, music of the people, will be found online, including newly developed forms of sound-based music for group creation and performance. Obviously live forms of sound-based music will aid in the creation of new musical communities as well, but my prediction is that the amount of online music making will increase hugely in the coming years.

Readers will by now have learned how expansive the universe of sound-based music really is. It is hoped that readers will listen to a number of excerpts from pieces representing the approaches listed above. The more you listen, the better able you will be to situate it fairly well. Nonetheless, if you are looking for recordings related to specific types of music to hear, this can sometimes be challenging. In *The Music of Sounds* (Landy 2007b, 145) it was suggested that a straightforward categorisation system is not always ideal. A flute piece can be categorised under flute repertoire, the performer, the composer, the genre, etc. Similarly in sound-based music, various aspects may be of relevance. In that book, I suggested that one look at three aspects of a work: 1) the context of a work (placement, how it is performed, where it is performed/presented/heard); 2) creative practice (how it has been constructed, composition intention); and 3) listening experience (which aspects of the music are easy to hold on to and how do we listen to the work [more focused on the sound sources, more focused on the sounds' musical qualities]). All of these can influence how one places a work and most works will be able to be classified in more than one way. This may sound awkward and complicated, but is in fact intended to make our lives easy. In our Internet age, being able to search for things is easier as they are not necessarily physically placed in a single location. Ideally, after reading this book, listening to samples of sound-based music and making your own, you will find your own ways of classifying and searching for what you hear.

This contextual introduction has been intended to delineate sound-based music and has been approached from a fairly high level to avoid oversimplifying things. The time has come to go to "Go" and start introducing sound-based music from the very beginning. Enjoy your journey!

2

DISCOVERING MUSIC
ALL AROUND US

The late experimental composer John Cage often said: "Music is all around us; if only we had ears," going on to suggest that concerts were taking place everywhere in the world, 24/7. His radical statement confronts all of us with that age-old question: what is music? His predecessor, Edgard Varèse, invented the term "organised sound" as a means of describing his own music. The difference between Cage's view of organised sound and Varèse's is that Varèse implied but did not state that the sounds were to be organised into musical works for concert performance, yet Cage needs nothing more than those two words. Another interesting challenge that Cage poses, by asking us to open our windows or go for what today are known as listening walks★ (or soundwalks—we shall return to these two terms in a short while) focusing on our aural experience of the environment including both forms of nature—that which we associate with rural environments and human nature-affected urban environments—is the assumption that sounds in nature are organised and worthy of our attentive listening. It has often been shown that there are geometrical patterns in nature (think of the design of leaves, rivers and the like) and we are all aware of birdcalls and how animals communicate with each other spatially. Sonic patterns and communication can be perceived musically. Therefore, Cage's idea is by no means odd to me.

With this in mind, I am personally quite comfortable with a very broad definition of music. The challenge that this book poses is: can one convey this view to young people and, perhaps more difficult still, to people with deeply rooted views of what music is and is not? One of the best ways to start confronting deeply seeded views related to music is by listening to nature. It is for this reason that increasing aural awareness and becoming more acquainted with one's sonic environment (or soundscapes) is the subject of this chapter.

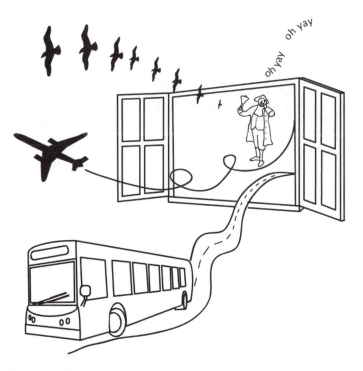

FIGURE 2.1 Sounds can be heard everywhere

Discovering Soundscapes

It is perhaps not surprising, given the clutter of our daily lives, that most people are oblivious to the sounds that surround them much of the time. The classic case in modern society is the omnipresence of the ignored television in some homes. I, for one, find the presence of the audio emanating from a radio or the image and sound from a television similar to a magnet. It is hard not to pay attention to them as they are requesting my attention. The notion of background music is anathema to me. I suppose it comes with being a musician, that is, a person sensitive to sensual input, in particular sounds. Tuning out is not part of this musician's vocabulary.

This not paying attention to one's environment can come at a cost. The most obvious is someone not paying attention to potential dangers, for example outside whilst riding a bicycle and listening to an iPod or the like.

Where does this tuning out come from? We all have thoughts about that. These may include people in urban settings attempting to combat noise by creating a permanent sound screen that is in fact not to be listened to, but simply to be hung like wallpaper. Another factor is a consequence of our consumer culture, a culture in which music was transformed from something with which one was involved or to which one actually paid attention to something to be perceived but not necessarily actively listened to, for example, background music or muzak in commercial settings.

Such omnipresent sound is a fact of life, but it is not necessarily either a form of progress or a particularly satisfactory state of affairs. After all there is a time and a place for everything and our relative loss of active listening, whether related to the musical experience or simply our environment wherever we are, represents a form of detachment.

The musician and acoustic ecologist* Murray Schafer has written extensively over this detachment, over the impact of what he calls sound pollution. His antidote, greater awareness, comes as no surprise. It is for this reason that he introduced awareness-linked concepts including soundscape and soundwalks. His view is that through greater awareness comes heightened understanding of one's aural environment. I would take this one step further. I believe that, as people become aware of their sonic world, this raises curiosity about sound and how sounds fit together. Heightened awareness allows the listener to flip-flop between what a particular sound is to what are the components of this sound, where the sound is in space, how the sound fits with other audible sounds, and so on. This experience can be life changing as those who succeed in this will often want to return to the type of tuned-in listening which is at the other end of the spectrum from the tuned-out background music that typifies today's consumer culture.

Given this context, I have found it extremely worthwhile to take people of all ages who have not consciously experienced this form of awareness into different aural contexts and share the listening experience in all its forms. A teacher might simply call such a session "Listening" and allow students to walk in a forest, sit and pay attention to the local traffic, go to an industrial building and realise how overwhelming sound can be in such a context, etc. In fact, Max Neuhaus created a series under the name "LISTEN", where listeners were taken to high-decibel environments such as a newspaper printing building, a hydroelectric plant and the like. The goal of such exercises is to discover as much as possible about a given sonic environment. The more such experiences on offer, the better people's vocabulary of description will evolve, and the more types of sonic experience will form part of the listening and evaluative experience and thus the greater aural awareness will be.

The one thing to keep in mind in such cases is to allow sufficient time to actually perceive a given environment and analyse it (but not so long that you lose the attention of those present) and adequate time to discuss things in detail. It is best to hold such discussions on the spot, allowing people to identify or return to certain sounds. The more listeners participate, the more the experience is owned.

Areas of discussion include:

- List the sounds that you have heard.
- Where did each sound come from? Which types of sound seemed to come from several places at once?

- Can you tell near from far; high from low; front from back; left from right?
- Can you describe each sound?
- Were there any sounds you could not identify and, if so, how would you describe them?
- Were there patterns to be heard in any given sound or amongst sounds?
- Were there elements in the sounds that remind you of musical elements, such as rhythm, melody, dynamic contrasts and so on?
- Can you help someone hear something that you heard that (s)he did not hear?
- Feel free to make up your own questions beyond those posed above that are specifically related to what you heard in the environment that you visited.

There is another aspect to this that is particularly interesting, namely, how one listens to a given environment at a given moment. It is possible, for example, to spend a great deal of time identifying sounds and then, suddenly, one notices that the listening experience is more about focusing on one or a few sounds and how they are evolving. This journey amongst different ways of listening is the theme of the following section of this chapter.

A Word on Various Types of Listening

Our ears and our brain are collaborating all the time, as are our other senses. That collaboration, however, knows many forms. Just think of what happens when you are drowsy. You miss something said in a conversation or emanating from the DVD that you are watching. If you arrive somewhere late after running, your attention is split between the fatigue related to that late arrival and that to which you should be paying attention. Even in a concentrated state, your mind and thus your attention can drift.

Perhaps we can speak of receiving sounds in different manners: the perception of sound, that is highly removed from content; hearing sounds, something that might be called passive listening; and listening to sounds, something that involves the highest amount of concentration, awareness of detail and understanding of content. Musicians theorising about the listening experience including Schaeffer (1977) and Smalley (1992) have spoken of "modes of listening" using a number of terms to describe different "listening strategies." We needn't discuss these authors' special terminologies as the three manners named above allow us to think along one dimension related to the type of attention. A second pair relates to the focus regarding what type of attention is involved. In this case, two terms are proposed that we shall use throughout the book: contextual and musical listening. Simply stated, in the former case, one is listening to sounds in terms of their own context; in the latter, the focus is on the sonic qualities of what is being heard and thus the aural experience is a more abstract one.

FIGURE 2.2   Some things can be heard as notes and as sounds

This pair, contextual and musical listening, brings us back to those people who cannot understand how opening a window could allow anyone to hear music (unless someone is playing music next door). The fact is that between listening to the sound of birds, the wind, planes in the sky, etc. and listening to different melodies, noises, rhythms, etc. there are many other points along this second dimension where the two are combined. This is analogous to our other scale ranging from vague aural perception to acute listening.

The clever musician can manipulate how one listens to sound-based music, for example by offering a very abstract passage followed by an abrupt, extremely recognisable sound. Most listeners will shift from one mode of listening to another rapidly dictated by that which they are hearing. This is no different from people engaged in the activities of their daily lives who suddenly hear a loud siren announcing that there is a fire in the neighbourhood.

Nevertheless, we, the listeners, control most such switches whether very consciously or simply due to circumstances that are not unrelated to our thoughts. We all have caught ourselves not paying attention to a piece of music when we think of someone we need to get in touch with or remember something that simply takes our mind off what we are doing. Conversely, we sometimes remember music when it isn't being played, as we are able to take the memory of the music with us. Similarly, if we make something that is based on context, the listener may still switch to musical listening. For our purposes, therefore, we shall base our creative activities in Chapters 3 to 5 on intention. We can always check how our listeners receive our work and change things accordingly.

In a sense it would be nice to gauge how we are perceiving things aurally at any given moment during our listening walks or any other situation where we are listening to organised sounds, but, of course, the act of monitoring our attention means that we are paying attention to something else simultaneously: multi-tasking, in today's jargon. However, not everyone multi-tasks in an equally efficient

manner and our attention can be removed from the music by paying attention to
... well ... what we're paying attention to.

One can also attempt to alter the focus during a listening walk from that of
contextual listening to musical listening. Schaeffer called the ability to listen to
sounds without paying attention to their source or cause "reduced listening"
and was therefore a great supporter of musical listening. In a sense the quest for
reduced listening is an acquired taste when the sounds involved can be recognised. We do experience reduced listening naturally when we are not paying
attention to an aural landscape, that is, when we are switched off or when we are
tired. In such circumstances this happens naturally; it is the conscious effort to
ignore sounds' sources and causes that Schaeffer sought and that is non-trivial.

I would suggest that, by way of listening walks, we should all be able to appreciate a given sound environment both in terms of its detail as well as in terms of
a purely sonic experience. Both can lead to satisfying results; these are potentially
both profound, yet different experiences. I would suggest that the appreciation
of music is always a combination of acute listening related to concrete detail,
whether it is a forest or a string section of an orchestra, and listening to the musical
sound that is the consequence of that detail.

As an aside, there also exists the case of the listener who knows how to make
sound-based music, who is neither listening to the context, nor to the music, but
to how sounds have been treated or generated by other musicians. This might
be called technological or recipe listening. It is a natural thing to do, but it does
often remove one from what (s)he intends to listen to due to an aural interest in
the work's construction—an occupational inevitability, I suppose. Suffice to say
that technological listening is not our priority here.

Our priority is instead the development of an awareness of passive perception
to active listening as well as from the contextual to musical reception of what
one hears. As we progress through our activities, one interesting challenge will
be to have people create sound sequences that offer two complementary aural
experiences: one related to what specifically is taking place and one related to the
musical result. In other words, the listener has two different ways of following
the sonic events: the contextual and the musical. Take note that in such situations
the eyes may have a major influence in terms of the listening experience. If one
watches an action that is taking place, it is very hard to ignore the specific detail
that is being interpreted visually.

Investigating Soundscapes

Thus far questions have been posed concerning how musical is the world in
which we live and how we listen to it. In the two sections that remain in this
chapter, I shall attempt to facilitate further investigation of those sounds we tend
to ignore in our daily lives. By the time we reach the final section we shall be able
to take this knowledge and apply it creatively.

Many involved in what today is called "soundscape studies," from Schafer onwards, have stressed the importance of people being knowledgeable of the sonic environment through its being studied, recorded and/or used creatively. Their rationale for this is simple: the goal is better knowledge and, through knowledge, an improved acoustic ecology, thus reducing sound pollution, for example. In other words, their goal is not only artistic, but also highly relevant to the quality of life in today's world.

This book does not have such ambitious goals. Celebrating the rich diversity of sound at our disposal towards creative goals is pretty challenging already! It is for this reason that from now on I shall not make the distinction upheld by many specialists between a listening walk and a soundwalk, the latter of which involves the use of a score or a map, as this is more relevant within the context of the field of acoustic ecology than it is to us.

Our interest is now in capturing the essence of a given sonic ambiance and being able to learn from the detail so that we are better able to apply some of these elements artistically. For example, how do we develop our sense of spatial awareness regarding soundscapes? The following discussion will not be comprehensive—a soundscape is, in the end, infinitely complex—but will attempt to offer some aspects of a sonic environment that can be discussed in isolation as well as in combination with other associated sonic aspects.

In an article I wrote in 1987 (Landy 1987) for a public whose interests spanned all of the contemporary arts, I suggested that one of the major innovations in twentieth-century music was the increased interest in terms of thinking of organising sounds, including notes in this case, parametrically, that is, in terms of isolable sound characteristics. In that article, I borrowed a definition of parameter for musical use from Josef Häusler and translated it as follows: "Musical parameters are all sound or compositional components which can be isolated and ordered." In fact our listening strategies discussion above involved two parameters; therefore, this approach is equally relevant to the production of music as well as the listening experience. Although centuries ago certain composers were known for creating rhythmical cycles and melodic cycles of different lengths, allowing them to repeat in a single piece, in the last century, this approach opened up to many more aspects than just pitch and time. The above-mentioned article was more concerned with experimental instrumental music, yet the majority of the elements presented are equally relevant to the current discussion and, whilst preparing this book, I discovered that very few appeared to be missing. Here is a selection from that article as well as those that I would like to add (the first and the last). We shall introduce these one at a time and discuss how they may serve our current purposes.

- Sound type/source
- Pitch
- Duration
- Dynamics

- Sound quality
- Space
- Simultaneity
- Density
- (Dis)order
- Recognisability of sounds

Sound Type/Source

As we are in the chapter focused on sounds from our daily lives, it seems logical to start off this discussion with the ability to determine what we are listening to as best as we can. Some sounds are unfamiliar; others unknown, but many are identifiable.

I admit that this first item is more like a huge list than one ranging from x to y as parameters normally do. In fact there are actually several ways in which sounds might be categorised or ordered. Fortunately for the purposes of what we are trying to achieve at this point, we needn't make things too complicated, as it is relatively easy to compile lists of individual sounds and group them into related sound types during listening walks. Other types of lists related to sounds from the point of view of musical listening will evolve from the other parameters such as those related to sound quality (see below). It is more natural for listeners to identify, or at least attempt to identify, the sounds they are hearing, particularly during listening walks, and it is this that we shall focus upon for the time being.

It has been my experience when taking people on their first (conscious) soundwalks that they are surprised by how many different sounds they are able to perceive. I always like to suggest that those sound producers all represent the musicians in the soundscape orchestra. The combination of which sounds they produce, when they are heard and how the sounds are produced is their score.

Soundwalk activity Write down all of the sounds that you hear at a given location or, in a particular area, at a small number of specifically set locations. Try to group these sounds into types. In some cases, a single sound might fit into more than one type—this is not necessarily a problem as long as things are clear. Compare your list with those of people who are with you and try to perceive those sounds that you might have missed. It is not necessary at this point to describe the sounds musically. This will come later. What you might consider is whether you can subdivide some of your categories in terms of sounds that have similar characteristics. This will prepare you for some of the other parameters that will be introduced below.

As the listing of sound types might be structured differently with different goals in mind, it might come as no surprise that we possess no single list, similar to our means of classifying instruments, for categorising sounds or how they are produced. Personally, I think that such systems might be useful towards educational goals. Still, of the ten parameters being proposed here, this is the most straightforward in terms of the vocabulary needed as decisions will be based on our knowledge of our environment and, therefore, making some sense of what we are listening to should not be too difficult.

Pitch

Pitch is easily ordered from low sounds to high sounds and can be grouped in terms of register (low, middle and high are examples, but one can choose as many registers as are required). Of course not every sound we listen to will have an audible pitch associated with it. For example, many noise textures span the entire register and will not have a highlighted frequency, although there are exceptions, such as the glissandi produced by the whooshing sound of wind changing speed rapidly. Noise sounds imply that we need two parameters here, one ranging from pitch-centred to non-pitch-centred sounds and the other related to pitch range or register.

Some sound sources produce more than one pitch, either simultaneously—think of the famous locomotive horns in North America—or in succession, like birdsong. This takes us well into the world of note-based music, at least at first glance (well, first hearing). However, many sounds do not fit well into the chromatic system, as you can well imagine. Having written that, it is surprising how many sounds in nature, including the speaking voice, can easily be represented on the chromatic scale. That is something to listen for. Another point is that many sounds in nature are not based on a beat. There exist some forms of traditional and contemporary music that work in this manner, too, especially within the contemporary art music world, but most music that we are familiar with does contain a clear beat. Therefore the absence of an audible beat does take many readers into unknown territory. And, of course, traditionally noises, beyond some percussion sounds, are rare in music. There also exist lengthy continuous sounds (for example, the sound of the wind, a jet, a stream) for which there is no obvious equivalent in the music of instruments and voice other than perhaps the drone.

Depending on the abilities of those involved, this particular exercise can become quite rich in information, thus encouraging the greater appreciation of the components of sounds in our soundscapes, and that is what this parametric approach is all about. Obviously looking at pitch without discussing time may seem awkward to some, but think of it this way: we are learning about how sounds fit within a given environment, just like we learn which instruments fit best in a given type of music. It is, in a sense, assisting us in creating a music theory for the sounds in our sonic environments.

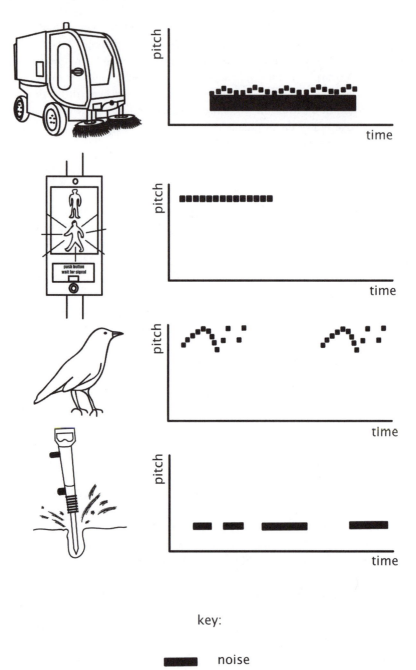

FIGURE 2.3 One way to notate pitch

Soundwalk activity After having written down all of the sound sources related to a particular soundwalk, you might add the first of a number of columns next to each name in which you might attempt to describe whether that source creates a pitched or non-pitched sound; whether the pitch is always the same or whether it varies; what register(s) it is in; whether it fits into the chromatic scale (an instrument or tuning fork might be helpful in this case; the opposite would be pitches that could not be related to the twelve pitches within the octave) or is chromatically related to another sound that is present; whether it produces more than one pitch at a time or in succession; whether all of the same sound source, for example, all birds of a single type, make the same sounds in the same way or whether things are at different pitches or varied; whether the pitches remain stable or glide upwards or downwards. In the case of noise textures, are they very broad or are they more contained, for example in a particular register; do they sometimes focus on pitch; if so, the questions above become relevant, too; are they static or dynamic; if dynamic, what seems to happen to these sounds in time?

Duration

We all know that, in most notation systems, pitch is indicated along the y-axis and time along the x-axis. In fact the time axis normally reflects individual note durations, groups of notes representing rhythmical patterns as well as tempo. For the purposes of this discussion, tempo will contribute to the time duration discussion instead of being treated separately, as was the case in Landy (1987). Tempo has to do with the basic speed of the beat of a given music. Much that we shall discuss has no apparent beat and, when it does, its durations will obviously be influenced accordingly, so for our cases one parameter covering the two is sufficient.

I would venture to guess that some sounds encountered in soundwalks are so short that we cannot hear them as individual sounds. Think, for example, of the rapid sounds made by cicadas in hot weather. Others are so long that they will have started before we arrive and continue after we leave. For our current purposes, I suggest we discuss all sounds that possess an audible start and finish and find a means of describing those continuous ones, including constant sounds consisting of rapid successions of ultra-short sounds, such as the individual rapid sounds of the cicada.

Can we investigate duration in a manner similar to pitch? To a certain extent the answer is yes. There is a time-based equivalent of register: very short sounds to lengthy continuous ones. Some sounds discovered in soundwalks will possess their own rhythmical patterns, whether based on a beat or not. In such cases this rhythmical pattern may well be linked to a number of pitches similar to melodies in traditional music. Some patterns will be constant, yet many may be more dynamic and will vary. This is similar to our pitch discussion where some sound sources do not sound exactly the same all the time, but may have similar pitch sequences instead. In terms of what you hear in a given environment, do all sounds coming from the same sound source emit patterns that are the same or similar?

Another aspect that is related to both time and space has to do with the acoustics of the space. Are there echoes present? Does the space in any way influence when things are happening? For example, sounds from far away take longer to reach you. And then there is the fact that, in some cases, sounds are related to a form of linguistic communication, amongst animals for example. What can we discover that is related to such phenomena?

Soundwalk activity Make a list with columns similar to the one presented under pitch or, better still, add some columns to the original one. Try to group the sounds into duration categories. There may be only three: short, medium or long, and you can decide where you perceive the boundaries to be, or perhaps use even more duration categories, such as very short, short, and so on. Too many such categories will add complexity to your investigation as you may then make subjective decisions placing durations arbitrarily as you simply cannot decide which is best. In such cases, I would suggest using fewer choices. State whether the sources tend to produce a single sound or groups of them. In the case of groups, it is worthwhile to attempt to describe or notate patterns that evolve from that source and discover whether these patterns are static or dynamic. Do these groups of sounds suggest a certain tempo? In some cases the end of one sound and the beginning of the next sound might not be entirely clear. How can you describe such sonic movement?

It might be worthwhile trying to create a time notation for single sound types or even for an entire environment if you dare. It is much easier if you can record the environment and listen again and again. You may want to combine this type of transcription with pitch (and soon, dynamics as well). The notation you choose is open to you. Perhaps one similar to traditional five-line notation is useful for some sounds; imaginative forms of evocative notation may better represent others.

We are most aware of frequency, related to pitch, and time when we listen to or play music. These two components can be a bit more complicated when discussing sounds, but are certainly fundamental to the listening experience, and that is why, after sources, they have been presented first.

Dynamics

If pitch and time are the two "lead" parameters in music, the parameter related to loudness or dynamics has to come a close third. Loudness has always been a formal aspect of musical behaviour even before the words piano and forte entered the vocabulary. In recent decades, loudness has become a hot political topic as our world has become an increasingly louder place in which to live. An important element related to this increase of loudness in our sonic environment, technology has allowed many sorts of music to be played at extremely high levels, music related to club culture and noise music representing two of many types of music that are at least as interested in high decibels as they are in any other musical aspect. A composer suggested to me recently that every concert should include a quiet piece, thus suggesting that people might be reminded that there are indeed two ends of the scale.

It is interesting to note that, in our digital age, many listeners do not hear a difference between a professional-quality recording and a compressed one. This is due to the music's sitting at the saturation level of dynamic most of the time. Music that does demonstrate significant dynamic contrast offers an audible qualitative difference when compressed. As the music involving a wide spectrum of dynamics, music that does not necessarily become extremely loud, is now in the minority, compressed audio has succeeded in becoming a fact of life. The irony of the story is that in real life loud normally means irritating, yet in music it has come to signify enjoyment. This fascinating fact is relevant to our investigation as it is quite important in terms of the understanding of our raised awareness, not only in terms of what sounds are being heard and how they can best be described, but also how we react to them. Certainly, subjectivity plays a role here and not everyone in a group will enjoy the same sounds. For example, the above-mentioned cicadas are found to produce an annoying sound to many; others will find that sound welcome.

Loudness does not only concern whether a sound is loud or quiet. It also concerns the evolution of loudness within a sound, also known as its envelope★, within a musical gesture★ or phrase and so on.

We are used to loudness being notated by way of relative dynamic symbols, such as *p, mp, mf, f* and so on. Alternatively we can notate loudness more objectively using the decibels (db) scale.

During soundwalks loudness can be perceived to be a complex issue as many sounds will represent diverse levels of loudness amongst themselves or individually. What is fascinating here is how, by a simple change of loudness, a type of sound can suddenly or gradually become more or less prominent within the entirety of sounds that are audible. Distance, of course, affects loudness; therefore something loud that is far away may appear to sound less explosive than one might expect. All such details should be taken into account during soundwalk activities.

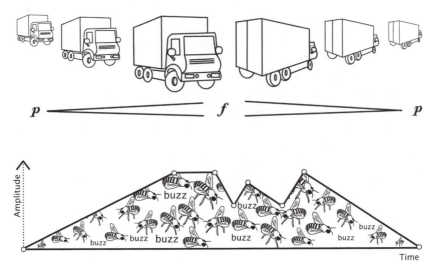

FIGURE 2.4–2.5 Two ways to notate dynamics

Soundwalk activity Using the list of sound types, we can now attempt to identify their basic dynamic registers. Some will be impossible to place into one category as they may range from very loud to extremely quiet or silent. Try to find a way to notate how loudness evolves in the more dynamic sound types. Is there an efficient way of demonstrating how different sounds have different loudness levels in different places?

Is there another way of classifying these sounds in terms of loudness than just whether they are essentially loud or quiet, static or dynamic? Perhaps sounds' envelopes may provide us with some interesting insights.

What are the dynamic contours or envelopes of various sounds? Are they fairly constant or do they have consistent characteristics (e.g., how they commence) or are they always varied and, if so, how? Are there particular envelope shapes that can be related to more than one sound source?

If you visit more than one sound environment, what are the key differences that you can perceive? Is one more pleasing than the other and why? Are there particular sounds or ways in which the sounds are heard that are more pleasing and, if so, why? Having investigated pleasant and alienating sounds, can you discover a pattern of behaviour, that is, characteristics that make something welcome or unwelcome to the ear?

Loudness is not discussed sufficiently in musical analyses. Murray Schafer apparently believes that we, in different increasingly noisy countries around the globe, are not discussing it often enough either. One of the great talents of musicians is the ability to use loudness and dynamic contrast to heighten the success of a given performance. Our understanding of loudness during soundwalks and evaluating how we react to different levels of loudness in different situations not only raises aural awareness, but also awareness regarding how we react to our environments aesthetically. The more aware we are of such things, the more able we are to reduce our blocking out of our aural landscapes. Consequently this offers us the opportunity to actively design and influence them.

Sound Quality

We now arrive at a parameter that is of fundamental importance in terms of the appreciation of sound organisation. It is also one of the most difficult to discuss and thus to comprehend. One of the reasons for this is that sound quality is based on information from several parameters at the same time; it is therefore a combination parameter. It is related to terms that are similar, but not identical, and often used incorrectly. On the EARS site, it is suggested that timbre can be related to "frequency, spectral content, sonic identity, and source recognition." The EARS site describes texture as "a highly useful term in describing the character of sounds and . . . of sequences of sounds in terms of their overall behaviour and internal details". However, not everyone uses the terms this way. Given the inconsistent usage, I have opted to use a safer, broader term: sound quality that is in a sense an umbrella term is most useful in our context.

Where it might be said that a sound source is analogous to what is normally placed at the left-hand margin of a sound-based musical score, like an instrument, sound quality is related to information that is traditionally given in a variety of ways above or below the pitch/rhythm/dynamics information on a score, such as different types of bowing on a string instrument. In other words, in this case, one sound source can possess a number of different sound qualities that may evolve rapidly or gradually from one to another in time. Whether we notate things in these ways is dependent on the particular use of the score and the sound qualities involved. They can also be represented in the form of an evocative score in which the representation of sound qualities appears as graphic images that can easily be related to the sound heard. What is important for our purposes is the ability to differentiate between various sound qualities, ideally finding clear means of verbal and/or visual description.

I have often written that, beyond technological developments related to music, the biggest musical revolutions of the previous century could be found in: a) sound qualities/sound sources becoming more diversified and often a central focus of works as well as b) the re-discovery of space (which follows below) as a potentially important musical element. Given its central importance to sound-based music, the understanding of sound sources and their related sound qualities must also play an important role in terms of the theoretical support that is needed to provide a foundation for the music's understanding.

Returning to early remarks regarding sound classification, it is here where some attempts have been made. In other words, although sounds have been classified by source for some applications, they have normally not been placed in a system for musical use. Sound qualities, on the other hand, have been documented in terms of classification to a modest extent. Although there is a considerable amount of literature that has been published concerning sound-based music, it is hard to tell how important these attempts have been. With so few categorisations available, some people have done their best to determine how useful these are to their own personal goals. Sound quality-based systems include Pierre Schaeffer's (Schaeffer 1977) in which sound quality typology and its evolution in time have been combined, Karlheinz Stockhausen's evocative adjectives (1974—in this case related to one specific score) such as whirring and buzzing and Denis Smalley's, which concerns the morphology of spectral sonic behaviour—his approach works best at the level of sound gestures (e.g., Smalley 1986, see Chapter 4).

The Schaeffer and Smalley systems, as valuable as they are at local level, are highly sophisticated tools, in the case of Schaeffer using terms to represent qualities, some of which come across as rather intangible to the uninitiated. I would suggest their being of use to people who have had some experience and are curious as to what systems have been proposed for musicians interested in sound-based music from a reduced listening point of view. The Stockhausen initiative, on the other hand, which involves a lengthy list of adjectives that describe sound qualities, can easily be used as a point of departure for beginners. By choosing descriptive adjectives we are invited to think about how sounds sound.

Like many things in art, subjectivity has to play a role in terms of our understandings related to sound qualities and in this case we are seeking to find manners of communicating what we hear in sounds beyond what they are or are perceived to be. This is, of course, no different from, for example, describing an orchestral phrase in which it is difficult to differentiate which instrument is producing which sound.

Let's take a simple example. Some trees create a sound like "whoosh" when their branches move in the wind. One could write this word with a small w and large internal letters and a small h at the end to relate to the dynamic curve of that sound, or write it diagonally if the pitch seems to go up or down, or much larger if a stronger breeze were to pass by. In this case we have found a word to act as a representation or translation of the sound and various means of writing it to reflect the specific experience of that sound. It is at this level of thought that we should commence. There is one exception, and that is when there are established words that already exist that describe certain sound qualities. In those cases, it seems silly to replace them.

FIGURE 2.6   An evocative way to notate sound quality

Soundwalk activity For sound qualities both our lists and our transcriptions are of equal importance. This is a great chance to allow ourselves to jump between contextual and musical listening as the contextual information will tell us where to look on our lists and the musical information will be able to be mapped to the contextual information, thus creating a correspondence between sources and their qualities.

Go back to a site where you have been before during these activities and take along the list made for that visit. Try to identify the sounds you have already discovered (and new ones if present this second time) and listen to their sound qualities. I have consciously chosen the plural here as many sounds possess more than one sound quality depending on circumstances, so you will need to be able to enter the varieties of sound qualities next to each entry. Please take note that some sound qualities are individual, that is, this sound source produces that quality. Some are sequential, some layered (there are many such sound sources and they make a similar sound at different time points, sometimes simultaneously) and some are combined with others (it is hard to differentiate an individual source's sound as it has been moulded into a sound quality coming from more than one source).

After doing so and sharing these with others present, the next step, and this one is slightly challenging, is to attempt to group sound qualities that you think belong together, such as pitch-based and noise-based sounds, and then compare these with the groups of sources you made earlier. The use of those descriptive adjectives might come into play here. Do they largely match up? What were the exceptions and, more importantly, why?

Having put these perceptions into words, how can we best translate this information on to a score? Is this in fact easier? Which form expresses the greatest amount of detail? Which is more efficient or helpful and why?

Share different means of notating sound qualities and evaluate what works well in each and where potential weaknesses can be discovered. Do you believe that when you go back to this score it will remind you of what you heard?

Try the above sequence of activities at another, contrasting site that you have already visited and see whether the same types of conclusions are drawn. Now that you have had these rich experiences of sound quality hunting, do you think you are more aware of your soundscapes in terms of both context and sonic qualities?

A morning chorus of birdsong is heard from the break of dawn.
These first sounds are overlapped by a train entering the station at 8.00. Three further
trains pass through the station during the day.
Rush hour traffic starts to builds up in the distance around 8.30 and at 9.00 the first hourly
church bell is rung, which continues until 21.00.
The birdsong continues intermittently and around 9.00 sounds from an industrial factory start up
and continue until 17.00.
Children make their way to school from 8.00, while shouts and laughter from their games in
the school yard are heard at lunch break and afternoon recreation.

FIGURE 2.7   A prose score of a soundscape

Key

Noise:

- Factory turbines
- Car engine
- Train
- School area

Pitch:

- Church bell
- Bird song
- Car horn

Motion:

- Train arriving
- Car
- Bird flight
- Children playing
- Water lapping

FIGURE 2.8   An evocative score of a soundscape with a key

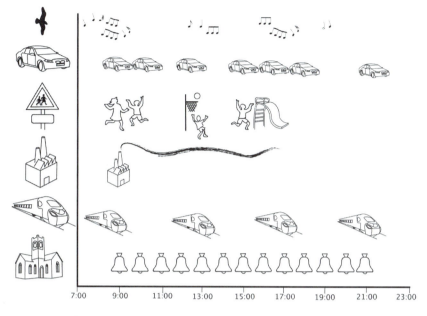

FIGURE 2.9   An evocative events score of a soundscape

In the field of music cognition, focused on how we hear and process musical elements, little work has been done in our area of sound-based music. I am personally impatient to learn what can be discovered in this field. One of the reasons for this slow start might have to do with the infinite potential sound qualities with which we are dealing. Hopefully, through this introduction you have found a means to express your perception of sound qualities in word and image. If so, your ability can only improve and your awareness will consequently be further increased. One way of really honing in on sound qualities in a particular sonic environment is by adding spatial position into the equation. This is our next stop.

Space

The composer Giovanni Gabrieli is known to have separated choirs at different sides of a cathedral in the late sixteenth century, so the idea of taking space into account within a musical context is by no means new. The combination of multichannel technology (think of surround sound systems) and the fact that musical events can take place anywhere have led to space being integrated in recent forms of music in several innovative manners. In this chapter, we have been focusing on sonic environments. One of the most exciting aspects of gaining awareness of sonic environments is our encountering where sounds come from in space and how they relate to where you are.

Borrowing the approach introduced by soundscape professionals and sound-based musicians like Neuhaus, requesting one to "listen" means, amongst other things, to realise how sounds come from left and right, front and back, above and eventually below, far away or very intimately, in the foreground, middle ground and background and so on. Similarly the discovery of spatial relationships between sounds can be a magnificent experience. For example, I find the sounds of a forest stimulating, as creaks from trees can arrive from anywhere; an animal may make a cry from afar whilst another swoops very close to where you are sitting. Insect sounds may surround you and sometimes you simply cannot quite tell exactly where they are coming from. A "conversation" appears to be taking place between two sounds, but this can be, of course, a coincidence of nature. Listening to such jewels of sonic events is a great way to familiarise yourself with a given space.

With technology, we can play with a space, just like we can play with sounds. We are able to morph one sound into another almost seamlessly and we are able to make sounds move around a space in highly sophisticated ways. That is technological magic, but there is quite a bit of magic in our two forms of nature as well: the nature of flora and fauna as well as environments that are the result of our human nature. We should attempt to discover as much of this as possible as part of this chapter's activities as this will enable us to consider its potential in creative circumstances in the chapters that follow.

Space is not only about where sounds are coming from. It is also about the nature of the space you are in, its acoustic aspects. In other words, the same sounds will sound entirely differently in different spaces. Think of a string quartet or a gospel choir in the quiet setting of a modest concert hall, the more reverberant setting of a small church or a hugely spacious train station or even an enormous car park in the open air. We are able to identify what we hear as the same piece, but it will sound hugely different each time.

When dealing with sound-based music, the space and where you are within it highly influence what you hear and also what you might miss. For example, today one speaks of public art, that is, art placed in a public place, as opposed to gallery, museum or concert hall contexts. There also exist site-specific works specifically prepared for a single site as well as site-type specific works (e.g., any harbour, car park, etc.). Our soundwalks are site specific as well—what you see, hear and experience are very much dependent on the given site. As to the aspect of where you are within a space, this may seem completely obvious, but no two people will hear exactly the same thing in a given space due to where they are placed. In surround sound situations, and any soundwalks will take you to one of those, there may be an ideal location to hear things in a certain manner. This is also known as a sweet spot. At a cinema, the sweet spot is, for example, the seat directly in the middle of the room. If you sit in the back corner, you will hear everything, but the loudspeaker above you may be quite predominant when it is used.

It is for this reason that one often sees people seek particular sweet spots during soundwalks to get the best "view" of the particular 3D sonic environment.

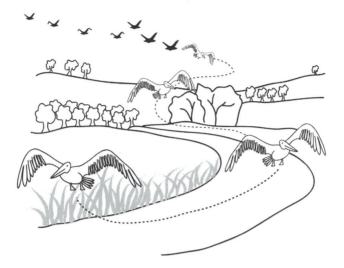

FIGURE 2.10   An evocative soundscape score offering a sense of space

Soundwalk activity Time permitting, visit a diversity of spaces, in terms of content, size, reverberant nature, loudness or other objectives. In this case the focus is not so much on evaluating which sounds are present; instead, take a selection of sounds and try to capture where they are in space in terms of direction and distance. Try, also, to find multiple appearances of the same types of sound and create a "map" of where they are in relationship to you and to each other. Whilst focusing on one type of sound, attempt to see when they occur and whether there is a spatial pattern to their occurrence. This can be done with combinations of sounds as well. Are there sounds that you find hard to locate? Why might this be the case? Are there sounds that are difficult to place in terms of distance? Again, why might this be so? Once you have done that with your selected sounds, can you add some of the other parameters we have visited before, such as loudness, pitch, how the sounds evolve in time, and so on?

Understanding and being able to articulate what makes that position special is part of the awareness development this chapter is seeking to address.

I was taught music traditionally and, understandably, space was not part of my musical study. It is hard to consider teaching people about sound-based music without placing spaces (venues, environments) and spatialisation (of sounds) in a prominent place in that curriculum. So much has changed. The word space has become so important to the vocabulary of sound-based music that one also speaks of the "inner space" of sounds, that is, their behaviour in time, something that belongs more to the sound quality discussion above than the current one. An

Internet search of "sound in space" and "sound and space" will lead to many sites related to sound-based music as the two go hand in hand in terms of sound-based musical thinking.

Simultaneity

The following four parameters are worthy of mention, but will not be discussed in the same detail as the others. Simultaneity and horizontal thinking (called layering in Chapter 5) go hand in hand and are analogous with what is traditionally called harmony and counterpoint.

Soundwalk activity Listen to a particular soundscape and focus on moments when more than one thing is happening sonically at the same moment or in rapid succession. Can you identify the sounds? Can you make associations between these sounds? When you hear the simultaneities, do they sound like two separate sounds or do they get fused into a new combined sound? Can you describe that sound and relate that sound quality or description to what you believe has been combined?

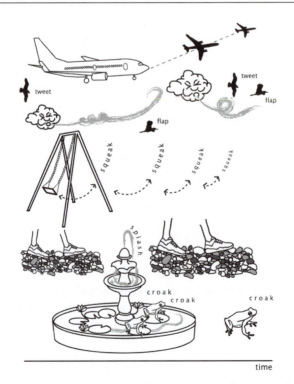

FIGURE 2.11   An evocative soundscape score demonstrating simultaneous sonic events

The parameter, simultaneity, concerns sounds heard at (virtually) the same time. In instrumental music one could say that this is a combination of pitch and density, our next parameter. In the case of sound-based music this concerns the conscious determination of what is allowed to happen simultaneously and where these are placed in time. Another aspect is to what extent the individual simultaneous sounds can be perceived as separate sounds or to what extent these sounds create composite new sounds that are created through their simultaneous audition. As this is not an obvious thing to do, predetermine simultaneities, I have decided to introduce it but not get into too much detail, as few will decide to use this extensively during the early stages of creative engagement with sounds.

Simultaneity and layering are going to prove to be very useful tools in terms of sound organisation. Works that evolve as a single voice tend to get rather boring. Being aware of how many sounds one can listen to at once before getting lost or, alternatively, turning those sounds into a fused new one is very important. Another way of discussing the presence of many sounds at once is by way of density.

Density

Some sonic environments may seem not only quiet but also sonically empty; others may involve so many sounds that it is hard to isolate or grab individual ones. Sometimes sounds occur so rapidly that they turn into one larger sound consisting of many smaller ones. The composer Iannis Xenakis was a propagandist of density and also the following parameter, order or disorder, in terms of music composition. He liked to formalise these elements in his works, but also used terms to describe density that are very useful to the current discussion, such as clouds of sounds and sound masses.

Soundwalk activity In diverse environments attempt to determine the evolution of the density of sound or of certain sounds that you hear. What ranges of density can you perceive and how do you best describe them or represent them in terms of the notation that you have been using? How do densities differ between the environments you have visited or within single environments at different times? How do they evolve in time? Stepping back from the detail, what influence does density have on the sonic environment to which you are listening and to what extent does it influence or even define what you hear?

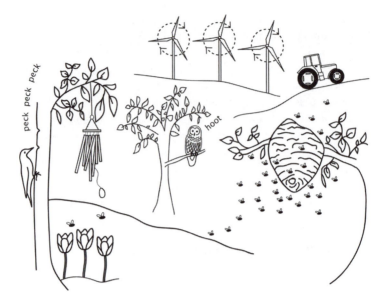

FIGURE 2.12 An evocative soundscape score including aspects related to density

(Dis)order

This parameter ranges from order to disorder and was an important element in Xenakis's music. He spoke of the amount or lack of entropy at a given moment in a given work or, in our case, sonic environment.

> *Soundscape activity* Sitting calmly in a given environment, what factors do you believe contribute to the orderliness of what you are hearing? Does this range from the recognisable to the anarchic (as I put it in the parameter article) or is there a better way of defining it? Does the amount of (dis)order evolve with time? How does this happen and what is the sonic result of change? What do you think the role is that this parameter plays in terms of the listening experience?

Recognisability of Sounds

This final parameter ranging from identifiable sounds to unrecognisable ones bridges a few gaps: that spanning the broad "grey area" between real-world sounds to more abstract ones and that spanning the area between contextual listening (where relevant) to pure musical listening. It will also form an important thread throughout the rest of this book.

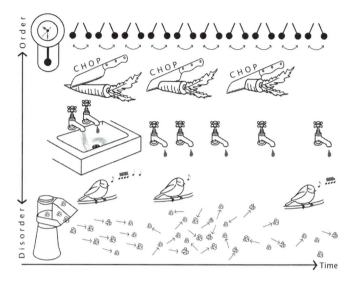

FIGURE 2.13   An evocative sound-based score focused on levels of order and disorder

Having introduced the notion of reduced listening, it has been the goal of many a sound-based music composer to obscure the origin of sounds as much as is feasible, thus making any given sound's source and cause unrecognisable. This can be done by way of sound manipulation or through the creation of new sounds *ex nihilo*. Neither is relevant to us at the moment, but it is nonetheless important to know that sound-based music concerns both recognisable and more abstract sounds and sound qualities. And there is, of course, the question concerning to what extent listeners are able to recognise sounds in the way a composer desires. This is of importance when investigating the loop between a musician's compositional intentions to the listener's reception back to the maker of the music so that (s)he can judge the success of a work through what is being heard. A musician may also create a sound that sounds like a real-world one, although the sound in question is generated synthetically.

Authors, of whom I shall name two, have created very useful vocabulary related to this subject. Simon Emmerson (1986) speaks of a dimension between mimetic and aural discourse, the one extreme based on recognisability and the other focusing on the sonic essence of what is heard. Denis Smalley (1997) has developed a number of levels of surrogacy from primal to remote related to the recognisability of source/cause, that is, the level of perceived transformation. In a sense, with this final parameter we leave the soundscape and need to enter the studio or digital music workplace.

But things are not as simple as they may seem, for most people will not recognise everything they hear during soundwalks and, in some cases, will not even be able to place a given sound into a broader sound type. If there is no experiential connection with a sound, it therefore is perceived as more abstract than a recognisable one. Although this subject will be one of the most important in the coming chapters, it is useful to introduce it more briefly in this introductory context.

Soundscape activity Going back to the sound source/sound type activity, were there any sounds at any locations where you were uncertain what they were? How did you describe them? Where did you place them or did you even simply set them aside? Return to one or more places you have visited (or a new one) and see whether there are any unidentifiable sounds and, if so, how do you best describe them? Are there any sounds where you think you know what they are, but are not completely certain? If so, how do you place such sounds: in one category, more than one or a category called "unsure", and why?

Beyond the Single Parameter and the Single Sound

It goes without saying that virtually everything we have been doing thus far is focused on the sound level or at very specific relationships between sounds. We have, nonetheless, also offered the possibility to transcribe or notate what we hear with regard to the parameters that have been introduced above. This part of the soundscape activities has a dual purpose: first to allow everyone the ability to imagine how it is best to translate an aural experience into a visual one, one not solely dependent on words. It also allows us to have an overview of what is heard and therefore look beyond the single sound or simple sonic relationship to longer durations that might parallel the notions of gesture or phrase in traditional note-based music. When we are able to segment music in this manner, we take the next step in time to looking at larger-scale structural issues. These longer time spans will form the focus of Chapters 4 and 5. Clearly, sonic environments will not normally demonstrate structures similar to those musical ones we learn at school, ranging from canons to verse and refrains to sonatas and fugues, and so on. Still, there are identifiable patterns in nature that go beyond the few seconds of a given bird call.

Soundscape activity 1 Go back to the scores that you have made thus far or, alternatively, go to a sonic environment and create a score that will allow you to discover the behaviour of sounds across time. It will most likely be difficult to speak of sections of the soundscape of certain durations as nature does not normally work that way, but some sounds may consist of separable elements. If you are in an urban environment, sections could be determined by a traffic light, for example. This activity is simply to whet the appetite for similar listening-based discoveries of sound-based works later on. Is there something that you have discovered that works like a musical phrase? Which sounds were involved? Which were not involved?

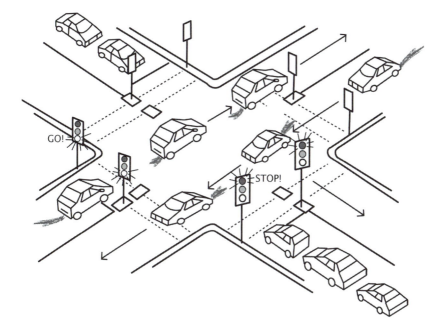

FIGURE 2.14

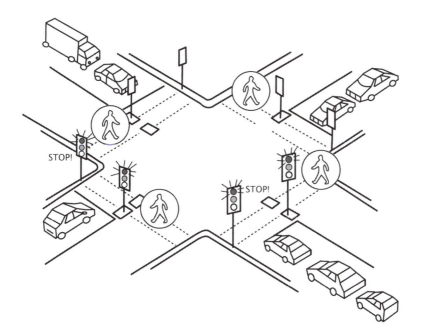

FIGURE 2.15

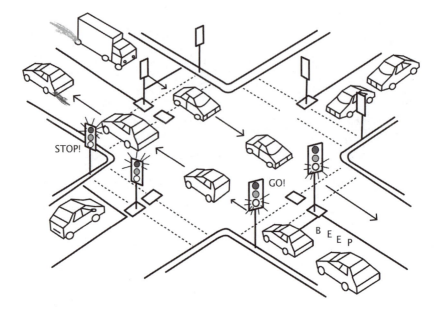

FIGURE 2.13–2.16   Three images representing the time-based structure of an urban soundscape

Soundscape activity 2 This activity may get a few younger people's laughing muscles moving as the aim here is to see to what extent we can vocalise the sounds that we have heard/are hearing. The voice is, after the computer, the most versatile instrument in the world. We have attempted to describe sounds in words and in images. Why not attempt to better understand them through vocalising them? For example, a group can choose a number of sounds in a sonic environment and perform them, as would a choir. This exercise may be seen to be silly by some, but some excellent reconstructions of environmental sounds have been made in this manner and everyone taking the trouble to participate knows a bit more about: a) what type of sound qualities are involved, and b) how these sounds actually do relate to each other.

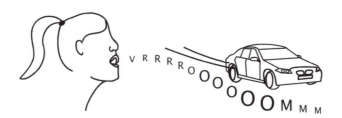

FIGURE 2.17   The voice can simulate almost any sound

Many music students at conservatoires and in universities dread to be asked to analyse a musical work, finding analysis too dry. However, much music is a treasure chest with loads of jewels to be discovered. Often the composer is not even aware of some of the jewels for which (s)he is responsible. The more we understand how music fits together, even that music one can hear by opening a window, the more one becomes aware of the multitude of creative opportunities offered by this wonderful art form. That has been the goal of this chapter's sound-scape activities thus far. Let's now move on to some thoughts regarding creativity related to sonic environments.

Composing Soundscapes

With the necessary resources, how might one compose a soundscape? It is inter-esting to note that some soundscape artists make a clear distinction between works involving shared knowledge (based on a specific place and made for people who have visited that place) and soundscape works for anyone. As defined in the book's glossary, we might speak of soundscape compositions being related to "actual environments, or . . . abstract constructions such as musical compositions."

Some will consider it a bit too simplistic to present an actual environment as a composition, although this is exactly what Max Neuhaus and others have done. In such works they brought listeners to a specific site, asked them to listen and thus presented the result as a composition.Alternatively, it is possible to make an excellent recording of a site and simply play it back somewhere else, again pre-senting the audition of the recording as a composition. Inevitably some may not find either of the two worthy of the name "music," but we have been through that particular debate already. These are examples of non-intervention in terms of soundscape material. This is, of course, not the only option.

I have sometimes had a few instruments perform in a given site material that was rather minimal and sparse. The reason for this was to allow listeners to pay more attention to the sounds of the site itself, as people's listening was clearly made active for the performance. In a sense my composition interrupted the soundscape or, alternatively, became part of it, as was my intention.

This is but one of many ways of composing soundscapes. Use sounds from one or more sonic environments and create a new one from that material; create sounds in order to organise them into what we have called imaginary sound-scapes, that is, mix the two.

It is a bit premature to start discussing exactly how this is done through using technology. That is all to come. We therefore should limit ourselves to the acous-tic world of soundwalks or performances at specific sites for the moment.

What is perhaps most interesting at this point is an activity related to all of those above allowing you to use your imagination in terms of what you might like to apply creatively, taking into account what we have learned thus far. This will be a means to get our toes wet in terms of sound-based creativity; this also forms

Final Chapter 2 activities 1 The two parts of this activity are based on sound-walks and site-specific installations or performances.

Soundwalks Some readers will have made their first soundwalks on account of their reading this book. After being initiated into the art of aural awareness through the activities in this chapter, the time has come to turn around the roles. You choose where to take some friends, family members, students and ask them to listen to the sonic environment of the site where you have gone. Once they are used to the sounds that envelop them, what would you like them to focus upon? If your public enjoys the sounds they hear, how would you approach the delicate discussion concerning what is musical about what they are hearing and, based on the responses, whether this is in fact music itself?

If you have the time to try this out on different types of people, see how they react and why. What is often very interesting is how individuals build up a sense of a sonic environment and how they react to it. When discussing these experiences with others, some of the individuals' ideas become influenced by others' experiences and a more consensual view of the majority, if not all of the participants, might evolve regarding what was heard.

Similarly, taking people to different environments may lead to different types of reactions and some of these reactions will be based on what you ask them to focus on as well as how much at ease they are with the sounds that they hear. For example, if a given environment is loud or contains a good deal of noise, then more people are likely to experience alienation alongside the excitement of becoming aware of some of the things about which you are enthusiastic.

Site specific installations or performances In this second case there are two options. You can write a description of an installation or a score for a performance or, more ambitiously, you can actually create an installation to be placed in a sonic environment or organise a sound-based performance at a given site. The installation should involve sonic objects that will produce sounds based on the behaviour of the environment, such as objects forced to produce sounds by the wind. In the case of a performance, musicians can produce sounds that take place at specified times in specified places.

If actually realising short pieces, they should be tried out beforehand and developed based on how successfully you and others find the installation, the placement of musicians, the score's realisation. An important attitude to have, particularly at this phase of our journey in sound organisation, is that one need not complete "perfect" works, but instead see how pieces or studies evolve as you try things out and evaluate them.

Questions to keep in mind include: are the sounds you are using effective? Do the sound qualities mix well with the local sonic environment? Are there factors that are outside your control (e.g., the weather) that (might) influence the success of these designs or works? If musicians are involved, what do they think of what you are producing together? They are, along with you, your first audience after all. What would you have to change if you did this at a similar site, that is, what is unique about this one?

For those who have the time to do this more than once, did you notice any patterns in your approach or in the sounds that you have chosen that are similar? This may have to do with things that are particularly of interest to you and might be worth keeping in mind in terms of future creative opportunities.

Final Chapter 2 activities 2 Imagine that you had access to any technology you might need to compose a soundscape. What would you use? (If you do not know the answer to this, don't worry. You will, after working through the possibilities in the next few chapters.)

Regardless of your ability to choose the technology you need, create a score or a storyboard that is intended to help you construct an imaginary soundscape. What types of sounds or sound recordings might you need? Would you involve either installed objects or people performing objects or would everything be recorded? Would you want to create new sounds? If so, how would you do so and how might they fit in? Would you want to manipulate sounds and, if so, what would you want to achieve? How would you like to combine the sounds that you have recorded or that are at your disposition and place them in sequences? What type of approach might you follow to structure the sounds and longer recorded segments that you have? Would this approach in any way be influenced by how you listened to patterns in sonic environments? How would you spatialise the sounds if you had the ability to do so, or would you prefer to make a stereo recording like the ones that you are familiar with?

What is "real" about what you plan to make and what is imaginary? Are there any parameters introduced above that will prove to be particularly useful here and, if so, why?

Where would be the best place to present such a work? Given the ease in terms of ability to use computers to create and change works, would you consider asking your listeners to remark on what they heard and possibly to change things?

our final group of activities of Chapter 2. Our next step in Chapter 3 will be to select, record, generate and manipulate sounds for creative use.

Remember, this is only a very first try and the goal is to identify what you would do when you start with a clean slate and infinite possibilities. The challenge may seem daunting, but once a couple of puzzle pieces are discovered and put in place, others seem to appear naturally afterwards. If that did not happen this time,

An ice cap slowly cracks and is sustained with reverb for over a minute.
At 0.15, a coconut falls from a palm tree which bounces and then rolls around on the ground.
The bounces echo into the distance while a snowmobile revs its engine at 0.30, getting louder
as it makes wide circles before taking a sharp right over the snow at 1.15. A swam of bees pans right
to left for 45 seconds and chirps of cicadas from 0.45 increase in loudness and quickly die away.

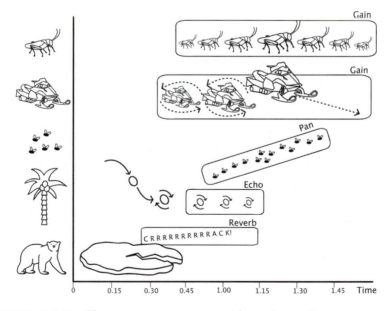

FIGURE 2.18–2.20   Three ways to notate a potential soundscape piece

it certainly will as a consequence of the introduction of means of creating sounds and ordering them in the following chapters. In any case, it is difficult to imagine a work without hearing it, and many readers will not have the knowledge and perhaps the means to realise their pieces quite yet. Ideally, some basic resources will be available to you as we progress, as that is all that is needed to achieve great results within the realm of sound-based music. These initial activities were provided to demonstrate that there are many similar processes involved between understanding a sonic environment and creating a new one. This is not unlike the fact that the research that went into my being able to write this book is hardly different from the way I do much of my creative work in sound-based music. Once we know how we think about things, listen to things and act creatively in terms of sound, we are involved with a greater understanding, not only about sound-based music, but also about ourselves.

3

THE SOUNDS OF
SOUND-BASED MUSIC

As we commence this third chapter, we move from a more contextual and aware-ness-based discussion to a focus on creativity. Chapters 3 to 5 represent a three-stage learning experience based on work at the sound level increasing up to the achievement of entire sound-based pieces. Creativity is not an isolated experi-ence. It involves a lovely combination of knowledge, awareness, analytical insight and imagination. Therefore, these three chapters continue to develop context and awareness whilst offering a variety of opportunities to be creative. The three chapters are dependent on one another. It might be useful to look at them all briefly before embarking upon some of the activities in greater detail.

In this chapter we shall start by imagining why one chooses some sounds above others when collecting sound materials for a piece of sound-based music when there are so many to choose from. After making these initial decisions, the ques-tion is, where best to find them? Can they be recorded or eventually downloaded online? Do they need to be generated synthetically? (Note, in some cases, this may not be an easy option.) Once our basic selection strategy is in place, we move up one notch by offering the option to tamper with the sounds, that is, sculpt or mould them. This is known as sound manipulation. As we are playing with words a bit, I have been known to say, when working on particular projects, that I move between the roles of sound hunter, sound designer, sound organiser and sound spatialiser. They are by no means independent; it is simply a question of focus at a given moment, all part of the creative involvement in sound-based music.

Finding Real-World Sounds

Not everyone making sound-based music is going to want to use sounds from our daily lives, but it is these sounds—as well as artificial sounds that sound like real-world sounds—that allow listeners to make connections with lived experience most easily. Real-world sounds were the focus of the previous chapter; they are also an excellent starting point for this one focused on choosing sounds for your music.

Let's jump into this subject with a bold statement: any sound is potentially useful within a musical context. In other words, when deciding to organise sounds, the question is not which sounds are and are not musical, but instead which sounds potentially possess the sonic or contextual characteristics, in the sense of musical or contextual listening, that are useful for the piece you intend to make?

Those characteristics were exactly what we have been attempting to identify in the activities in the previous chapter. It might have to do with a sonic quality, loudness, duration, another quality or a combination of two or more of these. A sound source might be specifically related to a given environment, grain-like, percussive, pitched, related to utterance or related to any other particular quality being sought.

Of course what is being described assumes that one already is aware of what one plans to achieve in a given sound organisation. Although this is an excellent goal, and the only way to fly in terms of the approach to learning as far as this book is concerned, it must be admitted that many people working in sound-based music simply collect a number of potentially interesting sounds and see what they can do with them. This is what might be called "bottom-up composition". Its counterpart, "top-down (also known as architectonic) composition", begins with a sense of a work's duration, its structure and so on and fills it in with content. We will work somewhere in the vast grey area in the middle as the serendipity involved in total bottom-up composition can normally only succeed after one has built up a substantial experience base. Top-down composition, on the other hand, might work easily in note-based composition—think of anything from a verse/refrain structure to sonatas and fugues—but in our case, there are few structures that are used by many musicians due to the lack of any given structure's proven track record. In other words, sound-based music exists largely as a phenomenon in which carefully chosen materials are moulded together, sequenced and layered into a well-structured entity, that is, more bottom-up than top-down. We shall discover that formalised types of composition introduced briefly in Chapter 5 can, in certain cases, be considered to be a key exception. We shall be working in this way in almost all cases throughout the rest of the book. As suggested, some will find that this means of working can easily lead to surprising results. Although this is indeed true, the current goal is to build up your ability to predict bottom-up behaviour.

As it is assumed that readers, or their students, have no experience making sound-based music, it is useful to create a miniature etude's storyboard to get the ball rolling. This will form the first activity of Chapter 3.

Sounds of sound-based music storyboard activity In Chapter 2 we made various forms of evocative notations and lists to describe what we heard. This time, the idea is to create a storyboard, that is, a description of a scenario, for a short sound-based musical study. Although the focus of this chapter is choosing materials, in this activity we can think in broad terms of what is evolving in time and, consequently, what *types* or *qualities* of material are needed, that is, sound sources, and eventually how they are made to sound. The choice of sounds should take advantage of those that you should be able to record should you have recording equipment available. For those who do not have this equipment, don't worry. We shall propose an alternative below. Adventurers amongst you can even try to put something together regardless of the fact that we have yet to introduce many key means of sequencing sound materials, but that is by no means necessary at this point. We shall have plenty of chances to do so in the coming pages.

This miniature should last for between one and two minutes. It should demonstrate some sort(s) of dynamic evolution, not restricting itself to one type of sound ambience throughout. How might you achieve this sort of evolution? You can evolve from one point to another gradually, make subtle or sharp contrasts or find other means of differentiation such as altering the focus from one parameter or sound type to another.

In terms of notation, what is the best way of symbolising your ideas? Do they involve text, representational and/or abstract images? How do you symbolise aspects of the sound such as register, loudness, etc. whenever relevant?

The number of sounds heard at a given moment might be important, as might sound density, general register, rhythmical information and so on. How might you best notate this information effectively without writing out a fully notated score?

Please note that this storyboard should not be overly ambitious. In the next activity you will be asked to acquire sounds that are related to this storyboard, so, again, you should choose sounds that you believe you will be able to record or eventually download. (For more on acquiring sounds over the Internet, see the following discussion.)

There are several advantages to a storyboard approach, in particular at this stage of the introduction. They are dynamic and can be easily altered. They allow for a good deal of freedom in terms of specific detail when translating them into a piece. They offer a good sense of the types and qualities of materials that are needed without overly prescribing exactly what is called for. The fact is that we do not always have access to every sound we might put down on a storyboard or a prescriptive score. Therefore, having the freedom to select something from

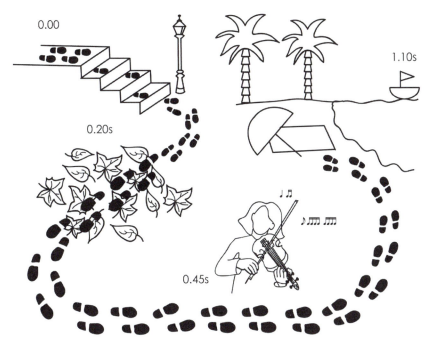

FIGURE 3.1 A potential storyboard

a group of options allows for greater experimentation offering an easier choice when there are few sounds readily available. The notion of a group of options is analogous to what we were doing in the awareness chapter, that is, bringing sounds together into groups due to their shared properties. Here we are looking for properties and then can choose from a group of eligible sounds.

Using today's vocabulary, we can speak of sound samples when we isolate one of these sounds. Traditionally they have also been known as sound sources and Schaeffer spoke of sound or musical objects in his theoretical writings. We will be able to mix samples or even remix them once used, place them in sequences or layer them vertically in time, play with their durations, dynamics, and the like and even manipulate them, perhaps even to the point that they become unrecognisable. For the purposes of this initial activity, the focus is on their remaining in their original state. This is important, as there are many circumstances in sound-based music where the original recording is preferable to one that has been altered by way of any of a number of effects.

Recording (or Downloading) Sounds

So far you have been asked to use your imagination in terms of creative aspects in our activities. We come closer to planet earth now as we introduce the manner of gaining access to our sounds, through recording them or by way of the Internet.

This is the first point where the alternatives suggested in Chapter 1 come into play. It cannot be assumed that everyone reading this text or being taught by one of its readers has access to a microphone or a number of microphones as well as something on which to make recordings. If this option is open to you, this presents the opportunity to select your sounds locally, not to mention the opportunity to learn about the recording process and strategic decisions associated with it. For those who do not have access to this technology, fear not! In today's world, where the word "copyleft" has entered our vocabulary as the opposite of the better-known "copyright", we can access sounds recorded by others who have not requested that these sounds fall under copyright law. In fact, the organisation called Creative Commons (creativecommons.org) is very useful in this regard, helping users understand the differences between copyright and copyleft and everything in between.

To start with the case where no recording equipment is on offer, inevitably one is most likely dependent on what can be found online. Fortunately the Internet is for sharing and there are many sounds that have been placed online for other users to download and use as they wish. Beyond the fact that it does limit what one uses, there is another potential hitch, again one that can usually be overcome. The quality of sounds can vary enormously, so some sounds that are downloadable might not sound as crisp as one might like. This may or may not be an issue depending on what you plan to do with the sound, of course. Not only that, but many novices end up making noisy recordings as they are not using the correct microphones, or are holding them up too close or too far from the intended source, or have the levels on the recording equipment too high or too low, or the equipment itself might not be good enough for what is needed. You will have to be the judge of sound quality for this and all similar activities.

We cannot be too idealistic about the sounds we can obtain. Having said that, high-quality sounds are available online; it is also true that high-quality equipment is becoming less and less expensive with time. More importantly, this process of listening and monitoring quality will increase your aural awareness, both in terms of your own music and your listening to anything else as well.

Let's look at an example, the Freesound Project based in Barcelona. On this site (www.freesound.org) you can search for samples or try to find them through popular tags. Tags can be generic, more specific or even geographic. There is a search engine within the site as well. Here you can specify sounds fairly narrowly and, if wished, include information about the sound quality as well. Typical of recent sites, users provide feedback about sounds, thus allowing other users to discover whether they have been highly rated. One should be careful about this as the reasons why they are highly rated may have something to do with quality as well as personal taste regardless of the quality. Naturally, freesound is but one of many such initiatives, and more will join them in the future. What is wonderful about this is how the Internet has provided people with a magnificent means of sharing information, in this case audio files of specific sounds or sound qualities that have been of use to those who recorded or made them and are offered to others to reuse, remix, rediscover and, as we move forward in this chapter, sculpt towards our own creative goals.

For those able to record, at least one microphone and recording equipment of any medium is needed. In this case we need to know whether we are trying to capture a sound or a sound in space, the difference being between a monaural and a multichannel recording, the latter of which involves more (expensive) equipment. We are all used to the standard of stereophonic sound. This means that in many cases making a mono recording might be disadvantageous. For those who have had the luxury of hearing multichannel playback, for example surround sound in a cinema, stereo seems like an historical compromise. The purpose of this book is simply to get things going. Readers who, like me, discover the magic of making music with sounds, equipment needs may increase with time. Amongst these changes, the means of making recordings may grow. I have seen colleagues go out into natural settings as we did in the previous chapter with cases full of different types of microphones and recording equipment—increasingly using laptops for recording—so that they can capture an ambience from as many angles as possible. Most people just go out with a stereo microphone or two mono microphones. Then there are those who try to capture surround sound in stereo on binaural★ microphones. This is a very special, although not a very well-known, manner of capturing sounds in space as a microphone is placed near each or one's ears, which together register the entire listening space in such a manner that the listener hears the recording as if (s)he were where the person who made the recording was. To listen back to binaural recordings, headphones are needed, which does limit their application, at least currently.

There is much to learn about microphone techniques and some people have a university-level degree in making optimal recordings in classical music, popular music or outdoor field recording circumstances. For now, the most important thing to say is: try to avoid equipment that will compromise the quality of the recordings you make. Once you have the equipment, try to make several recordings of your target sound taking into account sound levels, position (distance, angle) of the microphone, whether it needs to be covered due to outdoor wind and so on.

Recording/downloading activity In this activity sounds are to be collected either by recording them, downloading them or both. The sounds should correspond to those that were selected in the previous activity in which storyboards were created.

This is possibly one of the more challenging activities, as you will likely find it useful to record or download several sounds related to yours to ensure they have the right qualities that you are seeking. This may have to do with duration, sound quality or anything else. It may also have to do with the quality of the recording that you make or download.

Where you do not succeed, try and try again. If you seem unable to get exactly the sound you like, this may have to do with any number of reasons such as: the context of the recording is not right or even the weather conditions; you cannot find exactly what you are seeking online; the equipment you are using does not neatly or easily achieve the sound quality you are seeking; you are looking for a sound that is so specific that it may be hard to find, etc.

Without embarking on a sophisticated training course in recording, which would take us on a lengthy detour, the reality of give and take is the easiest path towards achievement. Alter the storyboard to take into account that which is feasible and try to stay as close to your goals as is possible. Art making is not a hard science; therefore, artists are always looking towards optimal solutions and recording/finding these sounds is just one part of doing as well as can be done in given circumstances.

Once you have collected the sounds, it is time to listen to them over and over again to become better acquainted with them in terms of what they represent on your storyboard and their individual sonic qualities. Although we are not going to experiment with these sounds quite yet, what is fascinating is that, once recorded or otherwise acquired, sounds can spark off new ideas, thus altering things that one originally planned to do with them. For example, perhaps you thought about placing some sounds into a specific context, but after listening to them, the context seems too obvious. You therefore think to place them in a (slightly) different one, thus making the combination of detail and context a bit more surreal. That can add a bit of interest to your sound organisation due to its being unusual, but also may add to its overall sonic impact. When we start combining sounds, even more options will start to open up. This leads to another challenge: when to say "Enough!" once the options start piling up.

Don't forget to name all of the sounds that you are collecting and keep a list of these names with special information (such as duration and particular sound quality aspects) so that you can easily retrieve them. It is one thing to write C-sharp in a high octave played legato at a forte dynamic for two beats and it is another to have a few hundred short sound files that have not been efficiently classified or grouped.

Don't worry if you have not found everything that you sought in this activity or that the sound quality of some of your recordings was not as you wished. Practice will make perfect and a better understanding of what you can achieve with the equipment you possess will certainly inform your proposals in the future. This is all part of the learning experience.

FIGURE 3.2–3.3 Learning where to place your microphone(s) can sometimes be challenging

Special Case: Sounds that Sound like Notes or Groups of Notes

The term "C-sharp" came up just two paragraphs ago. It is important to note at this phase of the chapter that, in sound-based music, sounds that sound like notes or groups of notes may appear or play a significant role. This implies that a given piece might be placed somewhere along the right-hand side of the scale between note-based and sound-based works. Just like the fact that hip hop artists look for the perfect drum break to insert into their scratching, we may just want to have snippets from note-based music or qualities derived from this music enter into our sound-based musical world. In extreme cases, where all material comes from the note world and the composition techniques are taken from sound-based music, I have often spoken of "music-based music" such as can be discovered in the world of plunderphonics, that is, music found at the middle of that scale.

The use of the voice or of music in a sound-based context as defined in Chapter 1 is a powerful tool as there is an immediacy of communication normally in such cases, mainly by way of familiarity, but also potentially by way of emotional reactions. Of course, this can happen with anything, but we have very intimate relationships with certain types of music and the smallest snippet or the briefest vocal utterance can trigger a number of possible reactions based on the listener's previous experience.

Therefore the use of notes or sounds which are heard as notes (any percussive sound, for example, played as one would hear percussion instruments played rhythmically) can easily be integrated into a sound-based context and play a significant role in terms of what is being communicated and/or experienced. It is when the notes start playing more traditional musical roles that the means of listening trip from one engaged with sound organisation to one related to note-based music. Many pieces will quite consciously slip between one and the other, and why not? What we are to discover here is organisation focused on sounds that are, in general, not notes. Once we gain some expertise in this, the challenges posed by moving from one to the other can be added to the many options that are introduced in this book.

For now, the main point to be shared is that note-like material can indeed be included in a sound-based work and, therefore, such recordings may be included on a storyboard. Key to the employment of fragments of music is the intention related to how recognisable they are to be due to the potential power related to their being used. (This could happen as well with the spoken word where the manner of speaking might well be less important in terms of the reception of the content than the words presented to the listener.)

This is a special case for which no activity is being suggested at this point as it may only confuse our progressive journey together. The aim of these paragraphs is to create an awareness of how mixing elements related to note-based and to sound-based music can affect the listening experience and, more poignantly, how using music known to the listener—ideally without copyright infringement—can enhance the listening experience, but it can also potentially derail it, too. In short, proceed with caution when using notes, musical samples and even the human voice.

Synthetic Sounds

The final two sections of this chapter take us directly into some of the most sophisticated and exciting aspects of how technology can influence sounds. The chronology is simple: we shall commence by discussing how sounds can be generated using technology and then move on to how we can manipulate both recorded and synthesised sounds technologically.

This first of the two subjects is perhaps the most difficult subject to introduce in this book as to do it well involves gaining a great deal of knowledge that goes for beyond the book's remit, in particular knowledge related to the field of the acoustical properties of sound. In fact, other than the Norwegian Centre for Technology in Music and the Arts, NoTAM's project in which digital signal processing is introduced to children (DSP for Children information page and Rudi 2007) and the Sound Organiser, I am not aware of anyone who has tried to tackle this subject in a user-friendly manner for beginners. Most introductions to synthesis are like the volume written by Miller Puckette (2007), involving high-level mathematics as part of the foundation for understanding synthesis.

Regardless of this worry concerning the complexity of the subject, the fact of the matter is that any sound can be created synthetically. Still, it is actually quite difficult to achieve the richness of an acoustic sound in this manner. Only the most experienced are able to construct such sounds "from scratch." Synthetic sounds are perhaps best known to us as the sounds we hear produced by most synthesisers today, not to mention on our computer games, many of today's toys and mobile phones. There are several other devices that use synthetic sounds.

There is an assumption regarding sound synthesis, namely, that the maker of such sounds is aware of what (s)he is doing. This need for detailed knowledge is in dire contrast to today's society in which instant gratification or at least understanding is almost assumed. It comes as no surprise that the famous book series has yet to offer a volume entitled *Digital Signal Processing for Dummies*, due to the amount that needs to be learned to achieve a high level of understanding regarding how synthesis works and consequently how to create sounds knowledgeably.

With all of this in mind, a user-friendly introduction will be provided here. For those readers who are interested in pursuing this subject further, literature in the areas of acoustics and sound generation and manipulation, our following subject, is plentiful.

Sounds can be created from the bottom up, from the top down, by way of the modelling of acoustic information, and by using interesting tricks or shortcuts also related to acoustics. Let's go through this list step by step.

Bottom-Up Synthesis

The unit measure in acoustics is the sine wave, a simple and pure sound that can be perceived as dull, or even shrill, to the listener depending on its pitch. Theoretically, every sound we hear can be reduced to one or (many) more sine waves piled up on top of one another. Their individual amplitude levels vary in time. The sine tone generator or oscillator was the piece of apparatus that traditionally was used to produce such sounds. However, if you want to make a complex sound such as that of the violin, the voice, leaves rustling and so on, you would need many dynamic oscillators, and in the case of the noisier sounds, the bow rubbing on the violin string, the sound of leaves moving in the wind, hundreds of oscillators. Thank goodness that digital technology has made this possible. Just like our CDs, a computer can create a sound consisting of several thousands of pieces of data every second that are perceived by the listener as a continuity (similar to the images projected in a film or on television, but the resolution needed by the ear in time is much higher than that of the eye in order to perceive continuity).

The main form of sound generation associated with this approach of piling up sine waves, or in some cases other types of waves, is known as additive synthesis★. It is at this point that I must insert a few words based on personal experience. Having discussed fairly "rich" sounds thus far throughout the book, I can assure

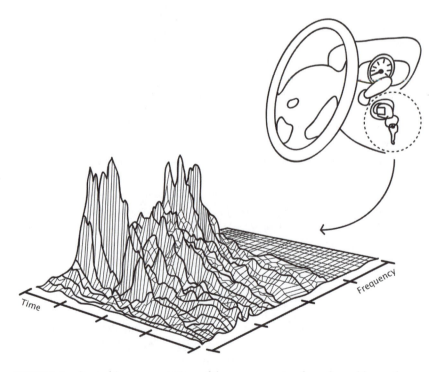

FIGURE 3.4 A graphic representation of the components of a real-world sound

you that I have heard extremely rich sounds, whether similar to real-world sounds or totally new, made in this manner. Some of these sounds have been generated serendipitously; most, however, are based on a thorough understanding of the acoustic principles of the sound that one is trying to construct or emulate. This is a laborious and, eventually, gratifying task. As said, what would need to be acquired in terms of the acoustic and even psychoacoustic bases of sound, the latter focused on how we perceive and hear things, is fairly substantial and is based on information that this introductory book need not offer.

To get through the negatives as quickly as possible, there is another potential problem for readers, namely, the choice of software to use when embarking on your first experience of additive synthesis. Although my intention as author has been to avoid naming alternatives in this book, thus time stamping its contents, an exception will be made here. The ultimate program able to do a vast variety of forms of synthesis is called Csound, the C representing the computer language in which it was programmed. This freely available software demands a complete understanding of what the user wants to construct. This program, the name of which has evolved since the 1960s, is well over forty years old at the time of this book's being written, demonstrating its robustness, and it continues to be taught internationally as well as avoided like the plague by many sound-based musicians due to the demands it places on its users. At the other extreme, the DSP for Children package, which is also free, is user friendly relatively speaking, but unable to handle hugely sophisticated additive synthesis tasks in comparison with Csound. For example, the number of oscillators and what they are tuned to are limited at any given moment, which is completely understandable in the context. As the children's package is a dynamic pioneering venture, as this book hopes to be in tandem with its associated website, it is uncertain how long it will continue to be developed and maintained. Technology evolves so rapidly; one can never be certain what the shelf life is of anything one uses. Between the children's package and Csound there are commercial programs that are intended for evolving musicians and professionals, but they often come at a cost. Two examples currently that offer a form of additive synthesis are Audiomulch and Reason. One need not be an advanced acoustics specialist to use these, but again, this comes with limitations, such as the lack of ability to enter in as much detail as a particular sound might need. Such programs are most useful in terms of searching to develop sounds that possess certain qualities that are difficult or impossible to achieve in any other way.

Additive synthesis activity As we are on a bridge between increasing awareness and working creatively with sounds and given the fact that it is uncertain which tools you may be using for this activity, the objective is quite modest. If you are able to synthesise sounds additively, try to create three or four short sounds and one or two longer ones that blend well. The sounds may be quite different or quite similar. The means of noticing whether they blend well is to allow them to be heard in a very short fragment of, say, ten seconds. During this time the shorter sounds can be repeated in some sort of pattern and the longer ones may be the context within which the shorter sounds are heard.

One idea that you might like to try out is to have the shorter sounds create a rhythmical pattern or, if possible, have their pitch changed. For the more adventurous, you can alter the sound quality of some of these sounds each time they reappear.

How would you describe or classify each of these sounds? Can you make a score to represent how you have put them together? Naturally, if you were able to place the sounds into a sequence, the software you used also created a score for you.

What types of decisions did you make when making and choosing your sounds? What were you looking for? What did you reject and why? How did you determine that the sounds blended well?

Every aspect of sound-based music is a world in itself and this one form of synthesis could keep someone busy and interested for life. We are therefore only barely touching the surface here. As we shall discover below, additive synthesis can be used when modelling acoustical phenomena, such as an instrument or any other sound, be it with great difficulty and not always leading towards a totally convincing result. For the time being, it is best to create sounds that do not sound like anything familiar; our sampling will take care of capturing our real-world sounds.

Before moving on to the next type of synthesis, one exceptional form of bottom-up sound generation is worthy of mention. It is synthesis based on what is known as microsound. One relatively well-known case of microsound is called granular synthesis. How this works is very intriguing. Although both additive synthesis and microsound have foundations in acoustics, the latter can be much more intuitive in terms of its musical application. The principle is this: create masses of tiny sounds, sounds so short that they cannot be perceived as individual sounds by humans. Present these tiny sounds, measured in milliseconds ($1/1000$ of a second) but longer than the single pieces of data used on CDs and digital recordings, in such quantities that a sound quality is built out of the collection and development of minute particle sounds.

Granular synthesis can use synthetic sounds or tiny pieces or grains of a sampled or recorded sound. Still, its principle is to create sounds from the bottom upwards, although in this case up is not solely vertical, but instead part of the means of creating sound masses from microsounds.

There are several freeware and shareware programs for synthesis based on microsounds. Some take a sound file and break it up into many tiny sounds; others allow the user to create these sounds from scratch and subsequently create

FIGURE 3.5   An evocative representation of microsound

sound masses. What results is normally a fairly homogeneous sound quality that characterises microsound-based synthesis.

Top-Down Synthesis

If the sine wave is the basic unit in acoustics, its opposite would have to be noise, as some forms of noise possess sound at virtually all frequencies. The notion of top-down synthesis is to take a very complex signal, often a form of noise, and reduce it to the sound quality that you seek. The most common form of reduction is through the use of one or more filters, something that we shall discuss at greater length in the next section of this chapter focused on various means of sound manipulation. As we shall discover, filters allow us to reduce high- and/or low-pitch information related to a sound or bands of information within a sound. This type of sound generation, known as subtractive synthesis★, normally is most effective when combinations of filters are linked together to treat a given complex sound in order to create and mould a resultant sound that possesses a (dynamic) rich sound quality. Similar to granular synthesis, subtractive synthesis is a more intuitive way of creating sounds. As the various types of filters have yet to be properly introduced, activities related to top-down synthesis will be included later in this chapter.

Synthesis through Modelling

The ability to generate sounds by way of modelling will be presented briefly for the sake of completeness, as this is truly an advanced topic. The understandings involved in this type of sound synthesis often rely not only on acoustics know-ledge but high-level mathematics as well—that is, it is something to aspire to, not to commence with. Many readers have heard digital voices in various aspects of their life. In some cases you may have heard pre-recorded voices that have been digitised and are heard at a reasonably high sound quality. Fortunately speech synthesis★ has become increasingly sophisticated over the years. The amount of information needed to hear digitised speech clearly is fairly high, so what we hear in some cheaper toys, for example, can make your hair stand on end. Nonetheless, we are able to simulate the complex activities of the human voice speaking and singing digitally, which is the result of a huge amount of research.

Similarly, through something generally known as physical modelling★, key characteristics of particular sound types and sounds are studied and simulated by way of a relevant form of synthesis, including additive synthesis. Physical-modelled sounds range from tones of, say, brass instruments to any number of sound types in our daily lives.

Analogous to physical modelling, sounds can be analysed in terms of what their constituent sounds are and then synthesised. This approach is called analysis/resynthesis★. The alert reader will be wondering: why bother analysing a sound and (re-)building it? There are, of course, commercial applications for these things and furthermore it leads to greater understandings concerning sound and how sounds evolve in time. For those involved in creativity, I would suggest that being able to build something real and then make something surreal or impossible (in the sense that without technology the resultant sound could not exist) out of it can be gratifying and great fun to listen to.

Synthesis Applying Other Acoustical Phenomena

In the history of digital sound, it did not take very long before it was discovered how intensive the calculations were that were needed when one was involved with, for example, additive synthesis. We must remember that at this time, the 1960s and 1970s, there was no such thing as a fast PC. People at my university in the mid-1970s only got to use the university's computer in the middle of the night as the sound synthesis calculations took up a great deal of its memory and thus we were given one of the lowest priorities. How things have changed!

To make things more efficient, people attempted to find new means of synthesising sound that were effective but less intensive. One of those attempts, one made famous on early digital synthesisers, such as the well-known DX7, is called FM or frequency modulation synthesis★. The musician John Chowning invented this form of synthesis by having a few simple sounds influencing one another and in so doing a host of new, complex sounds evolved. Here one signal is modulating another. When done slowly and with a low frequency, the result is a vibrato. Some FM sounds found on the DX7 were quite lifelike, such as the synthetic metal bell and some of the wood-like sounds. Others were only

FIGURE 3.6   An example of how cross-synthesis might work

approximations of what was being emulated. For many years, listeners became hugely accustomed to the sound of "presets", that is industry-provided sound types found on the synthesisers. Such presets offered on synthesisers during that period and afterwards represented a great advance and a step towards affordability, but also led to compromise by those musicians who could not take the time to master the potential of FM in order to create more successful, personal sounds beyond those preset sound qualities. FM synthesis is one of many alternative means of sound generation based on principles related to acoustics.

Another way of applying influence is known as cross-synthesis★, where one aspect of a sound, for example pitch or loudness, is used to influence an aspect of another one, albeit not necessarily the same one. Think, for example, of the pitch of the song of a bird being used to influence the amplitude of a sound with which you are working.

Some Interesting Alternatives

Before leaving this exciting yet somewhat complicated world of creating your own sounds, there is one user-friendly approach that deserves mention. The same Xenakis who was called upon in the parameters discussion was also responsible for the creation of a system called UPIC. This is a system in which the person designing a sound draws on a tablet that can read the input information. The further analysis of what the drawing represents is done by the computer. Many users of the UPIC system have created dynamic, somewhat noise-based sound worlds. This is consistent with Xenakis's personal goal to be creating new sounds all the time. This system evolved to accept sampled sounds as the basis of the user's input manipulation, but originally it was envisioned for the generation and further evolution of synthetic sounds only.

UPIC is not widely used although it was made available for public use. A better-known commercial product that is partially based on the same principle is called MetaSynth. In this case the developers' approach is known as "Image Synth", where users are encouraged to "paint sound" (their website). As with all such initiatives it is important to see what constraints are included to make the programs efficient. For example, are all frequencies available in such packages or only notes on a scale? Matching up the specification of such products with your own creative needs is advisable before deciding to invest in them. Still, such packages offer a much more immediate approach to sound generation than many others.

In the early years of computer sound generation, sound synthesis systems were mainly non-real time, that is, you had to wait for your results and, depending on circumstances, that could mean waiting for hours or even an entire day. Imagine making a typographical error before running a program of sound generation only to discover the next day that this typo ruined the result!

Today, non-real time is the exception, not the rule. Wonderful interfaces have been designed to make sound generation less of a burden and this is probably even more relevant in our next subject, sound manipulation. Along with the interfaces, there exist a wide variety of controllers, triggers and sensors that enable you to launch, modify or terminate a sound in real time. Such controllers can be used by musicians, people engaged with sound installations or performers such as dancers conducting the sonic aspect of performance. They can be applied in online environments or in networked multi-location ("telearts") performances. Ironically, in such situations another type of non-real-time issue comes to the fore, namely that when sharing sounds and images with others online, there is a bit of latency built in as the transmission of this information is based on the combination of information moving along at the speed of light and the capacity of the relevant Internet connections. Still, such delays, awkward as they may be, seem trivial when compared with the slow calculations of early sound synthesis due to our modern computers' ability to deal with the heavy density of calculation related to their musical production. What a luxury.

Sculpting with Sounds

When it comes to sculpting with sounds, the need to know what is taking place acoustically in detail is much less than in the case of generating sounds. Once potential sounds have been found, and some general ideas of how a musical project might evolve have been formulated, trying some experiments in which you attempt to manipulate your sounds offers the chance to make discoveries that can help shape the development of a piece of music. The following pages will present a fairly broad spectrum of means to shape sounds into exactly what you are looking for. Suffice to say that this is only the tip of the iceberg. The better one comes to grips with these items, the more advanced opportunities will unfold. Still, I am of the opinion that it is better to gain experience with a few such means than to have a superficial knowledge of many. It is through the gaining of virtuosity with particular techniques where the difference can be found between a good piece and a great one. Without the sense of knowledge of one's "instruments", one is left with a constant sense of trial and error. By attempting to learn too many of them, it is unlikely that such expert knowledge will be gained.

To Start

Here are some of the basic means to manipulate sounds. They include editing sounds, looping sounds and reversing them.

Before computers were an important part of music technology, this type of music was often made on tape, specifically reel tape (as opposed to cassettes). The quality was not perfect, although the more money one had to spend, the more professional the tape recorders that were available. Most people worked, at least to start, on ¼-inch stereo tape recorders. There were also multi-track recorders that were useful for pieces that were to be spatialised (e.g., four or eight channels). Sounds were isolated by way of what is known as splicing. The very start and end of the sounds were cut with a razor on a splicing block or with scissors and placed somewhere where they could be retrieved, often on another reel with white leader tape before and after it to ensure that the sound started and ended in silence. Splicing was the primary means of editing. Later, the sounds could be retrieved, eventually copied and spliced alongside another sound. In some cases, a musician might have preferred not to use an entire sound; only part of it was needed. This is called truncating. As long as one could make the start and end "clean," this posed no problems. In today's digital systems, things are ever so much easier and more efficient, not to mention cheaper and of higher quality. Many computer programs offer a visual form of a sound at a graphic resolution whereby you can find exactly where you want it to start and to end.

Some musicians have been able to create new sounds from existent ones by, for example, taking the very initial part of a sound, its attack (or transient), and separating it and then playing only the body of another sound afterwards. This might be fun for a party game or an exercise in aural awareness—name the original sounds—but it also can lead towards the creation of new musically interesting sounds, and that is what we are after.

Editing is the key way of preparing sounds for their use in musical sequences and eventually in musical pieces. If there is one technique that everyone needs to learn, it is exactly how to isolate a sound so that it can best be used towards musical goals.

The term, looping, is very much a term from the years when analogue tape was used. The idea was to take a sound or sequence of sounds and have it repeat regularly. If the loop was short, a simple rhythmical pattern evolved. Loops could be extremely long as well, although it took a big room to allow that to happen. In these cases it might be possible that the listener did not realise that a loop was involved at all. To create a loop, the front of the spliced segment was connected to the end of the loop using splicing tape. Care must be taken to ensure that the transition from end to beginning seems to take place naturally. Silence between sounds is one way around this; adjusting sound levels is another if a continuity is to be sought (see below). To jump ahead in this section a bit, loops could be played at normal speed, sped up or slowed down (thus changing the pitch and the duration of its contents) or even backwards as well as with other effects. For the moment, let's stick with its natural form.

To create a loop digitally, one has to find the starting and ending point of a segment of a single sound or a sequence of sounds. Many programs offer the opportunity to hear it as a loop; others simply allow you to copy the sound and paste it again and again, as many times as you want. As there are plenty of aspects of music that are repeated at least once, looping can be a very useful compositional tool.

clunk   clap   click   clunk   clap   click   clunk   clap   click

FIGURE 3.7   A score representation of a loop

FIGURE 3.8   A tape recorder playing a short tape loop

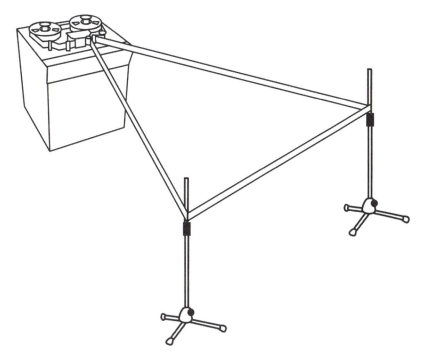

FIGURE 3.9   A tape recorder playing a long tape loop

Editing and looping activity Record or choose one or more sounds that you would like to use musically. This choice should be based on something that would sound nice as a rhythmical cycle either creating a single attack or a small number of attacks that as a collection create a rhythmical pattern. You can extend the sound(s) with silence to obtain the duration(s) that you seek. Make certain that the point where the loop ends meet sounds as natural as possible. Once you think you are ready, turn this musical passage into a loop and see what it sounds like. If the rhythmical pattern is not right, you can adjust it until it does sound right. In this way you will become familiar with simple editing and the creation of a loop.

The ability to reverse direction without any further changes to a sound is another very simple technique. What it does do is to offer a first real bridge from contextual listening to musical listening. Transforming sounds from their contextual state to a more musical state is actually also possible with clever editing and using loops, but it is fairly obvious when reversing sounds. I have already written in the last chapter that the speaking voice is more or less chromatic, that is, the pitches correspond to the intervals between notes on a piano. I used to demonstrate this to students starting to work in this area by creating a loop of my voice saying something along the lines of: "I have heard that the voice when speaking is chromatic, but I am not so certain that this is the case. Let's see whether it's true." This loop was played to students a few times, normally without anyone coming to any conclusion. To try to hold on to the pitch, I added reverberation★ as if I had spoken in a church (reverberation will be introduced below under "effects") so that the pitches would be sustained, but, alas, that often did not help. I then reversed the loop, playing it backwards. The pitches were too short; it still did not become clear to most, although everyone thought they could hear the pitches better as they could no longer pay attention to the words' signification. This was due to the fact that my voice played backwards, beyond sounding silly, became sound more than content. When I added reverberation for a second time, the pitches that I had spoken were sustained and there were no words getting in the way. It was only then that people heard that indeed the speaking voice was more or less chromatic. The fact that a loop was employed was extremely helpful, for it might have been difficult to decide this after listening to the text one single time.

When using a reverse function, it is not necessary to use entire sounds; instead it is useful to look for specific sound qualities. If the start and end points are not quite acceptable in terms of how sharp or clean they are, you can always adjust their loudness, our next subject, to ensure that the loop sounds seamless. Most programs that can be used for making sound-based music offer the option to reverse sounds.

Reversing sounds activity In this activity you can attempt to achieve an interesting sound quality (or sequence of sound qualities) or a rhythm or both. Similar to the editing and looping activity, one or more sounds are to be chosen, you having already listened to them backwards. If combining sounds, make your sequence first and then turn them into a loop, taking care that the top and tail point sounds as natural as possible once "spliced" together. Play back the loop several times. What is it in this loop that sounds attractive? Can you or others recognise what the original sound sources were? Which characteristics are most prominent: rhythm, pitch, sound quality, or perhaps something else?

Loudness-Based Manipulation

So far we have been focusing on sounds in their "as is" state. Although I like to represent existent sounds artistically that I have found during my sound hunting, most composers like to mould them to sound exactly how they would like. Before moving on to sound effects, one thing that is useful to anyone doing this kind of work is keeping an eye on the sound levels and how the sounds' levels work with respect to one another.

Some form of amplification is needed when we listen to our loudspeakers. This section is about pre-amplification, also known as mixing. All programs that allow for any sort of sound modification include the equivalent of a volume control. The more sophisticated the program, the more sophisticated the loudness tools. Having written that, almost any program allows the volume of each channel to be set at several points, and some even allow for changes to be made at the resolution of a single digital piece of information. Most offer an updated version of the envelope generator used in the "old days". When dealing with electronically generated (analogue) sound, older synthesisers did not offer the option to change the volume at several given points. Instead they included the possibility to indicate an attack time, a decay time to a stable state, the level of that stable state that was called sustain and a release time also known as ADSR. This offered a crude means of creating a dynamic shape that was feasible given the technology of the day. Clearly digital systems are infinitely more flexible, but still, perhaps for the reason of offering a form of simplified acoustic principle, some of today's programs still include an ADSR envelope equivalent based on analogue technology. Although learning how to use an envelope generator is a worthwhile experience, I believe it is much better to find the right levels of loudness for your sounds by defining their levels where your ears feel it is right.

One thing that you must keep in mind is that digital technologies do not like sounds that get too loud. This causes particular noise sounds as an unwanted side effect. If you are looking for such unexpected noises as an experiment, that can be illuminating, but most such noises mean that something has gone wrong. There are two ways around it: a) judge that your levels never go above the highest level that your system can accept or b) investigate whether your program has what is known as a limiter★. Radio stations use limiters to ensure that their volume levels never exceed a certain point. Limiters can be used just to ensure that things do not go awry. Please note that limiters may crush loudness levels in a way that makes

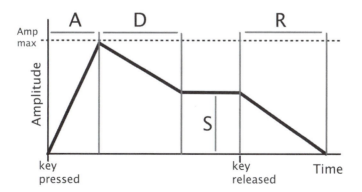

FIGURE 3.10 An example of an ADSR envelope image

your sound combination sound different from what you wanted. In such cases, it is perhaps more prudent to gauge levels within the limits of your system to avoid the need for a limiter.

Loudness activity Record or find three sounds or short sequences that you would like to hear at the same time. Organise the levels so that these three sound as if they belong together, where no sound is drowning out another one. This type of activity is known as layering sounds.

After succeeding with this, start this exercise again. This time change the loudness levels in such a way that all three sounds blend into one single sound. If this proves difficult, you can seek sounds that are able to blend into a composite one. It might be as if one melts into another and then into the other one. This can be tricky, so you may need to move the sounds about in time to make the transitions smooth.

Finally use the three sounds in a completely unexpected manner using only changes in start/stop times and other levels of loudness. Explain what you were trying to do with them and see whether others can actually hear what you set out to achieve.

Some Key Means of Creating Effects

Now the time has come to tamper with the sounds and their sound qualities. Effects are usually integrated into audio software programs. Alternatively effects are offered separately and installed within a program that you already have as plug-ins. The following effects are the most common and most basic. You can develop quite an expertise for sculpting sounds using these.

We shall start our tour of basic effects by looking at the most common types of filters. Filters are used to cut out or reduce part of the frequency range of a sound that you want to treat. (Some systems actually also offer the opportunity to amplify part of a sound; this is generally known as equalisation, but that negates the concept of a filter which only allows through that part of the sound that you need.) One type of common filter cuts off frequencies above a certain frequency or below a chosen frequency; these are known as low-pass and high-pass filters. Others focus on frequencies surrounding a central point; these are known as band-pass. Filters can be used in combination and there are several types of more advanced filters as well.

Low-pass filters were traditionally used to cut out the hiss from a recorded sound, as analogue recordings were imperfect, often containing some noise on the high end of spectrum. The use of a filter created an optimised sound; that is, the resultant sound did potentially lose some very high frequencies, but the offending noise was also (largely) removed. High-pass filters were traditionally used to remove audio hum out of the lower end of a sound. High-/low-pass filters allow one to remove unwanted sound from both ends. These days such filters are used to create a reduction of a sound spectrum in order to alter an original sound quality for a specific purpose, such as making a sound appear more distant. One technical matter of note is that some systems allow the angle involved at the low or high end to be altered so that some higher/lower sounds come through.

Band-pass and stopband (or band-reject) filters work around central frequencies. They are often used in series to re-shape a sound focusing on various frequency bands within the sound. A band-pass filter does exactly what it says. The more the band is amplified, the better it will be heard. These look like little hills. The width of the hill is often adjustable. In stopband filters, the opposite takes place. One starts with the entire sound and lowers the level surrounding a central frequency, thus making a shape like a hill standing on its head. An

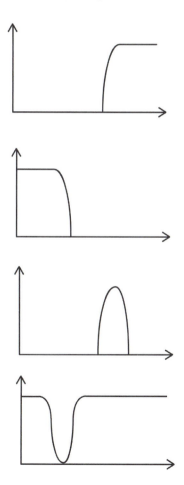

FIGURE 3.11   Examples of high-pass, low-pass, band-pass and stopband filters

extremely narrow stopband filter is also known as a notch filter. The illustrations in Figure 3.11 demonstrate the typical shapes of the above-mentioned types of filters.

When one has a series of band-pass or stopband filters, one can really play with the sound quality of a given sample. Some parts can be completely taken away, others reduced and some made extremely prominent. This is a great example of moulding sounds. In more advanced systems, you are able to alter the settings of the filters in time, thus changing the sound quality as the sound evolves. Such filters are known as time-variable filters. Remember that most sounds are quite complex. Many include a central pitch and its harmonics. With band filters, you can accentuate a variety of harmonics whilst ignoring others, thus creating a new sound from an existent one.

Filter activity Take a simple sound and then, later, a complex one and try out various settings of low- and high-pass filters on them. If possible use them in combination as well, varying the combination as much as possible to discover what happens to the sounds. Does the identity of either sound ever disappear? If that is the case, does it then start to sound like something else? It would be worthwhile to keep a list of settings used and try to describe the resulting sounds that are made. Although using similar types of settings with other sounds will often lead to entirely different results, a pattern of behaviour may emerge that could prove very useful when altering sounds using filters in various musical contexts.

For the band-pass/stopband activity, it is useful to focus on complex sounds or an integrated combination of sounds. Start by using only one filter at a time and try to describe, that is map out, the results you gain. Don't forget to alter the breadth of the bands if this is available to you. This can offer some big surprises, in fact. However, things get much more interesting when you are able to use a series of filters. You can place the filters equidistantly, in octaves or a number per octave. This is a fairly normal way of working. Some systems allow you to place the filters anywhere. In this case very unexpected and special results can evolve. If you are able to do this, start with equidistant filters and create various combinations. Again, take note how they influence the sound. In this case, patterns will be less relevant as what happens is totally dependent on the construction of the sounds that you are using. What you will discover is: the more you play with combinations of filters, the more interesting the differences in the sounds become and the more you are able to identify the ones you like and dislike and, consequently, you become more able to articulate what is special about certain sounds you are making and subsequently choose them for specific musical purposes.

As said, there are many other more advanced filter possibilities available. By naming just one, the comb filter, we have an opportunity to tie this filter section with the following one, focused on delay and echo. A comb filter does not just treat a sound, but instead treats it and a delayed version of itself. The technical term for what results is interference, as components of the sound seem to go into battle with each other. This can lead to the creation of very interesting sounds as well as some awful ones. The comb filter is so named as it creates a new sound consisting of equidistant spikes. This is a very specific sound as is the case in many advanced effects and is called upon when that sort of sound quality is desired. In a sense, the filters to which we have been introduced offer a great deal of possibilities, but no "typical" sound, but can be slightly cumbersome to use as there are so many options when using them. In contrast, many advanced filters have a characteristic sound and are called upon for that very reason.

Every young child is amazed when (s)he hears a convincing echo. Frankly, as an adult, I am still fascinating by them whether within a modest area or in the outdoors. Any echo offers an important climax of a soundwalk. Echo infers space and really is not effective if used on a single sound channel, although there are some who may disagree with this statement. Delay★, on the other hand, works in both situations. Their principle is similar: take a sound and hear it again (and again) after a given amount of time. Naturally, multiple echoes can take place depending on the geography of a given environment. Delays need not be equidistant. Furthermore, when the duration of the delay is very short, one does not hear that effect, but instead hears a complex sound created through multiple appearances of the original sound, eventually involving interference. Delays also need not follow the natural amplitude pattern of an echo that naturally fades out. Its dynamic can remain constant, act similarly to an echo or can be programmed to go up and down as one chooses.

Delays can be used to make a sound surreal. For example, by using delays the sound of a coin dropping can turn into someone being showered with money.

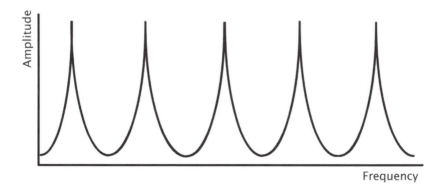

FIGURE 3.12   An image of a sound after going through a comb filter

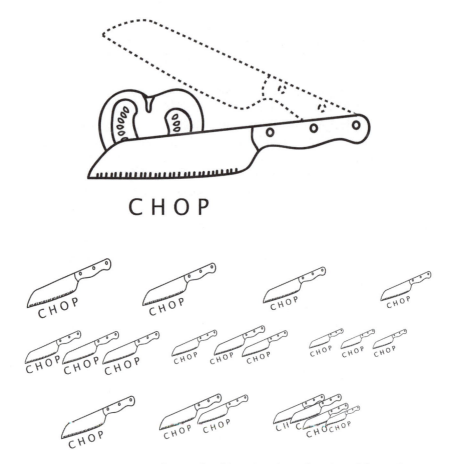

FIGURE 3.13–3.14 Images of a sound and its going through various delay settings

It can also be used to make a sound more abstract or simply to give it a more rhythmical quality. When the opportunity exists to use delays spatially, special echo effects can evolve which, too, can become surreal, such as sending a sound around a space, but the listener never knows where it will come from next. This takes some work, but the result can be truly gratifying.

Delay/echo activity Take a sound or a short group of sounds with a clear attack(s). Add a single delay to this sample and adjust the duration to see what happens. In some cases it can create what appears to be the start of a canon. In others the results can be quite odd. If possible add a second delay and try this again at some of the more interesting settings you discovered the first time and increase the number to see what evolves. Is there a point when there are too many repetitions and thus the resultant sound is too dense? How do you best set the volume of the delays? Is fading out like in an echo situation ideal or can you find other alternatives that lead to successful results?

Assuming that you possess a stereo system and your software allows for this, send the delay alternatively to one channel and then the other. If using loudspeakers and the cables are long enough, try placing them at different distances from one another to see what happens. Listen on headphones as well if you can as sonic games are played inside your head that may appear very interesting.

If you can set a variable delay, try dissimilar delay times. Alternatively you can copy the sample and place it at different intervals. A vast variety of results will be on offer. Play around a bit with the loudness for each one and see what happens and, again, if possible spatialise them and see whether some exciting sound scenarios evolve.

Evaluate the results of these different activities. By now you will be discovering the types of manipulated sounds that you prefer and the ones you don't like. This is useful, for the clearer you are about what you like to use, the more efficient and creative your composing will be.

I have sometimes alluded to sound manipulation as being a form of magic. It certainly appears to be this way to me when things truly work out. Such experimentation with sound is always a path towards discovery. That is why I prefer the verb "play" being applied to music instead of "work". The ability to use reverberation forms an important aspect of this magic as it allows you to create and change a particular sonic space, eventually creating totally unreal spaces. When one focuses on this aspect of sound manipulation, one can speak of the creation of a "composed space". Although a performance space can influence the final sound of your work, as it does in any concert situation, you are largely able to create the sonic space beforehand.

If that concept sounds a bit confusing, think of this. All children at one point will cup their hands over their mouths and talk in a muffled manner. This simulates the sound of something distant or perhaps even a tiny space. Similarly, children enjoy talking and, in particular, shouting when they are under a bridge or in a tunnel, as the reverberant space sounds larger than in normal circumstances. We rarely get a chance to be loud in a church, a truly reverberant space, unless we play an instrument or are singing, but this is another case of a reverberant space largely influencing what we hear. Clap your hands in a church and listen how long the sound takes to die away. With our sound tools we can create all sorts of sonic spaces.

Architects are becoming increasingly aware of how sounds act in the spaces that they design, whether it is a home, office or concert hall. A few concert halls offer a variable acoustic so that they can sound differently for different types of music. Purpose-built performance spaces at IRCAM (Institut de Recherche et Coordination Acoustique/Musique) in Paris, the music department of the Pompidou Centre, and at SARC (Sonic Arts Research Centre) in Belfast have means whereby the acoustic can be changed during a performance. Such spaces are rare, but the awareness of spatial acoustics has risen enormously in recent years. Beware, however, as knowledge regarding spatial acoustics is nothing new: church architects centuries ago were extremely aware of how speech and music projected in their buildings.

Reverberation allows us the opportunity to enlarge the space of a "dry" sound recording. The best way to attempt to make a "wet" recording appear to sound as if it occurred in a smaller space is through the use of filters. However, such reverse engineering is much more difficult (and sometimes it simply is not possible) than taking a dry sound and making it fit in any space.

We can use reverberation to make an entire segment of a piece of music sound as if it takes place in a given type of space; alternatively, we can change the reverberation to create the impossible situation of sounds being played in different spaces at the same time, again a bit surreal. This technique is used at times in pop music mixes.

Some reverberation programs or plug-ins are quite complicated. This is understandable when you think of everything that might be adjusted. This also allows for completely novel sounds to be produced. For our purposes, ones with few settings or ones that have types of spaces such as a "large hall" will do.

FIGURE 3.15

FIGURE 3.15–3.16 So-called dry and wet reverberant spaces

Reverberation activity For this activity a longer recording will be needed as a starting point as it takes a while to truly hear and get used to the potential and qualities of a reverberant space. Of course, one can determine a space's reverberant quality as children do shouting or clapping under a bridge, but to experience the characteristics of the ambience, time is needed. Ideally a recording that is fairly dry should be used. Play back this sound but change the level of reverberation each time. Does this take you into a different space? Is the space realistic? If not, what seems to be unnatural? Try to find some settings that place your recording in the 'wrong' space. What is your reaction to these and why?

If you are using stereo playback, see how stereo output of reverberation widens the space. Does your system offer means of controlling how this works?

If you are willing to attempt something that may not work, try to do the reverse. Take a reverberant sound or make a reverberant sound during the first part of the activity and try to discover a means of placing that sound in a smaller space using the filters that we have used already. Were you able to achieve a convincing result? If not, do you have the feeling that at least the space has been reduced somehow? Don't fret if you were unsuccessful with this part of the activity; this type of reverse engineering is difficult at best and, as said, at times simply impossible, unfortunately.

Now take a sound that clearly belongs to one space and another from a different, contrasting space and combine them. They need not start exactly at the same time and longer recordings might work best. How does this sound? Has this impossible combination turned into something humorous, irritating or something else? What might you do with them to make this combination even more interesting? Does one space mask the other?

Finally, take a short sound and make it last as long as is possible through setting the reverberation time at a high level. This example is useful as it demonstrates the extent of manipulation that can be applied to one single sound quality.

If you are curious, this is the moment when you can check and see whether your voice is chromatic. If you can record it, record just a sentence or two. If you cannot make a recording, grab a spoken text sample. Then create a copy of this sample in reverse. Turn it into a workable loop. Now add a good amount of reverberation and listen to the result. Did you discover that the result of the pitches you hear could be written on a traditional five-line score?

Other Forms of Time-Based Sound Manipulation

Beyond the use of an envelope to determine the loudness of your sounds in time, there are many other time-based forms of sound manipulation. Umbrella terms related to this are temporal shaping and spectral shaping, depending on which aspect of the sound is the focus. If it is the sound quality that is to be manipulated in time, and there are dozens of ways in which that can be done, one speaks of spectral shaping. An example of this was our using a series of band-pass filters to influence sound quality. When specifically dealing with time-based changes of sound, such as time stretching and time compression★, we speak of temporal shaping.

As far as time stretching and time compression are concerned, thank goodness for digital technology. In analogue technology there were very expensive means to changing the speed of a recording without changing its pitch, but the number of those machines was fairly modest and few had access to one. Therefore this activity meant changing the pitch and sound quality based on the amount of stretching

FIGURE 3.17 A visual example of time stretch and compression of a real-world sound

or compression, often leading to slow-motion or "Mickey Mouse" effects. (Such effects still exist today if one is applying a crude transposition method.) Today, we can stretch the length of a recording or shrink it according to our needs without these undesired side effects of altered pitch. Please note: when a sound is shrunk too much, it may well lose its identity. When stretched too far, it becomes grain-like and changes its sound quality.

Time stretching/time compression activity As suggested it is useful to gain experience in both time stretching and time compression to see how far you can increase or decrease a given sound before its identity changes. It is equally interesting to follow what happens to its identity as the change is augmented. Try this exercise with a variety of sounds of different lengths and qualities.

Now, for fun, let's take a sound and create a few similar sounds of different lengths using small-scale time stretching and compression. The resultant lengths should remain quite similar. Play them at the same time where the starting point is identical. Now shuffle them a little bit so they are all starting at slightly different times. Compare the results. Now increase the time differences without distorting the original recording and see what the best way is to use all of them as long as they overlap. How would you describe the sound of the combination that you have made?

Finally, combine stretched with compressed results and repeat the shorter ones as if they were rhythmical entities and see what this opportunity opens up. Do not make your total passage last any more than, say, fifteen seconds.

Before moving on, I would like to introduce a rather exciting, be it advanced, means of transforming sounds. In this case we want a single sound event to evolve from one sound to another, which is also known as morphing. This advanced type of spectral shaping certainly represents another form of magic and is one of the most extreme forms of spectral shaping. Many composers and sound designers find that as one sound gradually or even rapidly evolves to another one, there is a point where what you hear is neither the one nor the other and some form of masking is used in order to ensure that the listener keeps the two ends of the sound in the foreground of their perception. Masking may take on the form of the appearance of similar sound qualities to assist the gentle transformation from point A to point B; otherwise, the resultant transformation might sound less convincing. Just like visual morphs that we see in films, computer games and on the television, the creation of morphs has been possible in music for decades. The fact that this is not straightforward will explain why there are few software programs for the creation of credible morphs available at the time of writing this book and these are not widely used, most likely as they simply are not as convincing as one would prefer. Normally, similar sounds are easier to deal with than highly contrasting ones as the "in between" time (the time when masking might be necessary in other circumstances) tends to utilise characteristics of both. When there is little shared between the two end sounds, the transformation is simply that much more difficult to create or, alternatively, the sounding result is finally not terribly convincing. Given its complexity, no such sound transformation activity will be included in this chapter. Instead, you might like to experiment with the notion of crossfading, that is, reducing the levels of the first sound as you increase the levels of the second sound and see what types of results you can obtain. This is a good way of getting started and becoming familiar with means of gradual transformation.

Pitch-Based Manipulation

The following forms of manipulation were all created to support note-based aspects of music made with technology. They can equally be used in a sound-based context. Furthermore, in the note-based context, these effects are normally used chromatically; in a sound-based context, any change is possible.

FIGURE 3.18 A visual representation of a sound transformation

One of the most straightforward means of manipulating pitch is by shifting or transposing the pitch of a given sample by a frequency or an interval upwards or downwards. If the interval is very small and the original is played simultaneously, another form of interference may occur. If the interval is wide, the surreal experience of hearing the same item at two (or more) pitches is the result.

What do you think of a basso profundo birdcall or a chorus of several tins being opened at different pitches, perhaps in the form of an arpeggio? Experimentation using chromatic and other intervals including those very small ones can lead to wonderful discoveries and, of course, this need not concern hearing one or more copies of the same sound simultaneously; one can simply take any sound and place it in a given context at any credible pitch.

Similar to the tale concerning time stretching and compression, to shift a pitch in analogue technology, one usually equally changed the sound's length. Now this can be done without any durational change. If one wants to combine the

FIGURE 3.19 A basso profundo birdcall

FIGURE 3.20 Tins being opened at different pitches in the form of an arpeggio

two, they need not be related as they were with varispeed tape recorders. One can lower the pitch whilst compressing a sound, for example.

As mentioned elsewhere in this book, there is nothing awkward about employing aspects from note-based music in a sound-based context. Transposing and superposing sounds is one form of manipulation that can easily be used in traditional as well as highly novel ways.

Pitch-shifting*/transposition activity The composer John Cage wrote a series of compositions called "imaginary landscape". Although this chapter is focused on single sounds, the goal of this exercise will be to take a modest number of recordings and create a multi-layered imaginary landscape. Any effect introduced thus far can be used, but the effect used most often should be that of transposition. Try to create an evocative score of what you would like to happen and then work on the short sequence. If you are not satisfied, think about what is not working and try to determine what is wrong in your view. Seek alternative solutions until the sequence works for you musically or on any other level, including that of humour.

It might be useful to start by taking individual sounds that you would like to use and transform them into something you think might be useful. What effect does transposition have? Do the transposed sounds sound best on their own or do they work better when the original is heard at the same time or shortly before or afterwards? Combining longer, contextual sounds with shorter detail sounds should prove useful. Try to avoid making sounds too abstract by over-filtering them, compressing them too far or playing them in reverse.

Two other types of transposition, harmonising★ and chorusing★, will now be introduced. The principle of each is fairly simple. In the case of harmonising, a single sound can be heard at a number of intervals simultaneously or with very short time delays (in ms.) without any alteration of time duration. In this way the sound of a forest could be heard as if it were a major chord or a dissonant combination of intervals. The number of sounds and the intervals are usually programmable unless there is only a basic choice, mainly consisting of traditional chords, offered by a plug-in or a program.

The chorus effect occurs when sounds are heard simultaneously that share much the same sound quality and where individual aspects of the conglomerate sound cannot be perceived in isolation. In other words, one new sound is made up of the blend of a number of single sounds. The textbook example of a chorus sound is that of a string orchestra. The chorus simulation can also be created technologically using a sound and then applying mainly small-scale pitch shifting as well as delay to create a new, blended sound.

FIGURE 3.21   An image represening a harmonised lawnmower

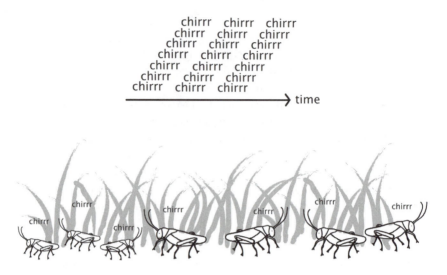

FIGURE 3.22   Two ways of illustrating a chorus effect

When the same sound is used with multiple delays, where it is in fact multiplying itself, the term flanging★ is used. In this case, the process is more controlled by the user and fewer delays are used.

Harmonising and chorus activities To come to grips with harmonising, choose a simple sound that does not alter in pitch and another sample that includes several sounds. Harmonise each one separately, first by using a combination of intervals that is very familiar in a note-based context. If possible, do this again using a much less conventional combination of frequencies. The simple sound should be heard to become "an instrument" as harmonising it is a fairly logical thing to do. The more complex sample when played harmonically is a fairly bizarre phenomenon. If you do not like the sound produced, try a replacement until you find something that seems interesting. If it took several tries, what was it about the one you finally chose that made it work and why did the other ones not work? How does it sound with the less-conventional combination of intervals? Does another one of your sounds work better with this new combination of intervals? If so, why?

To become acquainted with the chorus sound, take a sample that is not terribly short and consists of one single sound quality, eventually starting after its initial attack. Try this out using a chorus effects processor. If you can adjust parameters, for example how many layers of sound are produced or delays used, play around with these until you find you have created some convincing sound qualities.

Now find another sound that is similar to the first one and repeat what you have done in the previous paragraph. Once you have succeeded, combine the two best results, one from the first and one from the second sound. What do you think of the new sound that evolves from the resulting combination?

If your software permits this, you can repeat the above two paragraphs focusing on flanging. How would you describe the difference of the resultant sounds?

Modulation

There are several ways of having something acoustically modulate another sound. The two most common are amplitude modulation★ and frequency modulation★, also known as AM and FM. We are acquainted with both: when the modulation frequency is low, the sound that is to be modulated turns into what is known as a tremolo or vibrato. In the former case, the amplitude is fluctuating up and down relatively slowly; in the latter case, it is the frequency that is moving so that the "carrier," the sound being modulated is shifting up and down slightly in pitch. When the speed of the modulation increases, our perception gets overloaded and a new sound develops. This is, in fact, the basis of FM synthesis mentioned earlier in this chapter.

Modulation, like sound generation, is a topic best understood with a good deal of mathematics supporting it. For our purposes, the best way to start is to be able to create tremolo and vibrato effects and then discover what happens when the modulating speed or the extent of modulation increases to the point of altering the carrier's sound quality.

Modulation activity Choose any homogeneous sound of at least moderate duration as the carrier. A sustained or prolonged sound is ideal. Modulate this sound in terms of amplitude by a sine wave at approximately five cycles per second and do not make the breadth (how much louder and quieter the carrier will become) very wide. This is a typical tremolo sound. Now move the number of cycles per second (or hertz, hz) a bit either way and you will hear the tremolo slow down or quicken. If you alter its breadth, the dynamic differences will increase or diminish accordingly.

Following this, do the same thing, but using frequency modulation this time. Here you will be creating a vibrato effect. If you are using a dynamic carrier the result may be confusing, as what is being modulated might be changing all the time. That is why a homogeneous sound quality in the carrier is much better for this activity.

If other waveforms are available, such as a triangle or sawtooth waveform, you might try them just to hear the difference of the modulation effect. Advanced modulation can take place with complex waveforms as the modulator, but trying this now would be extremely counter-intuitive and therefore not advisable.

Now let's move forward into the unknown. Starting with amplitude modulation and a fairly modest breadth, increase the number of cycles per second up slowly until you hear the carrier's sound quality changing. Continue to increase the frequency of modulation and you may occasionally hear noisy sounds turn into more familiar pitch-based sounds. This may have to do with the relationship of the pitch of the modulator with the pitch of the carrier. Write down where those points are and see whether a pattern emerges.

As above, you can repeat this experience using frequency modulation. What happens to the sound quality in this case when the original sound is no longer recognisable? Are there any patterns here as you continue to increase the modulating frequency? Can you describe the resultant sounds in a particular way?

Making Things Noisy

Everyone has a particular feeling about noise. It winds some people up, excites others, brings pleasure to more listeners than you would imagine and is frankly detested by most people. Nonetheless, in the 1960s, distortion, feedback and other forms of noise crept into popular music—it had already been used in various ways in experimental forms of art music—in parallel with the increase of volume associated with pop music. An electric guitar player without a distortion pedal wasn't cool and the true guitar virtuoso knew exactly how to place the instrument in front of a large loudspeaker to create and perform feedback as part of the performance.

Distortion is created through modulation or overloading an amplifier and is therefore linked to the previous subject. Feedback is based on a sound modulating itself such as that guitar located in front of its loudspeaker or making a closed circuit of a mixer plugged into its own output. Be aware that things can get very unpredictable if not hugely loud if you are not careful with feedback. Noise music, introduced briefly in Chapter 1, is a genre of music that has been gaining in popularity over a number of years. Surprisingly, some noise musicians, not the majority by any means, make music consisting of quiet noises. Noise can be used as a contrast when "cleaner" sounds are a piece's focus or they can be a focus themselves. Distortion and feedback are just two of many ways of creating noisy sound qualities.

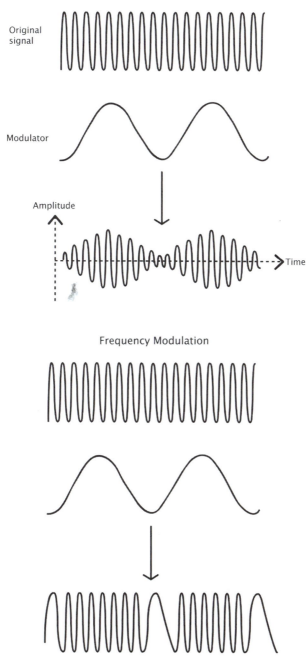

FIGURE 3.23–3.24 Amplitude and Frequency Modulation

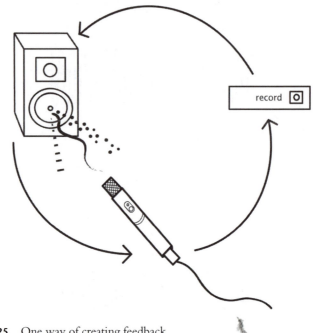

FIGURE 3.25 One way of creating feedback

A Few Advanced Possibilities

The large category "Sound Production and Manipulation" in the EARS site index is the equivalent of what this section of the chapter has been about. Key information related to this chapter can be found under the header "Sound Shaping." Many terms will seem exotic, such as convolution, which is somewhat analogous in terms of sound manipulation with what cross-synthesis is to sound generation. An example of convolution would allow for a sound to be heard in a series of "wrong" spaces as the aspects of one sound influence that of another. Brassage is the chopping up of a sound into many pieces and putting it together again in any order, taking care to ensure that transitions between the pieces are smooth, and freezing involves the creation of an effect as if a sound were "frozen" in time. The software approach to this is to select an extremely brief sound loop, which, through repetition, allows for an indefinite prolonging of a brief frame of a given sound. There are many more such advanced techniques that people who have mastered what this book has to offer will be able to learn afterwards.

How to Play a Sound Manipulation

This book is focused on things you can do with a computer in front of you. If ever there is a volume two of this book, it will focus on those advanced techniques that have just been mentioned and others like them as well as performing sounds, whether involving physical presence or online. One form of live sound manipulation all readers will be aware of is scratching, something we know from hip hop. This is not digital, of course. Many readers have been using software with a user-friendly interface to create sounds and manipulate them. Some such programs allow users to perform sound-based music in real time, for example during a concert, and allow for sound manipulation to take place whilst you are performing. Granted, a single person cannot alter too many aspects of sound live at once, but as time goes on, these tools become increasingly efficient and sophisticated. They often also become easier to learn and improved interfaces or other means of performance are developed. You may have seen people playing music on stage just using laptops. This is but one example of playing sound-based music live; often including deciding which sounds are launched or generated, and when and how they are manipulated. Even in the home studio situation, it is one thing to calculate a sound manipulation, but it is infinitely more fun to play it whilst you make it, for example by using something like a fader to decide the speed of the path from A to B, thus allowing for physical involvement in shaping the sound.

There are also commercially made and homemade controllers and even digital instruments that can be used to manipulate sounds, including digital scratching. I often find it more gratifying to influence sounds with something other than a computer mouse or trackpad. As efficient as they are, they are not the most obvious means of creating gestures for sound manipulation. Controllers and instruments can be programmed to influence sound quality in a similar manner to how they influence pitch. The result is the combination of how much influence a controller or instrument is capable of, the functionality of the system that is being used and the imagination of the user. For example, one can use sensors that can track movement with, say, one or more dancers, whose movements influence sound quality and also determine which sounds are playing. This is fairly advanced, but demonstrates something you can work towards once you have learned the basics introduced in this chapter.

And there is more. We have only glossed over the potential of space here, something that we shall return to in later chapters. At home we are used to some mono radios and televisions, but most are stereo. There are a few homes now with surround sound, too and this will most likely increase in the future as it makes the viewing/listening experience more realistic. With many of today's sound-based software systems we need not restrict ourselves to stereo. Just to cite one example that is only one or two steps removed from what we have been doing already, how about designing a sound, paying attention to how it evolves in time and then finding an ideal way to send the sound around the space as it evolves. That is an incredible sonic experience and is quite common in today's sound-based music, just like a bird flying around nearby during a soundwalk. It is true that to hear this one needs multiple loudspeakers, more than two, or some form of encoding that can generate a perceived spatialised sound even though it has been encoded into stereo, such as those binaural recordings mentioned earlier, when using headphones.

Generating or choosing sounds and then sculpting them are two of the most exciting aspects of the sound-based musical experience. Just as exciting is the activity of placing sounds together in time, first at the local level, for example a sonic gesture, and then at the higher level of sections of pieces and, finally, entire pieces. The next two chapters will apply what you have discovered in the last two as you move into increasingly longer durations and start to combine things, creating sonic magic of different sorts.

4

ORGANISING SOUNDS 1

Combining Sounds and Creating Sonic Gestures

In the fourth and fifth chapters we move forward from aural awareness and what we can achieve regarding the choice and subsequent sculpting of materials towards combining those materials at a small scale (this chapter) and at a larger scale (Chapter 5). The reader will discover that no tailor-made sound examples are being offered to illustrate the chapters' activities. The reason for this choice is quite important. Like many others, I was trained musically using an approach whereby I learned about and analysed the compositional methods of other musicians. If this had been a goal in itself, I would not have minded. However, I was subsequently asked to compose in the style of those composers too. I may have learned something by taking on someone else's style, but do not feel that my own music was furthered by such exercises. What I propose for this book's readers is to offer a large selection of carefully chosen works that can be found online to become acquainted with repertoire. This repertoire is intended to act as an inspiration, not to have readers make pieces that sound like others. These works will be categorised in a manner that corresponds with our overview of genres and categories in Chapter 1 as well as with some of the activities proposed in Chapters 4 and 5, that is, by approach or theme. The fact is that there exist very few commonly followed structures in sound-based music, but there are loads of types of musical gestures that one hears. It is for this reason that the approach is to allow a maximum of freedom for individuals to discover their own influences, techniques and, thus, their own personal sound.

Having introduced the notion of the storyboard as a means of envisioning how a sound-based piece of music might be put together, this chapter will focus on the bottom-up side of things. What this means here is that we shall be making a selection of materials with which we want to work and start combining sounds, both horizontally and vertically, working our way up to sonic gestures. These gestures might easily be considered to be the sound-based music equivalent to the phrase in note-based works.

To achieve this we need to start by choosing sounds that we might use in each activity. I have always liked to call this part of the work "sound hunting". Subsequently these sounds will at times need to be treated along the lines of what has been called sound sculpting. The next phase is sound organisation, that is, composition.

Placing Sounds in Sequences

Many of you will have a similar precious memory to mine regarding the first time you consciously sat down and started to compose a short piece of note-based music. Most people start with a melody. Those studying polyphonic instruments, such as a guitar or a piano, may throw in a few chords even at this very early stage. The excitement and the frustration of this initial experience (as well as any that may follow) are difficult to describe, but precious nonetheless.

It is a goal of this text that similar emotional excitement and a sense of accomplishment can be gained by organising sounds. Where in note-based music, novice composers are often asked to write a phrase with the idea that the phrase is itself a complete entity, we shall be doing this with our sequences and gestures in this chapter. The ability to create a short sequence or a sonic gesture can truly be seen to be an accomplishment given the huge number of choices available even when one has limited equipment.

It is understandable that some may have the view that the creation of sequences in isolation is a bit odd or goalless. However, we can still think of how such a sequence or sonic gesture can be used in a larger context, for example, as part of a storyboard. Therefore, there is a very strong connection between what will be built up in this chapter and how the results can be used and modified in Chapter 5.

Let's start with two pairs of activities that are at the extremes of our scale related to listening, from contextual to musical, where each pair involves a live performance and organising sounds using recording technology. These will allow us to focus not only on how to organise sounds, but also how we would like listeners to hear them. All of the tools offered in Chapter 3 can be used, but don't make your life too difficult at this stage. One can easily become wrapped up in the search for a succession of interesting sound effects. This can become tedious if you have not built up a repertoire of things that work for you. Therefore introducing effects when you believe they are needed is probably the best thing to do. What you will need for the second of each pair is some form of sequencing software, such as the Sound Organiser, that allows you to place sounds in succession and at least a few sounds simultaneously. The more you are able to adjust the loudness levels in these sequencers, the better, as you will definitely try to balance the relationships between sounds that you are using.

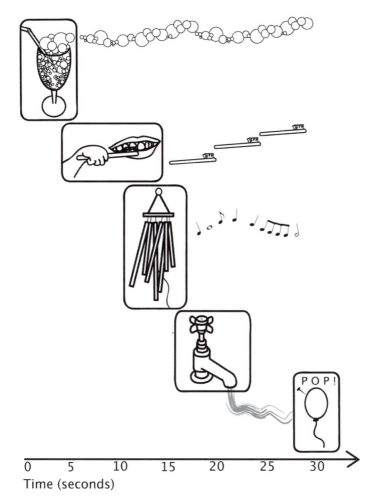

FIGURE 4.1   A sequence containing real-world sounds

Sound organisation activity 1a: Live contextual sequence Not all sound-based music has to involve digital technology. This first contextual sequence focuses on collecting objects that create sounds that can be directly linked with them just by your playing them. In other words, turning some attractive pieces of wood into an alternative percussion instrument is not the goal, as any wooden or hard object could produce a similar-sounding result.

This activity can be approached in one of three ways: 1) make a very short performance sequence that you have prepared in which you find interesting ways to create sounds that are either inherent to the objects or occur through your interacting with them; 2) similarly, perform the sequence behind a curtain so that the listeners cannot see what the objects are. In this case, their remaining identifiable is, in a sense, even more important than in the first option; 3) create an installation that can be played by its visitors. In all three cases, the aural link to the objects themselves is key. Therefore choices will likely be more difficult with this activity than the live musical sequence below.

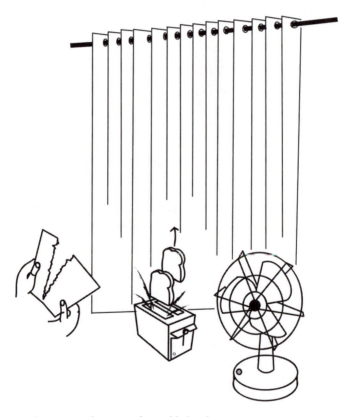

FIGURE 4.2   A sequence being performed behind a curtain

Sound organisation activity 1b: Recorded contextual sequence Try to make a simple sequence that takes us into an imaginary world. The key focus should be on how the used sounds are recognisable yet offer a sense that they do not belong together or could not ever be found in the same place. All sounds should be identifiable, or at least allow the listener to think that (s)he knows what is being heard. Although this is not completely necessary, you might decide to have a general contextual or ambient sound in which the more prominent shorter sounds are placed. If working in stereo, play with the placement from left to right of certain items. If you can, have them travel or jump from one place to another. Above all, make the impression that what is being heard could never be experienced in reality. Effects, if used at all, should be used sparingly to ensure that connections are made between what we hear and where the sounds originate.

One could think, based on the recorded contextual sequence activity's descriptions, that what is being made is literally a sound organisation as opposed to a piece of music. Let us not jump to such conclusions quite yet. First, we are not attempting to create a masterpiece for the time being, but instead are getting used to organising sounds in a way that might not deviate much from what one might hear through an open window. However, when you think about these activities, your listeners may be experiencing something different, perhaps more profound or unexpected than that. As time goes on and we evaluate what we are making (you, your friends, family, teacher, etc. together), the distance between the act of simply ordering sounds and making art will be reduced.

Sound organisation activity 2a: Live musical sequence Using the three options mentioned in the live contextual sequence, make a short sequence that is solely, or at least primarily, concerned with the sound qualities coming from the objects used. In the live performance and installation versions, it will be interesting to see how people react to objects from daily life being used more as an instrument than in terms of what they are. The biggest challenge here is not so much to obscure the sources, but instead to avoid these objects turning into a "junk orchestra" or some such where the key sonic foci are pitch and rhythm, that is, the foundations of note-based music. One interesting thing to explore is the interplay between continuous sound textures and more discrete ones, such as between one or more rasping sounds of some duration with a number of sharply attacked sounds heard simultaneously.

Sound organisation activity 2b: Recorded musical sequence Of the two recording activities, this one is slightly more difficult for beginners as the attempt to mask the sources of the sounds and the means by which they have been caused, such as striking, rubbing, pouring water into them, etc., might seem slightly challenging. Having worked on the live musical sequence, you may have already overcome this challenge. You do not need to completely avoid any identification of source or how sounds are produced in this recorded sequence; nonetheless, the listening experience should focus on the sonic result whereby contextual information is largely or even totally set aside. It might be worthwhile playing the sequence to others and then telling them where the sounds came from and how you manipulated them, if you did at all. Sound manipulation in this second recorded sequence activity is much more logical than in the first, although manipulation may serve both goals quite effectively.

Depending on the time that is available and how easy it was to create these two pairs of sequences, it might be worthwhile repeating one or more of them to gain greater experience at this basic level. What types of sounds are fitting together best? Why might this be so? Which ones seemed not to fit together and why? Did you find the musical sequences more related to what you used to consider musical or is it equally possible to do so when a contextual approach has been the focus? How does the act of performing a sequence feel? Did you get the idea that what you were doing was more like playing instruments or perhaps did it feel more like acting due to the fact that what you performed with was not a group of traditional instruments? Could you imagine using any or all of these sequences in a piece and, if so, how?; if not, why not? If the answer is "no," it would be useful to repeat the activity until an affirmative answer is the result.

The third activity to get things rolling takes us to a sound-based musical area that is close to my heart, as I often use it in my own works, namely organising the sounds of the speaking voice. Most readers will have experience of listening to rap artists using speech as part of music. The fact is that the speaking voice has been used in music for centuries. In terms of our exploration, there is a genre of music of particular relevance known as text–sound composition* that is based on organising the sounds of the voice, either speaking or producing other forms of utterance. In Chapter 2 it was already suggested that it is likely that the voice is the most versatile instrument after the computer. In this early activity, we shall not explore the huge repertoire of sounds that the voice can make, whether making utterances or singing, but stick closely to what you do with your voice most often: speak. By the way, in the following activities, there is no need to avoid humour. In fact, as you play with sounds, you may very well end up generating unanticipated and particularly interesting sounds.

Sound organisation activity 3a: Live text–sound sequence As we are working at the short sequence level, it is perhaps best to create a short text for one performer or a score of texts for more than one performer. Just performing a single sentence might be problematic; the content of the (repeated) sentence would most likely create such a focus that people would indeed have trouble finding the music in it. Instead, it might be useful to create something of the length of one or very few sentences that indeed does not make sense. You could do something along the lines of a child's mixed-up story activity where words of some type (verb, number, famous person) are chosen blindly and inserted by the person writing words down within a narrative that the others do not see, and they hear the product in the end. You could cut up all of the words and put them in a random order and try to pronounce them as if they were a normal sentence or become even more adventurous by interpreting the words slightly, giving them a "spoken personality" as part of the performance. This should be well prepared before sharing it, thus allowing you to improve your performance or correct things that do not seem to work well. When working with more than one person, you should attempt to make the individual parts work well and, especially, ensure that the totality sounds musical.

Voice 1	*Voice 2*
Banker...	...sss
	... sssssssssssssssssssssssssss
Take your money *(rhythmically)*	... sssssss ...money *(echo)*
	... money ...money
	... money ...money
Save your...	... money *(keep the beat)*
	... money *(reply)*
Save your...	... money *(simultaneous)*
Save your...	... money
Save your...	... money
Save...	... me *(simlt)* ... me *(reply)*
Save...	... me *(simlt)* ... me *(reply)*
Save...	---... me *(reply only)*
Save...	---... me *(reply only)*
---	--- Oh my!

FIGURE 4.3   A text–sound sequence score

Sound organisation activity 3b: Recorded text–sound sequence In this sequence, it is best to avoid effects beyond the basic ones such as reversing sounds, looping them and stretching or compressing them. In fact, using no effects at all can lead to some exciting results. You will either record one or more voices or have to find speech recordings and download them. For example you can download famous politicians' speeches or an interview with a celebrity. Using similar techniques to start composing with the spoken voice as in the live sequence above, you now have the opportunity to carefully cut up the downloaded recordings into short words and phrases, place the fragments of speech in time either using one single layer or more than one, as was the case with the performed sequence. If using more than one, see what happens when you place two voices or two words at exactly the same time. If you find that combination hard to follow, separate the two voices left and right and eventually add a third in the middle (same amount of sound left and right).

Listen closely to how smoothly the voices move from word to word. If things get too awkward due to the cutting and pasting, the sounding result can be quite disconcerting. What do you end up paying attention to? Is it the text or texts? The voices? The sounds? The pitches?

As in the case with this chapter's initial examples, there is nothing stopping you from returning to these text–sound activities and discovering the wealth of opportunities that arise just by using the voice. If you like, expand the activities' potential material by using unusual sounds that the voice can produce and this new speech-based music world will open up even more. Try changing the normal timing of how speech works, perhaps by adding an unusual rhythm, and create the vocal equivalent of our imaginary soundscape. The bad news is that there are so many choices; the good news is that these choices are as diverse as your imagination is open to adventure and discovery.

It is worthy to note that there exists a visual version of text–sound composition. Instead of poetry to be read transforming into poetry to be heard, in this case the transformation takes you to poetry to be looked at. A movement called letterism (also written as lettrism from the original French *lettrisme*) evolved around the usage of text as material for paintings and sculpture and, of course, digital media versions of letterism have evolved subsequently. Think, for example, of the word explosion. A letterist might portray this word by writing the ex in small letters, the p a bit louder and so on until the end of the word seems to blow up or get torn up.

Performers have been known to improvise using the images of letterist works as evocative scores, scores in which the level of interpretation is much greater

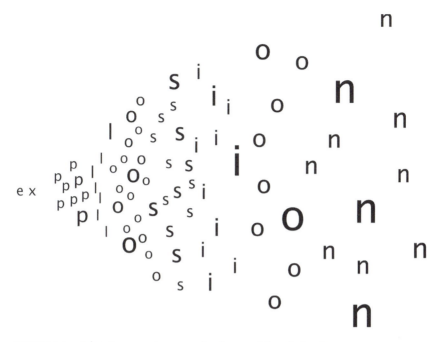

FIGURE 4.4   A lettrist evocative score for the word "explosion"

than that of a five-line score. Such performances can turn into a wonderful mixture of literature, song, acting and sound-based music. Of course digital means can be applied, such as effects during performance or, alternatively, one can make pre-recorded mixes of the interpreted images.

The following activities will introduce how you might organise sound based on a diversity of prescriptive materials. We shall follow up on the letterist approach employing a more abstract evocative score and a storyboard. These activities are unusual in that there is a different type of planning involved. You get the chance to create circumstances. By preparing an image that tells you or a performer what the inspiration is for a sequence or, even more specifically, what is expected within a sequence in time, a stimulus or some details related to aspects of the sequence are prepared beforehand. This is a very useful way of creating sound-based music. That said, traditionally most sound-based music scores are made after a work is composed for analytical purposes or as an aid during performance. In the following examples, we borrow the idea of using notation from the tradition of note-based music as a preliminary stage before performing or recording a work. One of the goals of these activities is to see to what extent these forms of notation support your own creative work or, if you discover you work best by going straight to your chosen materials, whether these forms of scores hinder your sound organisation.

Sound organisation activity 4a: Letterist score sequence In this first score-based sequence, we stay with our previous subject of spoken voice and add other forms of vocalisation this time by way of an evocative score consisting solely of the text. No instructions need to be given in order to leave open how the text is to be interpreted. The only interpretation information is how the text of the sequence is presented visually. As above, this activity can be turned into a live performance or, alternatively, worked on using a sequencer, thus involving a recording of the text eventually with some of the interpretation already worked out and then further worked on using any relevant techniques that you like that were presented in Chapter 3.

This approach is particularly rewarding when listeners can view the score as they listen to it. This combination is also very useful in educational as well as workshop situations as it offers participants something to hold on to.

If you want to be inventive in a different manner, you can create an instant score by taking something that was not intended for this type of use. For example, you could try to perform an advertisement from the classified section of the newspaper or one from a newspaper in a language that you do not speak. They tend to be filled with abbreviations. A humorous result is guaranteed. The advert is to the score what a sample is to sample-based music. Just be careful that you do not tread on any toes in terms of copyright!

As with all of these activities, you can try different scores or different versions of a single score or even mixing bits from different scores to create short sequences and evaluate what you find effective and what is unsuccessful. It might also be useful to try to evoke different moods in the various versions that you make.

```
Aantr. gedist. sl. j.vr. zkt.
discr. gener. rijk HEER 50+
Br. o. nr.          v/d bld.
```

FIGURE 4.5   A classified advertisement in any language can be used as a score

Sound organisation activity 4b: Evocative score sequence Taking a step further, we leave the word and move back into the world of any sound. An evocative score can be fairly literal. For example, you could draw the objects that are sounding and, as in letterism, treat them visually as you would like them treated sonically. Alternatively, you can make more abstract images that act as an inspiration in terms of your artistic choices, in particular any of our parameters or combination between them. What we are looking for in this sequence activity is a means of planting a seed to inspire the search for potential useful materials, enticing ways of treating them if relevant and successful ways of ordering and eventually combining them in time. Admittedly there is potentially so much freedom in this activity that individuals may decide that they prefer evocative scores that are less abstract. Others may like the more abstract images due to the opportunity to make diverse sequences based on one single image. Like the letterism activity, the goal is to trigger ideas as opposed to assigning them. This can be done more effectively by way of a storyboard, which is another type of score.

Sound organisation activity 4c: Storyboard sequence The storyboard was introduced in Chapter 2. Unlike our five-line staff, it can look like anything ranging from a recipe to a general description—in words or images—of a sequence of events. There is no better way to get an initial experience with a storyboard than at the modest sequence level. In this way, one does not need to get lost in terms of deciding about too much information at once. The ability to make a larger-scale storyboard comes with experience.

Using any form you feel comfortable with, create a storyboard of a sonic sequence. In this case it is quite important to be aware of your intentions as it is useful to discover that what you set out to create is received in a similar manner by your listeners. The storyboard can be as detailed as you want it to be or simply offer more general instructions or visual pointers.

The next step is to realise the sonic version of the storyboard ideally in more than one form. It is possible to create a performance based on a storyboard as well as a recording, so this activity is not exceptional as far as that is concerned. What is quite interesting in this activity is the ability to prepare information regarding all aspects of the sequence including content, manipulation and notated suggestions related to all of our parameters such as dynamics, density and so on.

After having tried one or more storyboards in one or more versions, you might evaluate how successful your sequences have been in terms of your level of satisfaction with them, how well the listeners were able to hear what

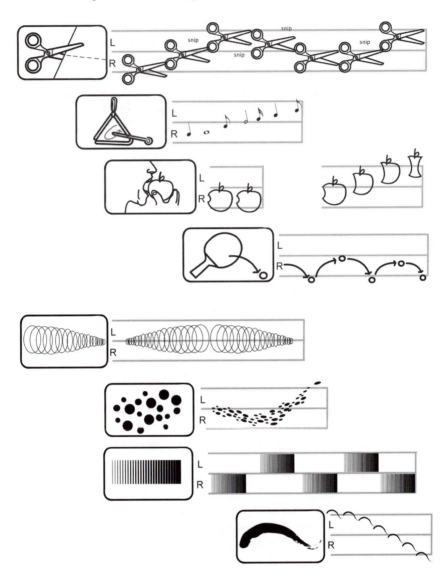

FIGURE 4.6–4.7 Evocative score sequences using contextual and musical symbols

you set out to achieve and how useful a storyboard has been in terms of aiding your creative efforts. The answer to this last question will be very dependent on each individual's way of creating and solving a challenge and will aid in finding efficient ways of working at the larger levels presented in Chapter 4.

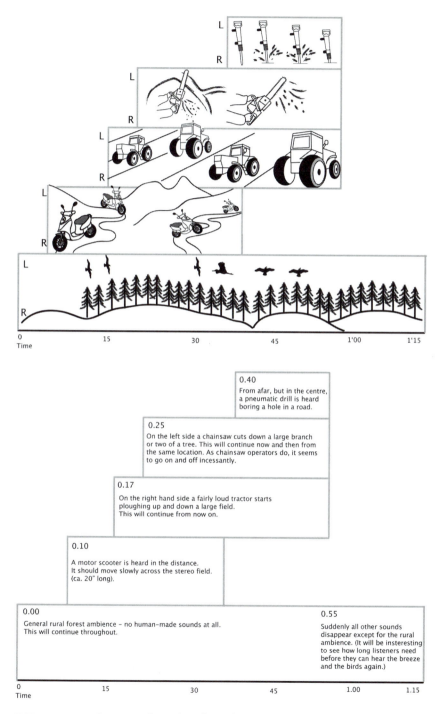

0.40

From afar, but in the centre, a pneumatic drill is heard boring a hole in a road.

0.25

On the left side a chainsaw cuts down a large branch or two of a tree. This will continue now and then from the same location. As chainsaw operators do, it seems to go on and off incessantly.

0.17

On the right hand side a fairly loud tractor starts ploughing up and down a large field. This will continue from now on.

0.10

A motor scooter is heard in the distance. It should move slowly across the stereo field. (ca. 20" long).

0.00

General rural forest ambience – no human-made sounds at all. This will continue throughout.

0.55

Suddenly all other sounds disappear except for the rural ambience. (It will be insteresting to see how long listeners need before they can hear the breeze and the birds again.)

0
Time   15   30   45   1.00   1.15

FIGURE 4.8–4.9   Image- and text-based storyboard sequences

Most musicians trained in schools and conservatoires will eventually learn notation. Having written that, most music made around the world uses no score at all. The music is prepared aurally and in many cases passed on from generation to generation in this manner too. Therefore literacy related to scores is not a must in many types of music. It is also not a must in sound-based music. Nonetheless, the use of notation can be extremely useful in terms of getting many ideas into perspective when taking on an artistic project. Some people never use any form of notation, as is the case in aural tradition. Others cannot work without them. Others still decide whether to have some sort of prescriptive score support based on the needs of the project itself. And, as said, some make their scores afterwards for a variety of purposes. Some food for thought: to what extent might one consider a saved session in sequencing software as something related to a score?

We will now move on to an activity that can be very rewarding artistically. It also can be rewarding for the listener, in particular the inexperienced listener, as it offers something to hold on to even when the music that is being made is extremely novel. I once published an article in which I suggested that much innovative music was not reaching a very large audience, not only due to the fact that the media do not give it sufficient attention, nor many of our schools, but also due to the fact that composers as well as improvising musicians do not offer their listeners anything in particular to hold on to (Landy 1994b). After studying a significant number of sound-based works, I discovered a number of aural cues that listeners can hold on to in terms of navigating their way through a work. Before moving on to a very straightforward thing to hold on to, the main categories proposed in this article were: a) many of the parameters that have already been presented, b) homogeneity of sounding materials or, alternatively, the search for novel sound materials, c) restricting the number of discrete layers of sound qualities to approximately four in general (to avoid getting lost in a complexity of information), and d) sound-based music's equivalent of a programme. A programme does not necessarily need to equate to a narrative story as such, but still may allow the listener to partake in a particular type of sonic journey. An extra-musical programme note or statement of the musical intention of a piece, also known as its dramaturgy, can also be something for listeners to hold on to. Getting used to four sonic layers or to a programme needs a greater duration than that of a sequence to take effect normally, so these will not be presented in the following sound activities. They will become important in Chapter 5.

Sound organisation activity 5: Sequence utilising only one single sound type For this activity, we shall focus on the notion of homogeneity of materials. In fact the goal will be to create a few sequences based on a single type of sound. Whether the sound type is "bird sounds," "sounds related to friction" or even "my computer mouse", the goal is to create a sequence in which that sound type is presented in various ways, where the listener is always aware that the same sound type is always present. In other words, it is not advisable to make sounds so abstract that they can no longer be related to the sound type that you have chosen.

Techniques from any activity thus far can be applied here. One that I believe is worth focusing on is the notion of placing your sound in different places within the aural space: far away, nearby, and so on. Another thing worth pursuing is any form of audible contrast.

Not only can you investigate the many sounds that are available from a single type, you will also discover how using one or more effects can aid you in creating variations on that theme. In this way you can actually start to collect sequences in this activity, as in any other, that you may very well like to recycle and use in a sound-based piece later on. This comes with experience and gaining confidence.

Our next step in terms of creating sequences is from one thing to hold on to, the sound type, to our parameter list as mentioned above. One could easily spend weeks on this one. Some composers have made a career based on focusing on one or more parameters as highlight features of their works. For example, so-called spectral composers⋆ focus on sound quality. Many of you will also be aware of musicians who seem to focus on loudness, particularly at the upper or lower end of the scale.

Sound organisation activity 6: Sequence focusing on one parameter or more
In this activity the goal is again to offer listeners something to hold on to by focusing on one or, at most, very few parameters as the key sonic element. To reiterate, beyond sound types and sources, our parameters consisted of: pitch, duration, dynamics, sound quality, space, simultaneities, sound density, (dis)order and, of course, recognisability of sounds. Let's now look at these briefly in sequence.

Pitch Although we are not seeking to create note-based sequences, a sequence can focus on a pitch range, one or more single pitches (and eventually pitches that are extremely close to one another to create interesting sonic qualities) or simply be all over the place in terms of pitch, thus asking the listener to follow how pitch moves about as opposed to following specific pitch movement at more predictable levels. In this case, the sound materials may vary greatly, as may the effects, but the pattern of pitch behaviour must be reasonably consistent and clearly the main thing to hold on to.

Duration At sequence level this may be a bit challenging. Running the risk of shortening or elongating our sequences radically here, one might envision a sequence solely consisting of very short or very long sounds eventually involving sounds simultaneously heard or presented in layers. Alternatively, sounds may have unpredictable durations, thus adding a level of uncertainty of what is coming next. Or, at the opposite end of the spectrum, sounds may be used that are hugely varied but all lasting the same amount of time. There is a pattern of behaviour evolving already that demonstrates by choosing something that is constant or consistent an enormous amount of freedom opens up for most other aspects of the sounds that you are using.

Dynamics As suggested above, we can work at any place along the dynamics scale including very quiet and exceedingly loud. We can also have sounds move about the dynamic register radically thus offering a listening experience that one is rarely offered. You have already guessed that the materials used may vary as little or as much as you like to ensure that the aural focus is loudness in the dynamics sequences.

Sound quality As in the case of the spectralists, our focus will be on sound quality above all. To achieve this, one can start with a certain type of sound quality and somehow turn this sound or group of similar sounds into a sequence or one can use effects to vary a sound but somehow retain relative spectral consistency. There have been many sound-based works that evolve in this manner and they are sometimes grouped as "timbral works." Such works sound particularly special when the varieties of the sound quality are projected spatially, perhaps around, above and underneath an audience. For our purposes, simply creating a sequence in which the sound quality is more important than source or any of our other parameters is key. For those who have been educated solely in note-based music before starting reading this book, you might note how far you have come from melody and metre in such a short time!

Space The experience of space is definitely something listeners can hold on to in a piece of music. Many of you will have listened to pieces of pop music in which the sound of an instrument seems to crawl through your head if you listen to the piece on headphones or zigzag back and forth when playing the music on your loudspeakers. In multichannel environments it can be fascinating to follow where sounds evolve from or how they move about in a space. Before we graduate to such complexity, attempt to allow space to come to the foreground in a stereo sequence. For example you could use a single sound and have it bounce left and right and slowly work its way to the middle and then go back again to the extremes. You can have a longer sound move about as if it were a helicopter circling or have a sound appear at unexpected places within a general ambience causing a sense of unpredictability as we have before.

Simultaneities We are going to spend a bit of time discussing vertical relationships in a few paragraphs' time. For the time being try to make a sequence that focuses on the presence of a number of sounds at once occasionally within a sequence. In this case you should ensure that all individual sounds are heard discretely or, if you like and are able to achieve this, have them mixed so that one creates combined sounds as opposed to a group of simultaneous sounds. A variation on this might be to have some groups appear simultaneously and others to be ever so slightly staggered in time and space. In all cases the simultaneities should be the main focus.

Sound density This parameter is a very good one in terms of things to hold on to and can be very useful in terms of musical listening, as was sound quality. If the density is high and the duration of sounds is short you might be able to create what could be called sound masses or clouds of sounds. You might opt to constantly change the density and, depending on the predictability of change, alter your sequence from order (predictable) to disorder. Although jumping the gun a bit, density and space make an excellent combination of things to hold on to. We are not particularly used to talking about note-based music in terms of its being full or empty, although it is a focus in some pieces, but when organising sounds, this concept is an obvious one on which to focus. One example: create a sequence of what might be called "overly full music".

(Dis)order A sequence coming across as orderly or as chaotic is indeed something that one can focus upon when listening. Perhaps order is expected, so "a well-ordered example" may not be the best thing to do for this activity, but if order emerges from chaos, it is sometimes like a breath of fresh air. A chaotic example will certainly offer a navigation tool for the listener even if the origin and destination of the chaos are not terribly clear. Still, this parameter works best when it changes. Try to create a sequence that seems to start off in a disordered manner and seems to end up somewhere much less chaotic or vice-versa.

Recognisability of sounds Of all of our parameters, this one has been most tried and tested. We actually focused on it already in our first and second pairs of activities above. You can well imagine how this parameter, whether at either end of the recognition scale or moving about the scale, can offer the listener a navigation aid.

Any other parameter that you might come up with The parameter list is not exhaustive and there are probably hundreds that have yet to be named that might be useful in terms of composition with sounds. Can you come up with one that is not only useful in terms of creating a sequence, but also aids the listening experience? I would be eager to hear about your discoveries.

Or any combination that works and still offers something(s) to hold on to We have already experienced cases where it is easy to combine parameters efficiently whilst still offering the listener something to hold on to. In fact some combinations, such as density and space, work very well hand in hand. Try to see which combinations can work effectively at sequence level. Can you achieve this with three or more parameters at once without their getting in each other's way? It is possible.

The achievement of offering listening tools whilst being able to achieve satisfying artistic results is a formula that works for everyone involved in the artistic experience. I personally believe that the something-to-hold-on-to factor is not a means of diluting one's artistic abilities; instead, it is a wonderful formula in terms of connecting with your public, including those who have never heard this type of artistic expression before or, at least, have not been conscious of it as a potential form of music.

Creating Vertical Relationships between Sounds

Before moving on to the gestural level, which is in many ways a natural step forward from the sequence—in fact, many of your sequences may already have been musical gestures—it is worth spending a short amount of time looking at vertical relationships. We have mentioned this option on many occasions already, but we are now at a point where it is useful to know whether a single line of sound can hold a listener's attention and for how long. One might think that the single line is similar to a melody, but remember, a melody can also exist as a foreground line in a score with many instruments playing an accompanying role. Similarly a foreground sequence can exist in the sound-based context where this sequence fits into the totality of sound that is being presented.

We have spoken thus far of three things that are all good starting points related to this subject. First, we have discussed placing sounds within a general ambience; this was a feature during the soundwalks.

There was also the notion of working in sound layers, something that can be very useful in terms of our sound quality parameter as well as some of the others.

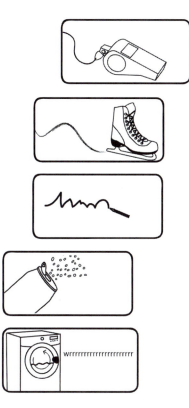

FIGURE 4.10   Working with layers of sound

Finally there was indeed the notion of sounds appearing simultaneously and thus these are similar to an interval or a chord in note-based music. We must be extremely careful when making such comparisons, as there is no obvious equivalent to a chord as this notion is entirely dependent on pitch.

Now that these initial three options have been introduced, why do we create vertical relationships? One obvious answer is that, through having sounds appear simultaneously, we can help to define the sense of space we produce musically through our positioning sounds in different places within that space. Another obvious answer is that music often works best when it offers the greatest contrasts as well as elements that appear and reappear. Therefore horizontal as well as vertical devices can all be hugely effective when organising sounds, just like they are with notes. A final answer to complete this brief discussion is that simultaneity is indeed one of our parameters. It offers a range between nothing ever happens at the same time to every sound heard consists of more than one sound. The moral to the story is that although note-based and sound-based music are largely produced in different manners and often do not sound all that similar, they also have many important commonalities. The musical aspect of vertical relationships between sounds is a very important member of the list of common traits. We shall encounter a few more before we are finished.

Creating, Analysing and Evaluating Sonic Gestures

How long is a sequence? Phrases in note-based music tend to be eight measures long, sometimes four or even sixteen, or something else. How long were our sequences, though? Answer: they were as long as seemed appropriate. A sequence has a length that is determined by our aural experience of it.

How long is a gesture, then? In note-based music it has no fixed length and that will remain so here, too. In fact a sound-based gesture may be as short as a single sound if the way it evolves sounds like the translation of a physical gesture. Conversely, it can be as long as a sound-based short story if that is how long it takes to arrive at the end of the gesture. As we shall discover, gestures need not take place in isolation. They may consist of 'mini-gestures' in succession or multiple (linked★) or even composite (at least partially simultaneous★) ones that form within themselves a single gesture (from Blackburn 2009a).

We are not quite ready yet for that gesture that lasts as long as a short story— we shall commence at a more modest level. The goal in this second section of Chapter 4 is to understand that any sound-based gesture is launched and completed regardless of its length.

Gestures are most obviously associated with musical listening. Can one therefore not create a gesture with more contextual or representative sounds? This is not only possible, but it occurs often in sound-based works. The nature of some sounds is gestural or the way that we are able to put them together turns these sounds into a musical gesture. Still, the majority of such gestures are, indeed, intended for musical listening.

Given all of the freedom that we have in terms of organising sounds, you may find it hard to believe that there are even some gestures that might be called clichés as they are used in sound-based works rather often. Just to cite one example that we shall return to below, many pieces start immediately or within a second or two with an explosive sound that diminishes fairly rapidly, turns into a rather stable, yet excited state before it explodes again and the piece continues. The few seconds leading to that stable state are a clear gesture; the following one commences when the stable state erupts leading towards the second explosive sound. This is just one example of potentially powerful, but now often-used gestures. As you listen to more and more sound-based works, you will be able to decide how effective such gestures are that you have heard many times before, and whether you like to use or possibly avoid them.

Nonetheless, to paraphrase Shakespeare, I am not here to bury sound-based gestures, but to praise them. Gestures are essential to bringing a composition alive.

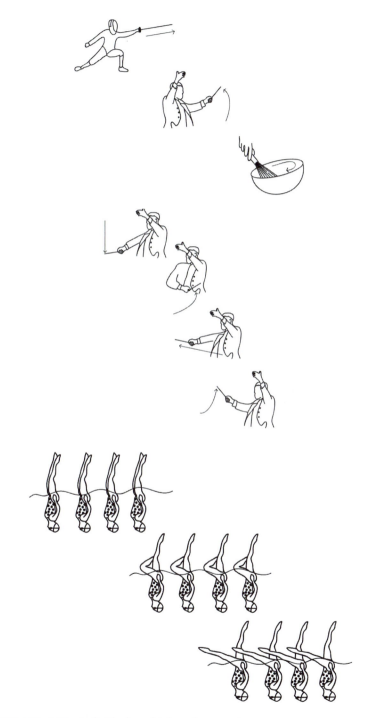

FIGURE 4.11–4.13 Individual, multiple and composite gestures

We shall present gestures based on two approaches: one more closely related to our storyboards, and one more based on abstract images intended for musical listening. In the former case, it is the people organising a storyboard in the form of a general prescriptive score who are to determine where contextual or musical gestures might be placed and how they evolve. Therefore they are creating images on paper related to how a given gesture is launched and resolved and how that fits within a given sound-based musical context. In the latter case, the more abstract images will act as a score suggesting sonic behaviour that can be constructed in many ways, thus truly focusing on musical behaviour, at least when such gestures are treated in isolation.

Gestures can be constructed but they normally evolve within a context, so it is a bit artificial to talk about them in isolation. The goal here is to work on a few by way of our activities so that we can all get a sense of how such gestures might sound and, in the next chapter, find means of creating contexts for them and means to link them up.

Following our approach the initial gesture activities will emanate from the artist's links to real-world sounds. This first step takes us to those storyboards that were constructed on the basis of identifying and, where relevant, sequencing sounds related to our everyday world. As said in this section's introduction, many sounds are, in themselves, gestural. Think, for example, of the sound of a squeaky door being shut. The sequence from initially setting the door in movement—a chill might go up your back at this moment related to the noise quality that would be heard—until the door is clicked shut represents a single sound gesture.

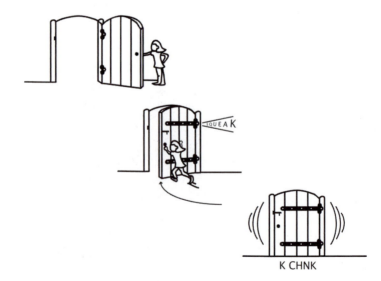

FIGURE 4.14 A gesture sequence involving a squeaky door

Still, not all sounds are gestural by any means. The sound of a hammer striking a nail is the result of a physical gesture, but the sound itself is a discrete attack as the movement of the hammer is probably silent. This sound is something that might be repeated in a rhythmical sequence. Here one might speak of an implied physical gesture when the cause, the person hammering the nail, is taken into account. However, the percussive sound itself is not gestural. A whip, on the other hand, involves the sound of its movement before its crack and thus does form a musical gesture.

Denis Smalley, the person who has written the most about gesture in sound-based music, speaks of gestures consisting of onsets, continuants and terminations (Smalley 1986, 69). These are not dissimilar from our attack/sustain/release (without the internal decay) that we associate with envelope generation. It boils down to how things are launched, how they evolve and how they reach some form of goal or, alternatively, move on to another gesture. As stated, gestures whose termination acts as a link to or onset of a following gesture form multiple gestures. Gestures that consist of smaller gestures within them, thus creating a complex sound, we can call composite gestures. Composite gestures are more difficult to create and are therefore at an advanced level. Obviously, the three-part model here is not needed in all cases, but does represent a great many sound-based gestures. For the sake of completeness, it is also possible to create two-part gestures or greater-than-three-part gestures, but for our purposes this three-part concept is by far the best starting point.

Contextual gesture activity 1: Identifying gestures employing identifiable real-world sounds In this first gesture-based activity, we shall not be creating gestures, but, instead, identifying them. The goal of this initial activity is to identify single-sound gestures as well as gestures that work with multiple sounds. Our next step will be to record single-sound gestures and construct multiple sound gestures as well.

You can go to one or more locations during this activity. The goal is to identify ten sounds that fulfil the description of a sonic gesture as well as five combinations of sounds—this is a bit more difficult—that together form a sonic gesture. Undertaking this activity with someone else or others can be quite satisfying as you can discuss gestural sonic behaviour amongst yourselves in order to gain both knowledge and confidence.

In the case of gestures consisting of more than one sound, can you describe how they fit together? Can you imagine how you would be able to construct such a gesture using a sequencer?

Contextual gesture activity 2: Imagining real-world sonic gestures In activity 1 we were sound hunters. In this second activity, we can use our imagination and memory to create mental images of single and multiple sonic gestures involving real-world sounds. As above, you are asked to think of ten single sounds (excluding those discovered in the first activity) that possess a sonic gesture themselves. If you need to add a sentence to describe the circumstances related to certain sounds, this would be useful. Furthermore, you are asked to envision five sonic gestures involving more than one real-world sound. This is perhaps a good time to return to our storyboards. How would you create a symbolic or descriptive notation for these five gestures? If you can, try to vocalise these gestures to see whether they would fit together. You will get a chance to make them in the next activity.

Contextual gesture activity 3: Creating real-world sonic gestures The time has come to translate the knowledge that you have gained in the first two activities to doing these things yourself. Similar to the other activities, the goal is to make a number of real-world sonic gestures, both based on one single sound or more than one. In the former case, it is a question of recording or finding sounds that you find appropriate and making certain that they are isolated in such a way that the result offers a clear gesture. In the case of multiple sounds, perhaps those you just conceived of in the second activity, you may want to refer to some form of notation, storyboard or otherwise. Here one has to be careful to ensure that the flow from one sound to another seems natural to support the contextual emphasis. You may need to use some of our means of sound manipulation to achieve this, but do not attempt to mask the source's recognition from your listeners. We shall get to more abstract gestures soon enough, but for now, allowing listeners to react to your efforts by offering contextual responses is the goal. If you are making these gestures combining sounds by ear, it might be nice to create a notation for them, beyond what is on the sequencer, after you find the resultant gestures satisfactory.

Some readers may find this last word, "satisfactory", a bit loaded. Obviously, when starting out, just being able to create a sonic gesture with more than one sound is quite a feat. I have found with most artistic activities in which I have been involved that there is always a phase of placing things into a basic sequence—with the ability to reject or change things later, of course—and a follow-up phase involved with refining the detail of those things that I placed in the sequence beforehand. Here, too, once you know that two or more sounds together form a sonic gesture, it is good to place them in general sequential positions and then ensure that they end up flowing together smoothly. Perhaps "naturally" would be a better word here, but of course, your placing some things in a sequencer and moving them around is not quite that, but the intention is clear. A good gesture is one that seems to fit together. When this is the case, they usually sound satisfactory. Taste plays a role here too, of course, and may contribute to a satisfactory outcome. This is normal. What is most important is the attempt to learn how to envision a desired sonic gesture and then, with time, to find the means to achieve it.

Contextual gesture activity 4: Creating multiple and composite real-world sonic gestures Our last activity before moving on to more abstract sonic gestures is to create multiple and composite gestures using real-world sounds. Let's start with multiple gestures that I believe most readers will not find too difficult. Here the termination of the first one is somehow involved with the onset of the next one. There are many roads to Rome. For example, a first gesture may end with a disappearance that reverses itself and becomes the onset for the next sound. Another example would be to have a short termination that, when repeated, is the attack for the following one or is even itself the attack for the next part of the gesture. There are hundreds of possibilities.

Try to create three or four such multiple gestures using real-world sounds only. These shorter gestures may consist of a single sound or a sequence of sounds like those we have been dealing with in all of these activities. As above, it is worthwhile evaluating your results and thinking about what makes a gesture successful and what can get in the way. Again, sound manipulation tools might be useful from time to time. By using a hit-or-miss working method one builds up a collection of skills and things to avoid, so a failure is in many ways useful in identifying risks that might be avoided in the future.

We have not really dealt with composite gestures yet and it is an advanced topic as far as this book is concerned, so feel free to skip it if it proves too challenging. The image I often have with composite gestures is a cluster of a few onset/continuation/termination combinations together forming a single gesture. An example might be an old-fashioned cuckoo clock where you get a sonic announcement that the hour is about the be heard followed by the combination of the sound of gears turning, bells being chimed and a reverberant termination when all ends, possibly including the cuckoo disappearing into its home. Similarly, if you think back to the soundwalks where we spoke of sounds fitting together, creating a single sound quality: these sounds may have created a single linear gesture such as those that we made in the previous activity or, alternatively, may have been composite gestures within themselves.

The creation of a composite gesture is best served by way of some form of notation, at least during the early stages. Try to envision sounds that fit together that, as a totality, create a single gesture of smaller gestures. The richness of this sonic gesture is the result of the simultaneous appearance of its constituent parts. Once you have one or two such composite gestures in mind, try to realise them through the use of recordings or downloading sounds and placing them in sequence. In this case it might be useful to think of how to spatialise them so that the component parts can all be heard clearly at separate points or areas within the sonic space. Sound manipulation tools may be useful to make the result seem more balanced. Once completed, you should again take the time to evaluate how successful these are, how they can be improved and what you particularly like about them for future use.

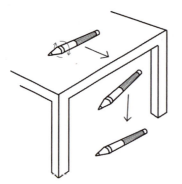

4.15

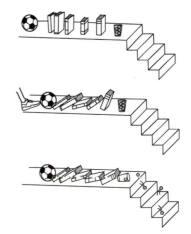

4.16

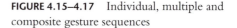

4.17

FIGURE 4.15–4.17   Individual, multiple and composite gesture sequences

These four activities should have provided you with an idea of the diversity of potential gestures related to contextual listening. This diversity takes into account the sound sources that you use and also how sounds are being caused. Cause is relevant whenever the contextual listening experience is important to the gesture. This is a huge area and a fundamental one in terms of creating music by way of sound organisation. Nevertheless, most sonic gestures are not necessarily related to their original source and/or context and, as always, there is that huge grey area in between. Let's now move on to the more abstract side of making gestures, namely that associated with musical listening. This, again, is an advanced, yet valuable topic that readers may choose to postpone after becoming acquainted with its opportunities.

To introduce this more abstract side of sonic gestures, the use of abstract images will be important. We can symbolise aspects visually using geometric shapes; this was a focus of Smalley's theory related to gestures. These shapes will be evocative of the more detailed content of the gestures. In this case we want our sounds to be heard for their musical values more than contextual ones.

Sometimes whilst writing a book like this one you discover that someone else has already been involved with one aspect of the book's contents. In such cases the person who got there first deserves the credit. The book's illustrator, Manuella Blackburn, has used evocative graphic symbols associated with Smalley's writings on sonic gesture construction in an experiment to see whether university-level music students with little sound-based musical experience could use these graphic symbols as a stimulus towards the creation of sound-based musical gestures (Blackburn 2009a, 2009b, 2010).

Blackburn created a set of images related to the combination of onset/continuant/termination using different words and symbols for each of the three, again to demonstrate the diversity of potential musical gestures. The following image contains potential onset, continuant and termination images (left to right) as well as one potential resulting combination. Obviously, simpler images can be used for more straightforward sounds.

Before readers panic, I must reiterate the point that these symbols are inspirational, not overly representing the sounds to be chosen. The idea is to create a musical sonic gesture that relates to a geometric abstract image. Look at any of the above images and try to create a vocal gesture based on it. It is actually not that difficult! I am certain that once you have succeeded vocally, imagining sounds that could be used to create a sonic translation of the image would not be too taxing either.

In another (previously unpublished) example Blackburn has created an image that is a perfect rendition of what has been described above as an often-encountered sound-based music gesture that might even be called a cliché. After an initial "explosion" a sound develops and reaches a steady state that, in turn can be used as the onset for the following gesture, thus creating a multiple gesture. The fact that this type of behaviour has become common is

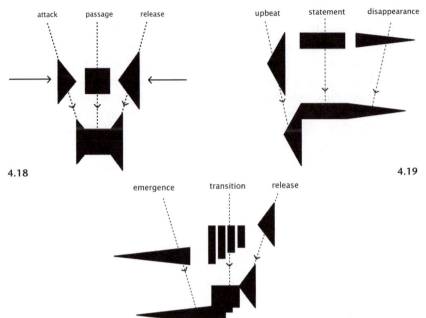

FIGURE 4.18–4.20 Three examples of onset/continuant/termination gestural sequences

FIGURE 4.21 A host of potential onset, continuant and termination images

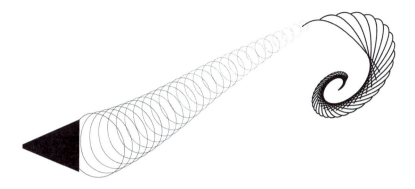

FIGURE 4.22   One combination taken from the previous illustration

FIGURE 4.23   An often-encountered sound-based musical gesture

naturally partially due to its effectiveness. It is simply comical that, during a concert of ca. six works, two or three might begin or include such a recognisable gesture.

The following image is an example of a multiple gesture in which the release element of the first part of the gesture is equally the upbeat part of the second part, similar to the description of that explosive sound. In this way, a single gesture consisting of two interlocking gestures can be constructed. Its six constituent parts merge into five, creating a gesture of two overlapping gestures.

Before moving to the chapter's final activities, it is worth noting that in Smalley's discussion of gesture, the term "motion" comes into play. Motion can be related to pitch and to space. It can also be related to other elements as long as they can be perceived as motional. An image introducing composite multi-directional motion might look like this:

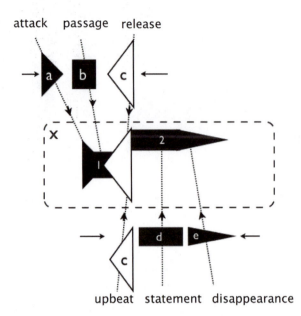

attack passage release

upbeat statement disappearance

FIGURE 4.24   A multiple gesture consisting of two interlocking individual gestures

FIGURE 4.25   An image representing multi-directional motion

Note that such images are not necessarily literal timelines. They are instead inspirational.

This discussion with its associated images provides a strong foundation for the activities for this second half of the gesture section of this chapter. We need not use these specific images as they have been provided primarily to give a taste of how such abstract images can be made. In fact, different people would come up with entirely different sounds when offered such images. And, of course, any individual could come up with dozens of sound scenarios for any of the above as well.

Musical gesture activity 1: Envisioning musical sonic gestures whilst using your imagination Similar to what we did with real-world sounds, we shall now attempt to imagine how to make diverse musical gestures. Create abstract images for five different musical gestures and then write a description of how they might sound, what types of (manipulated) sounds you might use and try to consider an alternative group of sounds for the same image. Can you vocalise what you transcribed?

Musical gesture activity 2: Creating musical sonic gestures Blackburn's image with the selection of onsets, continuants and terminations should act as an inspiration for this activity. Use similar combinations of your own to create five images and two different sonic gestures for each image. I have always found it useful to vocalise these gestures to get an idea of the type(s) of sounds and sound qualities that I am looking for. You may find this helpful, too. Which aspects of the sounds are you concentrating on? Do these have anything to do with our parameters or combinations of parameters? Can spatialisation be helpful here? Which common characteristics coming out of these examples seem to be related to the development of your own sonic signature?

Musical gesture activity 3: Creating multiple and composite musical sonic gestures Similar to Contextual gesture activity 4 related to real-world sonic gestures, the goal here is to create at least three multiple and, if you are willing, composite gestures focusing on different types of relationships. This activity not only raises your game in terms of the level of challenge, but it allows you to broaden the spectrum of types of sound qualities you can fabricate and apply in a gestural manner. People able to create gestures related to this activity are well on their way towards creating sophisticated sound-based music. Again, can you tell which aspects of sound you are concentrating on at various moments in these complex gestures? Is spatialisation a means of making the gestures more powerful? Don't forget to evaluate your work regarding the last two activities; self-evaluation is a great tool in terms of your being aware of the talent that you are developing. Obviously evaluation from outside people, especially those with more experience, can also be of at least equal value.

We have now been introduced to real-world and abstract gestures and it takes little imagination to realise that these are the black and white poles of a long line in which the grey area in the middle is quite wide, offering at least as many opportunities as those at the extremes. Hopefully, you will now have a sense of how we can put sounds together at the local level. This will prove invaluable when working with longer time durations working up to full pieces of music. A gesture can be anything from the musical equivalent of the short breath to what has been called a sonic short story. It is one of the key means of construction between the individual sound and a complete piece of music.

Before departing this fourth chapter it is important to re-emphasise the importance of the evaluations called upon in many of these chapters' activities. Evaluation is something that goes beyond criticism. It is also the investigation of a number of intertwined aspects of your creative work: what was intended and to what extent has that been enabled; how was it made and what commonalities does it have with other examples that you have created; and how has it introduced new opportunities to you, plus how did you react to those new opportunities? Evaluation is an important aspect towards having an analytical understanding of your work. I expect my creative music students to understand the "how" and the "why" of their work just like any teacher would. I also expect them to have some understanding of where their work fits in terms of other music or art, thus placing it in context. We have not dwelled on this point of musical placement in this chapter, but there is nothing stopping us from looking at our gestures and further work in terms of repertoire with which we are acquainted, such as those types of sound-based music introduced in the first chapter. The combination of a detailed knowledge of your work and a knowledge of whose work it is somehow connected with allows you to be able to identify and participate in communities who share your interests. The advantage of an analytical understanding is that you will not only be acutely aware of what you are doing, but also of what many others are doing who share similar music interests with you. Music may be seen to be spontaneous by many, but behind that spontaneity is a good deal of experience as well as skills and creative imagination. The thinking musician is aware of her or his abilities as well as aspects that can be improved upon. Such musicians are aware of the strengths of their work and thus often perform it with authority as they gain confidence through the knowledge of those strengths and the underlying unique creative ideas. This type of empowerment is one of the most attractive aspects of music, as well as the other arts, as creativity is, as already stated, not a question of answering a question, but instead finding your own best solution to the challenge of the day.

Evaluation and analysis will be returned to in the following chapter in which we, at last, can look at entire pieces. Please note that a piece of sound-based music need not be long, so we shall start with some short etudes to make the step from our gestures to the piece not too daunting.

5

ORGANISING SOUNDS 2

Composing with Sounds

The time has come to think big. All right, think at a larger scale, as we are still working our way up a ladder of creative potential. In this chapter we shall develop the ability to create an entire entity of sound-based music. Thinking modestly, perhaps the terms short studies, miniatures, movements or short works should precede our working on large-scale pieces.

It is here where our skills in finding, manipulating and synthesising sounds as well as creating sequences and gestures will all come into play. It is here where we shall start thinking about what types of structuring principles will prove useful and attractive and which will be found to lead to less-successful results or to be a hindrance in terms of creating pieces.

This chapter evolves from creating to analysing and evaluating work; however, it is hoped that analysis and evaluation are never out of the peripheral view of those working in the initial creativity-based parts of Chapter 5. Virtually all of our activities will be continuations of those that we have experienced already. In other words, no completely new approaches will appear out of the blue as the step towards creating an entire work is already probably fairly daunting for readers. It would be unfair to say that structuring works is approached in a similar manner to structuring gestures and sequences. There is much that is the same, but within a sequence all detail is within the memory of the maker and, most likely, active in the listener's mind when heard, whereas when dealing at work level we must be very clear what we want our listeners to retain in their memories. Therefore, what we consider to be important goals, whether musical or related to extra-musical dramaturgy, will be something for us, the makers of sound-based music, to hold on to whilst working creatively.

So what types of things should we be thinking about here? A quick run through the first four chapters will help. We shall need to keep an eye on awareness issues, that skill that we tried to enhance through the Chapter 2 activities. On this basis we may also decide to use some forms of prescriptive notation to help us design how we choose and manipulate sounds, create sequences, order them, place them into layers, structure them and so on. We shall need to make decisions concerning a more contextual or musical focus as well as decide to what extent our parameters or other tools will offer listeners something to hold on to. Associated with this, and perhaps decided upon first, is the communicative intention of what we make. What is a piece about or, alternatively, what would you like your listeners to hear or feel when listening to your piece? Finally, we were provided with a sense of the breadth of sound-based music towards the end of Chapter 1. Readers can discover key characteristics or approaches of some of these genres and categories and use them as part of their inspiration in terms of creating your initial small-scale works.

After these preliminary decisions or starting points have been determined, we can start looking at a level of greater detail involving thoughts related to how to record, find or generate our sound material; what sorts of effects may enhance the sounds or make them easier to combine with others; which (types of) sequences will be useful; and how do musical and contextual gestures fit in? What role might spatialisation play?

Many of these questions cannot be fully answered beforehand. There is a clear give and take between trying something out and then deciding whether any of a project's ideas deserve to be altered. Only very few actually formalise what they do beforehand. We shall talk about such approaches later on, but for now we can assume that most people involved in creativity related to sound-based music use their ears as the final judge of what works or is less successful.

Placing Sound Sequences into Structures (or Sequencing Sequences)

Instead of making any radical leaps forward, it is suggested that we start off with a few activities working at the level of miniature studies. Some may feel that this might be disappointing, but there are two important things to be said: first, a reasonable amount of works of contemporary music that I have heard left me with the feeling that they were perhaps too long. There may be excellent material being used, but keeping it interesting over a period of time is no small feat. Therefore there is something to be said for a short piece where that risk is minimised. Second, it is actually challenging to follow through an idea in, say, a minute or so. It certainly confronts you with how to tell a short story without reducing it too much. More importantly, a short piece asks the creative artist the same question (s)he would have with a (much) longer study, namely, how to create a convincing structure be it in this case within a shorter time span.

This question is something we need to discuss before commencing with our first Chapter 5 activities. It has been said in the previous chapter that there are, understandably, few commonly followed structures in sound-based music. Taking this one level higher, there are no forms in sound-based music that have established themselves that might be seen to be the equivalent of the verse and refrain form of song or sonata form in classical music. Even simple forms, such as the ABA form common to, for example, many piano works of Chopin, have not evolved within sound organisation. Why is this the case?

Unlike note-based music, there are infinite possibilities in sound-based music, relatively speaking. Furthermore, sound-based music does not entirely share the same musical traditions as note-based music. For example, although the composer Lejaren Hiller composed an "Electronic Sonata" in which, if I remember it correctly, the two themes contained the sound of horses and the sound of rain, the sonata form is by no means an obvious framework to use here as it is deeply rooted in the tradition of tonality.

One of the things that I find most fascinating about sound-based music is that many composers do indeed make their work from the bottom up, that is, collecting materials and building things upward based on constructing small-scale items, such as our gestures and sequences, into larger-scale ones. This is similar to how many choreographers work with movement material. Although dance often receives an implied structure based on the music being used, this type of bottom-up work in dance has been common for decades. It is a relatively young musical approach, in contrast.

For the time being we shall place our sound sequences into structures in this manner, as it is a fairly natural way to work. This may come as a bit of a relief to readers as it means that we continue to work as we have in Chapters 2–4, starting with sounds and building upwards.

So the time has come to take the step from the gesture and sequence to the miniature piece. For those who have little background in composing, think about some of the note-based music you are used to and how shorter pieces, a pop song, a short movement in classical music or anything else, are put together. Many pop fans will probably realise that a good number of pieces do not really end; they just fade out. It is as if the musicians just did not know where to stop. Unless there is due cause, we should avoid that structural cliché. A robust structure is like a good story: it may send you to places you did not expect to visit, but once it is done, you feel you have had a complete experience.

It is for this reason that what is sometimes known as a chain structure, an ABCDEFG . . . form as it were, is not really robust as you seem to just be continuing down an ever-changing path with no milestones to look forward to or iconic items to hold on to and return to from time to time. When we speak of sequencing sequences, including our gestures, we are not thinking of a linear walk through a passage of new ideas. Sounds return, not necessarily in the identical form in which they have already been heard. The same holds true for gestures and, in some cases, entire sequences. Variation is the spice of life in any form of music, or even a good comedy routine, short story, play, and so on. We shall focus on this type of variation below. How we layer and spatialise sounds is the result of our virtuosity regarding these aspects of structuring and placing sonic events. The development of tension and release, if a sound–based piece is not process driven, is another very common and effective tool. All of these will be presented as part of this section.

Clearly, in our miniature studies there cannot be a huge amount of variation. You will remember our activity in the previous chapter in which only one sound type was called upon. We shall return to it to start off, as this restriction, depending on the sound chosen, may end up not limiting terribly much given all of the means of ordering and manipulation we already have at our disposal.

Miniature study activity 1: Single sound type This is the follow-up to sound organisation activity 5 in Chapter 4 in which a number of sequences were to be constructed based on a single type of sound. What some of you may have done in that activity might have been in the musical tradition of theme and variations. The goal here is to make a short study of about one minute's duration based on the same challenge. You may even decide to recycle some of the material you put together in Chapter 4.

After choosing your sound type, two things should take place in parallel. First, you should gather your potential sound materials eventually categorising them in terms of some of our parameters. Second, you should plan how you would like to structure your one-minute work. This can take the form of an evocative score or just some basic notes that might be useful in terms of putting together a storyboard. The more familiar you become with your materials, the more able you will be to create the score or storyboard.

This can occur in reverse order where the searching for materials is based on the ideas for the work's goals and structure. Both options can be applied equally effectively.

Obviously, one of the major decisions that will define what you do here is whether you will be leaning toward a more contextual or musical focus. It would seem logical, given the activity's focus on a particular sound type, to involve the contextual, but the extent of this choice is entirely free.

The second phase of the operation takes us to the next level, as it were. At this point, we start manipulating some sound material to increase our options or simply improve that material. We also need to find means to achieve the basic structure that you have envisioned. If there are sections within this mini-opus, do they happen in succession? Do they move from one to the next gradually or is a contrasting bridging passage perhaps useful to move from one to the other? Which materials might be useful to achieve these chosen transitions?

By now you should have an idea about how many sequences are needed to complete this first work and how they evolve from one to the next. You can then start looking at what will be useful or needed to construct each of the sequences as well as investigate what the sequences have in common— in particular since we are dealing with that single sound type—and what the unique qualities of each will be.

How do sonic gestures fit in here, if you used any gestures at all? Are some gestures equivalent to a sequence or do the sequences involve multiple gestures? Might one or more of the sequences avoid gestural motion?

Fortunately, it will be difficult to avoid some sort of homogeneity given the sound material that you are using. The key here is to experience interesting development in general terms as well as variation in detail (such as density), contrast where relevant and, once complete, the sense of having listened to an entire very short story, be it one without a particular linear narrative.

As there is no single formula concerning how to make such a piece, don't be surprised if you encountered a few relatively unsuccessful attempts here. Do not despair! No one is an instant maestro in sound-based music and most do not succeed in their first attempt either; so we are simply trying to start climbing by taking on a relatively small hill. The more satisfaction that you achieve here, as do your listeners, the more confidence you will gain.

Accept feedback from your peers and those with more experience and see how that may influence your further work with this activity or future activities. If you are up for it, try to make another piece with the same sound type or an entirely different one.

Before moving on, it is useful to stop and think about the question of what was successful in the work of this initial activity and why? If others listened to your work, what did they react to and what was the reason stated that supported that view? Although I was never asked to do this as a student, I realised later that keeping a diary of reactions to aspects of creative work is an excellent way to document a number of things. First of all, and possibly most importantly, you should create a guide to where all of your sound files are, including where the raw materials can be found, the recordings of manipulated sounds, trial sequences and so on. This is the catalogue part of the diary. Then there is the aspect related to evaluation of aspects of your work. You can keep track of the types of effects and their settings that you have used. You can also keep track of remarks that you make regarding the quality and potential value or use of certain actions or sound files. Furthermore, you can document which aspects of structuring—within sequences or within entire works—you found more or less challenging, more or less successful, and why. The diary will then be a catalogue of your archive as well as of your developing skills and ideas all at once. Through the collection of those developing skills and ideas as well as challenges, a development of virtuosity-related traits will evolve with time. Another consequence of the information you retain, especially if score and storyboard information is available as well (where relevant), is that you will also have evidence of patterns of behaviour in your work that will inevitably lead to an increasing analytical understanding of what you are doing. Once you start discovering how your work is being put together, it might be useful to listen to others' works in the same analytical manner to see what their techniques and vision might involve.

Miniature study activity 2: Two sound types Our second activity in Chapter 5 is very similar to the first one. In this case you should carefully choose two sound types in order to ensure contrast in this miniature study. Depending on the sound types, it may be difficult to create an ambience in which sounds of higher predominance are placed. As this activity is not specifically aimed at creating a credible soundscape, the emphasis again will be on the two sound types and what can be organised with them within the span of about one minute.

Interesting issues arise when using two sound types. Is it more logical to attempt to have the two types act as opposing sides in a competitive sport or is it better to look for ways to synthesise them into hybrid sound qualities? Do their contextual differences dictate much of what you can do with the sounds or do you have to manipulate them a great deal to make them more compatible with one another?

The work and evaluation methods in this second activity are virtually the same as the one involving the single sound type. The main exception can be found in the fact that homogeneity may not be the focus at all, but instead contrast may be sought based on two groups of sound qualities being made to relate to one another. This notion of making sounds relate to one another is therefore the key aspect to be developed in the construction of your second study.

Readers may have noticed that our axis between contextual and musical has only been mentioned briefly in our first two exercises. This was consciously done in order to focus on those single or two sound types to see what kinds of challenges would evolve without any other information being imposed. A logical third activity might be to use four or more sound types, but this is a huge leap and might make the work much more challenging and eventually frustrating, so let us now remain with a limited set of sound types and combine these with other aspects of or tools related to sound-based music that will make the activities incrementally more sophisticated.

Miniature study activity 3: Few sound types—contextual focus As we have done before, the goal here is to construct an imaginary soundscape. It may be a bit sparse due to the restriction related to material. The word "few" is used to allow a bit of give and take here and a general environmental sound or a group of ambient sounds may also be included. Although not every sound source needs to remain acutely recognisable, the general effect should be contextual in this case. The surrealistic nature of an imaginary soundscape should make your work interesting as you create at least a few "impossible" sonic combinations. The challenge will be found in going beyond the creation of a soundscape. In other words, you should also focus on making this miniature study offer an interesting artistic experience as well. Effects will not be a focus in this activity, as over-manipulation of the material might lead the listener away from being able to hear things contextually. Still, some effects such as reverberation and the like might be useful in terms of the creation of space, position, distance, and so on. Care should be taken to avoid a progressive narrative in which things are always changing and sounds are not returned to. This might lead to an imaginary soundscape—one that not only ignores the general rules of any normal landscape but also fits into that one type of structure, ABCDEFG . . ., that should be avoided at all costs as, even within one minute, things might become dull or simply difficult to follow. That said, if you really wanted to create a soundscape in dictionary form, try it out and see what evolves.

In this particular activity you run the risk of making one large sequence with smaller detail sequences within, that is, a composite sequence as this is the nature of a soundscape. In fact this makes total sense here. You might like to pay particular attention to how to construct gestures that will provide something to hold on to from time to time. When your gestures are not the focus, what other elements offer the listener a navigation aid through this miniature study? As you can see, being aware of the answer to this question is highly valuable in terms of understanding the expected listening experience and forms an integral part of the intention/reception loop that will be introduced below.

Miniature study activity 4: Few sound types—musical focus Not unexpectedly, we now jump to the other extreme. In this activity sound manipulation and, for the first time, sound synthesis may both come to the fore. In fact activities 3 and 4 are focusing on our final parameter, recognisability of sounds. Most of the other parameters will get their chance later on.

One parameter that is also of great importance in this activity is sound quality. Therefore, sound types need not be taken as pertaining to real-world sounds, but instead refer to types of sound qualities. Although a narrative piece can easily be realised focusing on musical listening, it is the treatment of sound quality that will be the main focus of this study regardless of whether the goal is homogeneity, contrast or something else. One aspect that works nicely with sound quality, as it does in contextual circumstances, is space. You may therefore want to spend extra time figuring out which sounds come from where, which are stable and which move, and so on. In other words, structuring principles may become extremely audible depending on how the sonic materials are presented and how they evolve as well as how the various types are treated. This activity therefore typifies a bottom-up approach to composition, just like all others have thus far.

It may be that the entire minute becomes one large composite gesture, as opposed to the composite sequence in the previous activity. It may be that there is nothing gestural about this miniature study at all, in which case other structuring principles will be taking the lead. Nonetheless, there should be some sense of an opening at the beginning of this study and a closing, even if it is abrupt, at the end.

As with all of these exercises your (digital) diary is of great importance as the activities are becoming increasingly diverse now and aspects related to sound hunting, sound sculpting, decision making and evaluation are all extremely important, not to mention the recordings themselves. Having just undertaken two almost opposite activities, are you finding that you have preferred ways of working and that you have other approaches that you are avoiding? If so, do you know the cause of the avoidance? Is it due to taste or is it due to the challenge? If it is due to what you like and don't like, there is nothing to fear. If it has to do with certain things being too difficult, you might consider returning to the activities in the previous chapters where those particular issues were discussed and developed and see whether you can at least come to grips with it at a level of basic understanding and ability. Do not shun things that you consider to be too difficult as closing doors will limit your opportunities as these activities progress and finally when you choose what types of sound-based music you want to create yourself.

Miniature study activity 5: Score or storyboard-led piece Our fifth activity focuses on our being able to conceptualise a piece before starting to make it. We are all aware by now that making a piece involves a good deal of give and take, as it were. It is only the genius or fool who believes that a piece can be totally predetermined without allowing the ear to act as final judge.

There are different ways to conceptualise creative work in sound organisation. We have focused on two thus far and it is those that we shall return to here. We shall add a third later on in this chapter, involving formalisation, but as that is a truly different approach, it is best to remain with our more familiar ways at this point.

In fact the main difference between a score and a storyboard is dependent on how you approach each and what you might put on them. A score is image-based with eventual extra notations and can be evocative in sound-based music. It can naturally be fairly specific depending on how much information is communicated in those images and accompanying details. A storyboard normally offers more predetermined details, can involve more words than images and is often a bit more flexible or dynamic than a score. Obviously, both can be altered as a part of that give and take process. Perhaps the best way of attacking this activity is to do both, eventually both related to the same miniature study, and discover which works best for you.

Try to design a one-minute study that you have worked out beforehand in terms of basic materials and the work's evolution. Some will find that they can indeed hear what they have drawn and written down. Others may find that they have prepared good ideas, but the missing detail turned out to be more important than they thought and this deserved to be added to their scores or storyboards afterwards. Others still may take more time to be able to conceptualise a piece and finally prefer the method we have been using thus far of collecting sound materials and building something with them with or without any written support.

There is an advantage to being able to work in the way this activity suggests. When you work collaboratively, there are some shared or imposed aspects of the piece that need to be included. These are preconceived aspects, similar to what we are placing on our scores and storyboards. In other words, developing an expertise to work in this fashion can be useful in a number of creative circumstances, such as working together with a visual artist, a dancer, someone involved with theatre, and so on.

It is true that some scores can be evocative in an abstract way, as were our images related to musical gestures. There is nothing against making a score in this manner here. As we have already discovered, such scores may end up generating more than one piece. Perhaps with this in mind it might be useful to take on both contextual and musical aspects as part of this fifth miniature study activity.

Do not forget to keep track of your experiences gained here. You can take into account how the score or storyboard information was helpful or, alternatively, a hindrance or how the ambiguity of more abstract information was a stimulus or complicated things. More importantly, do you feel that having some sort of image and text information beforehand assists your creativity? If so, knowing why this is so may prove invaluable as you polish up your favourite techniques when it comes to longer studies than these initial ones.

Miniature study activity 6: Focus on gestures This study is to be highly gestural. There is no restriction regarding the number of sound types. Similar to some of our earlier miniature study activities, a conscious view concerning local contextual or local musical behaviour will be important here.

Of all of the activities, this is perhaps the most construed. One can speak of having heard gestural music, but does one consciously construct gestural pieces or are gestures simply just the way things are in certain types of music? I would assume that the latter case is closest to the truth. Still, these are studies and sometimes in studies you are asked to do something that would not normally be called upon in normal creative situations just to come to grips with that one thing. If you are an instrumentalist, I am certain that you will remember some studies that do just that.

The best way to approach this study is to create a small number of simple, multiple and/or composite gestures that you think might be able to be placed within a short piece. Having done this, try to find ways to bind these gestures together so that their appearing together not only makes sense, but also creates a miniature study that hangs together well, in fact forming a self-contained unit even though those gestures were perhaps created independently.

Remember that gestures may take many different things into account, such as a spatial gesture that simply moves around. Therefore, the gestural material in this activity need not be homogeneous at all.

This is an activity that may allow you to call upon your diary notes to see which types of gestural material you have been composing most naturally or with ease or discovering that you have been composing certain types of gestures without actually realising it when you were involved with one of the earlier studies. In such cases you may notice that you are already developing part of your own sonic signature, that is, part of your own sound when you make sound-based music. You may think that this takes years of work before particular patterns of behaviour and expertise evolve. But this is not always the case; sometimes habits are created almost spontaneously and it is our awareness of these that is truly important.

Don't forget to evaluate the gestures: how well they work where you have placed them and how well their combination works as a short piece. If in doubt, try out something else, replacing some of the material or moving it about. There is nothing stopping you from applying the old adage: if at first you don't succeed, try, try again.

Miniature study activity 7: Text–sound composition The following two activities might be seen to be an interlude in this sequence of composition exercises. There is a clear structure in the first six activities as more opportunities are added. Activities 9 and 10 will focus on parameters and other things to hold on to. These two, in contrast, focus on two particularly powerful forms of sonic material, the voice either speaking or involved with different types of utterance and chunks of music as sound material.

Unless you feel you are an excellent improviser, it is suggested that scores are used in the preparation of this piece. This does not mean that we are abandoning technology; it simply means that the work can be partially preconceived, recorded, manipulated (although this is hardly needed in this activity) and placed into a structure.

Any of our parameters, not to mention context—words with meaning are contextual, after all—can be used in this study. Remember the remarks about the flexibility of the human voice, so you may want to make abstract sounds instead of or alongside the use of meaningful words. All of that is open. What you should avoid is the score turning into a note-based score where the notes are simply spoken or uttered. Such pieces are valid, too, but ideally this study should fit more with the others made thus far.

Above all this activity should be fun. Suffice to say that if I were to make one to show to readers, it would probably be funny, too. We don't need to be serious all of the time.

You might choose to vocalise sounds that sound like something else or use words that describe something but then hear them in a particularly musical manner, and so on. If you have time for this, try to work both with speech and with vocalised sounds. There is so much that is possible here.

Do you note any parallels between this activity and all of the others? If so, how can you describe them? Such discoveries are ideal for your diary of techniques. Have you done something different because you felt more comfortable using your voice or asking others to use their voices? If so, what might that have been and how might that be useful in your other sound-based creative work?

Miniature study activity 8: Music-based music This activity is a bit tricky as it straddles the border of note-base and sound-based music. The idea is to take one or more recordings of note-based music of any kind and cut it or them into smaller pieces that are reorganised. This cut and paste technique is generally known as collage*.

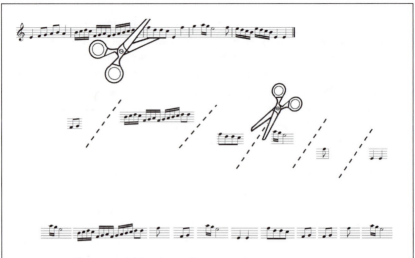

FIGURE 5.1   How one might make a collage

The result should be a sound organisation in which the new piece of sound-based music is made entirely of note-based musical fragments, using sound-based techniques with note-based materials, thus most likely yielding a hybrid piece. Sound manipulation can be applied and fragments may take on a microscopic duration up to a few seconds.

The rights problems with such music are indeed extremely complicated, as they are for other types of recycled music such as hip hop, and you should never use a sequence of more than eight measures of an existent recording to avoid the worst sort of plagiarism unless you have permission to do so.

Beyond the complexities of our legal systems, this can also be one of the most enjoyable activities, as you end up with multiple creative artists: those who made the original music and you who have made its reorganised or recycled version. If you did find this enjoyable, think of other things that you can plunder: radio, television, DVDs, church towers, games, etc., and see what you can achieve with these forms of sample-based music.

As always, it is worthwhile to see what is entirely novel in what you have achieved working within this activity and what seems to be familiar, what has worked especially well and what deserves improvement. Another thing that is worthwhile your taking into consideration here is how you are treating your materials: with respect, ironically, unemotionally or something else? Why might this be the case and can your listeners hear what you intended? There's nothing more satisfying than making a musical joke or creating a musical "whodunnit" that others can understand.

Miniature study activities 9: Focus on our parameters Activities 9 and 10 are not single activities as were the others, but multiple ones, as we have introduced a number of parameters in Chapter 1 and can return to most of them again at this point. In fact, some of these parameters are easily combined and one, recognition of sounds ranging from the contextual to the musical, has been a focus throughout all of our activities thus far. The parameter of space is going to be treated separately below. There will be a pattern of behaviour in these parameter-focused activities, so the descriptions will be limited to remarks pertinent to individual ones.

This activity will follow the parameters, excluding those discussed elsewhere, in the order in which they were introduced: pitch, duration, dynamics, sound quality, simultaneity, density (these last two can be easily linked with the subject of layering introduced later in this chapter) and (dis)order. When a parameter is a focus of a piece, it does not mean that other elements are tossed aside or ignored. It simply means that the parameter in question offers a focus, a navigation tool and that other details can be used to enhance that focus. Again, studies are allowed to focus on something specific in perhaps unusual ways. What is interesting in today's sound-based music is that a particular focus of a given study may become the focus of a much more ambitious work.

Pitch When pitch was introduced as part of our soundwalk discussion in Chapter 2 it was not spoken of in terms of pitch being attached to rhythm in the form of a note, but instead the presence of pitch relative to others in a given soundscape. For our purposes, we can think of pitches in relation to one another in the sense of intervals; we can also think of pitch relationships in terms of general groupings such as pitches belonging to the mid–high register.

Pitch may be introduced with one single type of sound material. In such cases, the sound material becomes increasingly taken for granted and pitch possibly becomes the unique focus. In cases with different types of sound materials or greater variation of the original sound material, the evolution of pitch and, for example, sound quality could form a dual focus.

In this study, whether your aim is more contextual or musical, the key thing for the listener to hold on to is pitch. Examples may range from drone textures that are harmonious or, alternatively, interfere with one another to combinations of shorter sounds where the primary salient feature is pitch. The former case has to do with simultaneous pitch combinations; the latter could focus on the succession of pitches. Both are equally valid here. As with our music-based activity above, this one may evolve into a study that is a hybrid between note-based and sound-based musical behaviour.

Our visual aids may be useful here: scores and storyboards in which pitch can be plotted. Our manipulation tools may also be very handy as they might be able to transpose certain sounds to a variety of pitches or highlight certain pitch bands in more complex sound qualities.

Duration This parameter is a fairly tricky one as far as acting as the lead parameter in a short piece is concerned. For duration to serve as the highlight it will have to be enormously predictable or largely unpredictable—when will the next sound be coming? To state the obvious: to create unpredictability, one minute is rather short. If dealing with lengthy durations, the parameter may be perceived, but not act as something to hold on to within this short time span.

Although these two extremes are the obvious starting point, I would suggest, for the purposes of this short study, using a fairly wide range of durations—either in terms of how long a sound lasts or durations between when sounds are initiated—whereby there is a sense of familiarity in terms of those durations, but one never quite knows what is due to happen when. Think of the pitter-patter of rain when it just starts and its density is low. You know what type of sound to expect, but never know exactly when you will hear it.

If you have difficulties with this one, don't worry. Duration works very well when the total length is longer. If uncertain, combine duration with density and/or (dis)order and you are certain to succeed!

Dynamics This parameter can be loads of fun. You can celebrate today's world of loud music; celebrate the "counter-culture" in today's world, that is, those who make quiet music; or avoid sameness by creating a piece that moves all over the place when it comes to loudness. Again, this can work quite successfully when only one sound type is employed. It can work equally successfully with several sound types or a single sound or few types taking on several characteristics. It can work extremely well when space is added. In this case, the focus would be the distribution of quiet to loud sounds as well as the various sounds' patterns of movement throughout space.

If you choose to do something with our imaginary soundscapes, all we need to do is allocate the "wrong" dynamic to the constituent parts. For example, one could place quiet jets and extremely loud insects; quiet motorcycles and extremely loud curtains moving in the wind; quiet pop bands but the musicians all breathe too loudly. Many remarks have been made related to expectations. Expectations have to do with our lived experience. When using synthetic sounds, there are relatively few associated expectations, so in a sense you are much freer to choose what you do with them. However, when dealing with real-world sounds, you can easily play with the listener's expectations and turn that into a focus.

It is not too difficult to turn dynamics into something to hold on to, although in fact few pieces of sound-based music use that parameter as the main one with the exception of much noise music and a form at the opposite extreme, lowercase sound works. The following parameter, sound quality, is probably the most obvious one to use, and this certainly is a focus in many sound-based works.

Sound quality The focus on sound quality and on space must be the two most radical developments that helped sound-based music to evolve in the previous century beyond the ability to use new sound-based material. One of the great challenges and opportunities in organising sounds is to learn about and work creatively with these two alongside some of the more traditional musical aspects.

As important as it is, sound quality has to be dealt with carefully. For example, if too many sound qualities are heard at one time and they do not form perceivable composite sounds, it is likely that the listener will miss a good deal of the information that has been provided. Use sound qualities too sparsely and one runs the risk of boring listeners.

Approaches to this study can include anything such as focusing on the evolution of a sound quality, multiple sound qualities, interwoven or composite sound qualities and so on. Keep in mind that the dynamics and pitch parameters and the like all support the quality, not the other way around.

Clearly, this study can be approached from a totally contextual approach (and, in this case, sound quality will work in tandem with sound recognisability) or from a totally musical approach where the sound quality is on its own. As we are singling out parameters, this latter case may be the better choice.

Of all of the parameters, this is the one that deserves more than one study to be realised, giving you the chance to look at sound quality from a number of points of departure. Anything to do with sound shaping is potentially of relevance here and, of course, the focus on sound quality can be combined with any other parameter if so desired.

As with all of these parameter-based studies, your entries in the diary are of importance. Perhaps this one is the most difficult to notate. How can you best describe your chosen sound qualities and the manipulations related to them? Which combinations of sound qualities do you find particularly successful and why? Which sound qualities seem to be easy to combine and for what reason? How did you deal with contrast in terms of this parameter? All of these answers may prove themselves to be of great strategic importance in future larger-scale sound-based musical endeavours.

Simultaneity The final four parameters are all of relevance and can be beneficial when used as compositional tools. However, they are fairly difficult to work with at the level of very short durations or, in the case of density, perhaps too obvious. Learning how to deal with them is all that is needed at this point. It has already been noted that simultaneity and density, the parameter that follows, can easily be combined with the subject of layering that is presented below.

The goal with this parameter is to play with different sounds launching or, at least, appearing at the same time in a manner similar to chords in note-based music. Although some sounds in this miniature study may occur on their own, the focus will be on what is heard simultaneously and what the audible effect is of hearing them at the same time. Can you hear the separate sounds or are composite sounds generated? Do some sounds seem to mask other ones and, if so, does this serve a purpose or is it simply annoying? What happens when you create a "chord" of similar sounds or the same sound at, for example, different pitches?

Although this is not an obvious subject for a study, it does allow you to gain important experience in terms of seeing how various sounds can work together when heard at the same time, which types work most effectively, and so on. Once you possess this knowledge, you can employ simultaneity as an important parameter throughout or at any given moment in a longer piece.

Density This study may appear a bit tricky at first appearance, but should not end up being that difficult in terms of conceiving what you want to do. First we need to come to grips with how one might approach density in this context.

Density, for our miniature study, means how many sound events are being heard per unit time, whatever the unit may be. It has to be admitted that a miniature is not ideal if the development of density is fairly dynamic as there will be very little time to get used to any level of density. In other words, gradual changes in density are only possible in a short study within a process piece going from one state to another as there is too little time for many changes to take place. Another option, one more logical in this case, is to change density levels in a sudden or extreme manner.

How does one achieve this? The most likely answer is to involve a number of shorter sounds when the density is high or, alternatively, a number of similar sounds where the density of longer sounds alters the general sound quality of what is being heard. When the density is low, shorter sounds will offer a sparse sonic portrait. Low-density passages featuring longer sounds will perhaps offer a "thinner" sound quality than when there are many such sounds present.

At higher levels of density there will most likely again be simultaneous sounds involved; there will also probably be more than one layer of sound involved if one looks at horizontal sonic development. These aspects can be your point of departure. Changing the speed of a rapidly repetitive sound is an alternative means of dealing with this, but I often warn students to be careful if all focus is on a single "voice", that is, a single line of sound through-out a study or a more formal piece as this can easily lead to transparent, somewhat superficial results.

To state the obvious, a focus on density works best over a longer period of time. With this in mind, it is probably best to work on a single challenge in this piece and see how you can best achieve it. If you do succeed with this challenge, the availability of a longer time span will allow you to navigate through more complex or more sophisticated density-related passages. It is fortunate therefore that we are calling these activities studies, for that is probably the best we can achieve within a minute's duration in particular when concentrating on density.

(Dis)order To create a study in which the level of order or chaos is the focus is not something people are normally asked to do. Most readers will normally attempt to create well-ordered sound organisation, and, frankly, why wouldn't you? Nonetheless, it comes to mind that if everything is well ordered, how can we determine how well ordered things are? This reminds me of an anecdote that John Cage shared from time to time. He felt that there were too many masterpieces in the Museum of Modern Art in New York City. He claimed that if there was at least one lesser painting in each of the rooms, viewers could better appreciate how special masterworks really are.

The same holds true with our order-based study. If order = comfort or "the known", we can better appreciate that comfort or familiarity by being confronted with its opposite from time to time. Clearly there are musicians who find comfort in the opposite of the known, such as today's noise musicians. They make pieces with material others find unwelcome. Still, most musicians do not work that way and want things to fit together nicely, moving about within various areas of order, comfort, that which most listeners will have already experienced.

So how do we take on this unusual challenge? If one makes "an ordered piece", I do not believe that order will be the focus. In contrast, if one makes "a disordered piece", it is likely that the disorder will be a focus, but then the question will be: how long can one sustain interest when what one hears is always disorderly? You might try to produce something short and see whether these are your reactions, too.

The more appropriate alternative is to move about between order and entropy. This is where our short time duration comes in again and is not our best friend, for how many such switches would one want to develop within about sixty seconds? As with density, the solution is simply: try to alter the level of order a few times, either gradually or suddenly, and see to what extent that can lead towards an interesting musical experience. Do the sounds work better in this case when they are more contextual or musical? I believe the answer to this question is directly related to what makes those sounds appear orderly or not. If one is dealing with contextual sounds, they are most likely to sound disordered when combined in impossible manners or manipulated in ways that are unnatural. If the sounds are more musical, then disorder has to do with the total aural effect of what is being heard. Both are equally valid, so it is down to your own personal intention in the case of this (dis)order miniature study. Obviously, switching from contextual to musical may act as a catalyst in terms of determining different types of order and disorder; this might pose an interesting option.

As in so many cases, it is very useful to make notes about both process and the finished product investigating how you have been approaching these challenges, collecting and working with sounds and putting together your pieces. It is also important to evaluate what you find you are doing repeatedly, what is most effective in your view and what types of things do not work, including a remark on why this is the case whenever it is feasible.

Combinations of two or more parameters The next step in our journey is not the longer duration, but instead the combination of any two or more of our parameters. It is likely that in many of the activities thus far, you wanted to do something, but had to step back as it was not one parameter that you were developing, but instead two or three at a given moment. This is natural and, therefore, it was somewhat unnatural to make you create something with only one for such a long time. Why did I do this? The answer is simple. The more you are aware of the issues related to each parameter and some of the means of working with them, the better able you will be to work on them in a specific context with other parameters with which you have gained some expertise.

Let's take a simple example. Working with density on its own may have felt very abstract at first. Now consider a request to make a sound-based piece in which density is to be developed alongside pitch. This second dimension might complicate things in other situations, but here it actually simplifies it, for the alterations in density will probably go hand in hand with the increase of pitch. In such cases, adding many other details may take away from a listener's ability to follow this parallel development.

Thus miniature studies with two or more parameters will certainly be easier in most cases. Of course you could choose two parameters that do not work that easily together. For example, it is probably not very easy to combine dynamics and order effectively. Combining dynamics and density, on the other hand, is an extremely logical thing to do.

Try to make five studies that combine two or three of the parameters here, eventually including the two parameters that were not included above: recognisability of source and space. Choose combinations that make perfect sense to you for the first four and one that you find a bit more difficult.

Evaluate each of the five in the same way you have with all other studies. The only extra aspect that is worth documenting here is how the combination made your work easier or more difficult and why. This will inform you of the types of things you like to work with and which combinations you find either more challenging or perhaps find less comfortable to work with. In the long run, those items on the latter list can be worked on in order to improve your ability with them or can be avoided, as they simply do not interest you in terms of your creative vision. We do not need to be equally agile in terms of all aspects related to sound-based music. No one is. We are not equally agile in terms of any of our other activities in life, either. A goalie is by no means necessarily a good centre forward, after all. In other words, discarding or simply being extra careful with some of these parameters or other aspects related to these creative exercises is by no means a sign of defeat. Instead it allows you to narrow things down to those approaches, just like your favourite sounds or favourite means of manipulating and structuring sounds, that you feel you "own" or with which you feel some virtuosity. The more you are aware of these strengths and limitations, the more able you will be as a sound-based musician.

Miniature study activities 10: Focus on other musical elements related to the something to hold on to factor This tenth activity is similar to the previous one in that it deals with a number of things to hold on to. Our parameters have already been proven to act as something to hold on to in sound-based music and should be seen to form part of these musical elements. One exception here is any non-musical or extra-musical thing to hold on to such as a musician's dramaturgy or a programmatic work. That will be the basis of the eleventh activity below.

Perhaps after working with these things to hold on to, you can come up with one or more of your own. If so, please let me know so that it can be added to the list. The two presented below have something in common, perhaps with the exception of the special case of the search for new sounds, that is, the ability to avoid a given work's becoming so complex that the listener gets lost in information overload.

Homogeneity of sounds and the search for new sounds We shall now investigate sounds that have similar characteristics aurally. When we started this chapter, the first activity concerned the use of a single sound type. This is not identical to this activity's focus as a single sound type, let's say bird calls, can be highly diverse and yet have that single thing in common.

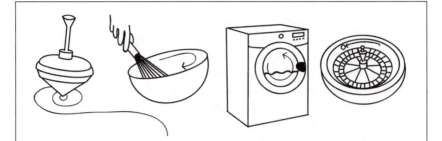

FIGURE 5.2   An example of homogeneous whirling sounds

Our goal here is one rooted in musical listening where perhaps different sounds may possess similar sound qualities or, alternatively, are homogeneous due to one of our parameters, such as pitch. You may recall that there have been some attempts by musicians to classify sound quality ignoring cause, including those evocative adjectives, such as grating or ringing. Although there are other ways to achieve sonic homogeneity, for the purposes of this first experience, you can choose one such characteristic and find, manipulate and/or create sounds that fit into that category and then create your miniature study based on these materials.

You may discover that, although there is a limited scope of the material that you will prepare, the limitation does not immediately ensure that the material will work together. This is where our tools introduced in Chapter 3 related to manipulation and spatialisation come in. Furthermore, homogeneity does not necessarily mean that one always makes sequences of a particular duration. You can be as gestural with this activity as any other or as sectional within the about sixty seconds as you like.

If you have found this assignment particularly easy or rewarding, try out another, contrasting sound quality. The term that is in use currently that is most likely pertinent to what you make is timbral composition*, that is, work in which the sound quality or qualities form the focus in terms of the listening experience. This approach is quite different from the programmatic ones that will be investigated in the next activity.

Several artists have pursued the opposite approach to the above for over a half-century, namely the *search for the new*. It is conceivable that in developing new sounds one ends up with a particular sound quality that is presented in a homogeneous manner as described above. My experience, however, is that once people seek the new, their ideal is to create or invent as many new sounds as they can and attempt to offer them in a coherent manner in their works. What happens in such cases is that the listener ends up following the novelty of the sound material more than what is actually transpiring within the piece. This *is* something to hold on to, but not necessarily the most user friendly in my experience. This type of experiment is being mentioned for the sake of completeness. It is probably premature to have readers attempt to create a study in this manner and, most likely, many will find this search fairly difficult if not alienating as well. So for those who would find the invitation to create a short work based on sounds they have never heard or made before enticing, feel free to try this out. Using synthesis, it is not difficult to come up with new sounds. Turning such sounds into a successful composition, on the other hand, is a fairly sophisticated task and possibly beyond the level of ability that we have reached thus far.

Restricted number of sound qualities heard at any given moment Where homogeneity clearly serves the purpose of seeking coherence, the investigation of the amount of information one expects listeners to be able to process is a good way of ensuring that the perception's fuse box does not blow during the listening experience. I have spoken with many composers and most agree with me that limiting the amount of material presented to no more than four textures at once is a good means of helping people navigate their way through a work. This advice works best in pieces in which there are clear lines of sound material being heard in time, something we have called layers of sound thus far. If layers fuse and become composite layers, then they can be counted as a single layer. Similarly, if music involves the combination of lengthy sound material and shorter sounds dispersed in time, the short sounds may or may not be heard as a single layer.

In cases where the sound material develops greatly over time, the number of total sound qualities may be difficult to follow, so the implication here is not only that not too much should happen at once, but also that the total number of sound types remain limited so that the listener becomes increasingly familiar with the sound material being used, in particular when it comes to musical as opposed to contextual listening. Try to create a piece now with no more than four different types of sound qualities present at any given moment and with no more than, say, ten sound qualities in total. You can reuse any sound material you have created in the past or further develop it. This is possibly the first time that you will have considered so much taking place at once. If you work carefully, you could involve approximately four levels of sound during part or most of your study and discover that, through careful development of your sound qualities, the end result is not too complex due to the distribution of those sound levels.

There is nothing worse, in my opinion, than getting completely lost in a piece and not knowing any longer what you are supposed to be listening to. By creating a well-defined set of sound qualities and not varying them too often or offering too much to listen to at any given moment, the totality of your material should become something to hold on to. When you are able to control this much material at differing levels of density, you know that you have made a giant step forward in terms of what you are able to handle within a single piece.

As we have stepped up a level in this activity given the number of sound qualities and potential number of layers involved, it is of particular value to make notes about what you have chosen, how you have chosen to put things together, which methods were needed to achieve that, which strategies were used for gestures and sequences and how the entire study was put together. Along with this, it would be useful to know what types of things have been rejected and why and, again, whether any particular decisions seem to remind you of actions that you have taken during any other activity as part of the discovery of the evolution of your own sonic signature. Once your study is complete, it might be worthwhile to create a score that is useful to demonstrate where you have placed which types of sounds and how the structure of the entirety looks. The reason for this is that, in this manner, you can start to identify what your architecture as a sound-based musician looks like and, when comparing this score with others, thus discover to what extent you have a signature at this level, too.

Miniature study activity 11: Focus on intention Before we finally increase the duration of pieces made in these activities, two more will be introduced that have specific foci. In this one, intention comes to the fore and therefore one might say that this is closely related to our activities in which a score or storyboard was important. The next one will take existing compositional approaches to sound-based music and use one or more of these as a point of departure.

This first one offers some things to hold on to that are based on extra-musical elements, each of which is related to intention: the specific, more traditional one, the musical programme and a more general one, relevant to cases in which any form of dramaturgy is involved.

Programmes It is one thing to write programmatic note-based music and perhaps another when organising sounds. A nineteenth-century programme symphony can be about a story or a natural setting. With sounds a story can range from the real to the more abstract; a nature setting can be as realistic as you like.

Let's work close to the two ends of the axis ranging from the realistic story to the acousmatic tale. At one end it is conceivable that one takes a sonic voyage from point A to B or one by way of points B to C, D and E remembering that when taking a voyage there are aspects that return again and again. So the voyage can be constructed, but represent a potential aural experience of a trip. The acousmatic tale may be more dreamlike but still be about some-thing, but it is not like a story that you can read any more. This latter case is in a way similar with instrumental programme music where, without a meas-ure-by-measure story or some sort of timeline, it is fairly difficult to discern exactly what aspect of the programme is being related. Note-based music is a fairly abstract art form after all. The vast majority of acousmatic works tend to relate an imaginary tale that is not a narrative in a literal or linear sense, but is instead an abstract narrative with many points where one can relate what one is hearing to aspects of lived experience whether this is related to source recognition, emotion or any other meaningful experience. In other words, the notion of tale is not used in the sense of plot, but instead has to do with the personal navigation through a work containing abstract materials.

Ideally, you should attempt to make a more literal and more abstract pro-grammatic study for this part of the activity. In both cases it is entirely valid to assume that your listeners know about your programme beforehand. If you consider this to be unfair, you can allow them to listen to your work first and see to what extent they can hear what you set out to do. We shall return to this type of approach in a few paragraphs. If you choose the latter approach, you should be open to alter and improve your work up to the point that what you are intending people to have your listeners hear by way of your programme is indeed audible and therefore something to hold on to.

Unusually for these activities, you can have friends listen to your work whilst you are making it for feedback regarding the relationship between what they hear and what you are trying to achieve, but then the work must be in such a state that there are sufficient clues for them to be able to reach a conclusion. If you want to wait until this short study is complete, that is fine too.

One thing to avoid, although it does occur in sound-based works, is the presence of a narrator telling you what a sound-based piece is about as you listen to it. An actor's voice is a powerful thing to hold on to, but for now, our goal is to have the sounds do the talking themselves.

Programmes are not for everyone, although it is worth stressing that one of the strengths of sound-based music is its ability to link contemporary art to lived experience. There are, of course, other ways to achieve this, but in fact programme music is an obvious way of working when organising sounds. Hopefully, making these two studies will demonstrate this well.

Which one of the two did you find more demanding to make? Why might this be the case? Which one of the two did you find more satisfying in terms of its musical result? Were you able to make the less-demanding piece more successful? If so, this combination is possibly a good way to work in the future. If not, investigate why this may have been the case. Understanding why this is so should lead to the more challenging becoming less so in the future. Your aesthetic taste may evolve as well and the more abstract or the more overtly contextual may become a taste you acquire after further exploration.

Dramaturgy The programme work is just one type of composition involving dramaturgy. We have also discussed dramaturgy in terms of musical intention in the previous chapter. Music has never developed its own word for this common aspect of theatre, dance and other performing arts related to the communicative intent of an artistic work.

But how much music possesses this type of intention? Songs are about something, in particular when there is a text telling you what they are about. Programme pieces are about something, too, but what about a piano sonata or a fugue? In fact they can also be about something, be it an emotion, an ambience, or something closer to a programme. Having said that, there are many pieces that are about nothing at all, particularly amongst those composed in the last century. There is even a term for such pieces: art for art's sake. There is nothing that says that such works must therefore be no good. Such a remark would be ridiculous, but the more divorced from experience a piece of music is, the harder it is to appreciate in general. This book is about opening doors, not closing them. If one hears many art for art's sake works, also known as absolute music, ideally more than once, one can start to come to grips with them. Some readers may opt to make absolute music works in the future, but in terms of our work, it is suggested that this be avoided for the time being.

Instead, for now, the goal is to have an intention and for that intention to be able to be received by your public, at least to some extent. I have been involved with a project with Rob Weale called the Intention/Reception Project (Landy 2006; Weale 2006) in which we discovered through the use of various questionnaires that when there is a dramaturgy offered by composers of sound-based music, the vast majority of inexperienced listeners find it helpful to discover their dramaturgy aurally as part of their introduction to this music. It helped them to better understand the music's motivation and finally understand the music itself.

So what might a work be about if there is no programme? It can be about a type of inspiration such as a particular type of landscape or setting. It might be about something you particularly like to do, such as a particular game you play, and you can potentially include sounds related to that game. It can be dreamlike or it can even be about a way to illustrate an emotion. More concretely, similar to some of the more contextual activities, it can be about something. The UN's cultural organisation Unesco once asked children around the globe to make music based on the theme of water. This was very clever, for some countries have too much of it and some far too little. We all have several forms of experience and thus a complicated relationship with water and can perhaps convey that relationship musically, especially when there are recordings of water or things that sound like water included.

If we go back to our storyboard activity, it is likely that most of you already had an intention when you thought about what types of sounds you wanted to put together. In this sense you have already had experience with dramaturgy. Dramaturgy is also about why you choose to do things as long as they are related to a work's intention and meaning in general.

In this activity, you should make very clear entries in your diary about intention. You should also include feedback from your listeners and document how you decided to resolve any issues. By this time you will be developing a shorthand system for this diary that is increasingly efficient and clear in terms of finding things again that may be of value to you in the future.

Music is about communication; at least I believe this to be true. It is about sharing and all of our activities have been constructed to allow for this to take place. When discussing dramaturgy, this sharing becomes more explicit. It is part of every piece of music I create and hopefully, after working on this activity, you will find it of great value as well.

Many teachers of music are strong believers in what is known as pastiche, that is, the creation of a study or a work in the style of or at least employing the techniques of another musician or musicians. There is something to be said for this. In my case, it made me understand the techniques and how they were used. However, to me this was more a musicological activity, one related to understanding theoretical concepts more than a creative one as I was not writing my music, but instead something that seemed to be an imitation of someone else's music. It is for this very reason that I have not proposed that readers listen to specific pieces throughout this entire book, but instead prefer to have the wealth of sound-based music's diversity discovered by way of the online repertoire support that the EARS II site offers, taking our Chapter 1 overview of genres into account.

With the exception of the compositional methods of the formalists (see below), there are few tools that have been developed beyond those related to synthesis, manipulation and gesture. Therefore, instead of taking the pastiche route in this chapter, a more reasonable approach is to look into works that fit into our genre list that share musical characteristics. To achieve this you should develop a sense of which musical aspects are related to the genre of your choice. The definitions in the glossary on the EARS and EARS II sites should help as well as your own exploration of repertoire in a given genre.

Terms that we have used thus far that represent genres are: acousmatic music/ musique concrète, ambient music, glitch, lowercase sound, noise music, plunder-phonics (a form of what has been called music-based music) and timbral composi-tion. There are also several genres with roots in popular music; most of these tend to have a note-based bias but may also embrace sound-based versions. This list is not intended to be complete, but does demonstrate the breadth of potential gen-res. As suggested in earlier chapters, sound-based music, still being of a relatively young age and covering a vast horizon of approaches, has yet to have a sophis-ticated genre-based terminology developed for it. This is not ideal as it impedes access (although tagging systems can be useful). It is hoped that this vocabulary expands in the coming years, allowing anyone interested better opportunities to search for repertoire and supporting information in the genres of choice.

Miniature study activities 12: Focus on existent genres You can choose one or two of the genres listed above or one that you have discovered and make a miniature study that fits within the general style. It is extremely important to choose a genre that you find attractive to ensure that this activity is ben-eficial to you. In contrast to all other activities where there have only been suggestions proposed for your diaries, this exercise involves a compulsory component, namely that you present an overview of musical aspects that you believe are indicative of the genre with a description of how you applied them in this study as well as how you integrated them with your own evolv-ing musical techniques.

There is a "hidden agenda" in this activity. As stated, it is advantageous to know how people place themselves within current musical contexts. This activity offers you the chance to try out working within one of today's genres, perhaps even identifying what your own take or departure is related to that genre. All of this naturally forms part of your sonic signature that by now should be unveiling itself slowly but surely.

Increased duration activities Some of you will be pleased to finally take the step beyond the boundary of the miniature study. Others may have done so long ago. We have now arrived at the point where we should start looking at longer durations. This will be quite challenging to some, but offer comfort to others who simply had too many ideas for a short duration.

I have mentioned gestural clichés in this text already. Another type of cli-ché is the fact that many compose works that last between ten and eighteen minutes as if this were an ideal duration for sound-based works. In fact, one needs to be quite a strong sound organiser to fill up a quarter of an hour, retaining the interest of the listening public. Although such durations are ideal for a certain type of narrative, a complete tale can be told in a much shorter time span. In my personal experience I have found it quite gratifying to offer "almost too much" information in a shorter time span. In this case listeners may actually hope to hear more as they have the feeling that they are just getting into the work. This is in contrast to experiences one can have in longer works during which interest can fluctuate as the combination of sonic materials, development and structure are simply not sufficiently substantial to fill that many minutes. Suffice to say that this issue is equally relevant to all other time-based art forms.

With this in mind, it is proposed that you go back to any of this chapter's activities and create a piece lasting from two to four or five minutes to start. As you gain confidence, you can attempt longer durations or, alternatively, make shorter pieces that you intend to reemploy as sections or, in traditional terminology, movements of a longer work. I personally believe that the latter option is an excellent way to work your way up the time scale. You will know when you are ready to attack a longer work.

Documentation here is extremely important, as you should not only continue to log which decisions you are making, but also look into why you are making them and evaluate how well the sonic result works. If others offer feedback, you should consider investigating to what extent their attention was held and look into a pattern of behaviour in terms of dips of interest regarding the listening experience. Naturally a piece need not be equally engaging at all times—that would probably lead to an awkward listening experience—but losing the listener's interest can sometimes be fatal. You should have an idea of an ideal listening strategy throughout these longer works and it will be interesting to see whether your intention or desired listening experience is actually reflected after other people have heard your work.

Does offering the associated dramaturgy influence your listeners' experience? Another interesting question is: do you find that with a longer time span you continue to use the same techniques that you found most useful with the short studies or did you discover new ones that were more pertinent given the particular context? Have you used a storyboard or evocative score to assist you to create a more robust structure for your longer piece(s) or have you used a bottom-up approach based on your ear as sole judge? Regardless of the answer to this question, do you feel that the structure of your piece is as strong as the materials that you have used? How do you judge the success of either and how might you seek to improve things in the future?

This last question has now become very important. It would have been unfair to ask it earlier as you would have had too little experience to be able to respond with any confidence, but now you have been taken to many points on the map of sound-based music and have sufficient making and listening experience to be able to come up with an informed judgement. Please note that your judgement may not be the same as someone else's. The fact is that art is not a science and there are no universal rights or wrongs. What is important is that you gain confidence in your ability to make such judgements and that you are able to back them up with clear criteria beyond "I liked that" or "I didn't like that". Experience therefore leads toward greater confidence in terms of your creative endeavour, understanding and your value judgements. That is why one speaks of the thinking practitioner these days. With such powerful technology, an infinite amount of source material and also endless manipulation and structuring possibilities, a holistic approach towards this music is ideal.

The increased duration activity was hardly an activity at all. It is in fact your graduation certificate. This final activity was in a sense a carte blanche to make any piece that you feel you are capable of making. From now on you can determine your own creative projects as a graduate of this book's activities. Congratulations and best of luck!

The rest of this chapter will focus on aspects related to composition and the understanding of composition that should prove valuable to you. The activities proposed are top-ups to what you have been presented with thus far and are intended to round off the progression of activities introduced above.

Varying Sounds, Gestures and Sequences in Time

The following sections all consist of useful tips related to creating sound-based music. Much of this may already be known to many readers or may seem reasonably obvious. To others, some of these hints may simply improve your promising efforts into more well-rounded ones. The choice is based on shortcomings I have regularly encountered listening to works of my students and others. You should simply see these discussions as being related to other tools of the trade.

Remarks have been made throughout this book concerning the importance of items appearing in a work more than once—not necessarily everything, but key items that can serve as signposts in a piece of music. It is the chain form that is the structure that deserves to be avoided as much as possible. Therefore, reusing or varying material, structural devices, spatial movement and the like can help listeners find their way through a work.

Let's look at the notion of reappearance of materials in a bit more detail now. If something reappears in a work, is it necessary that it comes back as it originally appeared? This can indeed be effective at times, but is by no means a necessity. We have also discussed theme and variations from time to time as well as varying things whilst ensuring that their association is clear to the listener, one of the most important tools we have as sound-based musicians.

Any comedian knows that, time permitting, returning to a joke that has been successful as part of a routine and perhaps varying it based on circumstance can help pace a performance and offer it a clear structure. This approach is no less pertinent in our art form.

Think of it another way. When looking out of the window during a train journey, you will notice many unique items, but some will come and go depending on where you are, such as green fields, smaller towns, churches, train stations and so on. These markers help you know where you are if you make the journey often or offer the journey a sense of coherence if you are making a trip for the first time. It is these general and specific types of markers that can be extremely useful in helping you structure your work and make it coherent as an artwork.

Please note that you can vary something to the point that it is no longer recognisable as being associated with its former manifestation. Think, for example, of some of our manipulation techniques. You can transform a contextual sound into a musical one fairly easily. That forms part of the magic of the tools that we have on offer. However, the resulting sound is not necessarily going to be connected with the original one. This is fine if that is what you are seeking; problematic if that is not the case. For our current purposes, let us accept the restriction that when the word "vary" is proposed it means that it can be associated with its preceding and succeeding forms.

When varying a sequence, does the resulting sequence need to be of the same duration or involve the original in its entirety? The short answer to this question is "no". It is the association that is more important than the recognition of what has been done with the original or any other variation. Returning to our train journey example, green field areas can be of any size; they are all green fields. Even detail items such as a church can be of all shapes and sizes, too.

I often call on the train journey as an example in such discussions for I like to see how sounds are placed in time in a form of a map. The notion of map ties the two together. Maps have larger regions and smaller specific details, just as do our sound-based works. There are also different ways of mapping a given area, as there are different ways of scoring our pieces. The similarities are in fact quite striking. The understanding of the potential of variation can be extremely useful when working on structural aspects of any piece.

Layering Sounds and Sequences Horizontally

Most people think of structure in music as a time-based affair in which significant vertical signposts mark where sections commence or demarcate some form of alteration. Structure is also of extreme importance when looking at music horizontally in time. Many people studying note-based music will study harmony and counterpoint at one point. The former is looking at chord sequences that,

FIGURE 5.3–5.4   Two evocative scores of sequences with markers indicated

Variation activity Create a piece of ca. four to five minutes' duration in which your structure is largely based on the reappearance of sequences, gestures and sound material. Some form of evocative score should accompany this in order to demonstrate how the structure looks. It should be altered if changes are made to strengthen the piece. Therefore, a computer-based image might be useful, as this tends to be more easily altered.

It will be useful to receive listeners' feedback regarding the audibility of what you have set out to achieve, both in terms of varying sequences and the like, as well as in terms of the work, its detail and its structure.

To what extent is the outcome of this exercise comparable with your work thus far? If it does demonstrate significant difference, do you believe that using these markers and applying this approach is a means of strengthening your work? Why is this the case, or why not? If you have found this to be a promising approach to your work thus relating structure to any type of bottom-up approach you will find that you will most likely be applying it consciously or automatically from now on. Please note that what has been called upon here is a type of storyboard approach as a storyboard can easily portray any form of material and its variations.

to an extent, are similar to our notion of simultaneities, although one can play a chord horizontally in the form of a melodic curve. One normally determines where a chord starts and which one it is in terms of the key in tonal composition. Counterpoint is based on two or more voices moving concurrently. Although the vertical relationships at any given moment are relevant, the key aspect to such music is the development of layers of horizontal movement.

Sound-based music naturally can also be analysed and described in these two ways as well as others. The key reason for singling this subject out here is that much sound-based music involves the creation of horizontal layers of sound, often sound quality-based. The layers' identities, their interaction and their eventual merging, similar to a composite sound or gesture, are all important in terms of the listening experience as is the interaction between layers of sound and shorter detail sounds. Layers of sound are therefore related to various things to hold on to including sound quality, the number of layers heard at any given moment, eventually homogeneity, pitch and other aspects.

Even the presence of contextual material must be carefully looked into when investigating sound layers. Do more contextual layers seem to act as magnets to the ears or do they, at times, act as a general ambience? Can they combine easily with less contextual sounds over time?

Layering may appear to be a ninety-degree turn from our simultaneity parameter. This is in many ways true, but what is of great interest here is how layers can be made and listened to as a key aspect of a work and can be combined with those vertical signposts, thus combining the vertical with the horizontal.

That is the bigger picture. For now, the intention is to focus on sound layering in isolation.

Layering activity Create a piece of two to four minutes' duration in which the treatment of layers and the relationship between the changing numbers of layers of sounds is the focus. The term "layer" here implies the presence of long sounds or sonic gestures that might be seen to be a "voice" in a score involving several "voices". A layer can consist of a single evolved sound or several sounds that together form the content of the "voice" in question. The use of contextual sounds is permitted. The creation of a composite layer of sound is also encouraged. The result might be a timbral composition focusing primarily on sound quality and eventually pitch, but this is by no means the only way to approach this activity. A surrealistic soundscape of disparate elements could equally be created. In either case, the musical result will be of greatest importance. The way it is listened to may vary depending on the elements you choose to include and how they are treated. To make a link with the following subject, the way the layers are placed or move about the physical space might be worthy of investigation.

Keep a diary of the materials used, information regarding how well they sound together and what changes when the sound quality of one of the layers has been altered or any other aspect of it. Some questions of note might be: how does the listening experience change when attention is drawn to particular layers of sounds? Is the presence of contextual material different when the main content consists of items of longer duration? Is the sounding result different from most pieces that you have made thus far and, if so, how? Is music based on layers easier to make or to listen to than some of the other types made thus far and why? Answers to these questions will help you determine to what extent horizontal thinking might be important to your developing sonic signature. It is my experience that listeners in general do find layered pieces largely accessible. This remark regarding accessibility actually also holds true for timbral instrumental composition that focuses on the horizontal development of layers. This type of note-based music comes perhaps closest to sound-based music in terms of its sonic result.

Spatialising Sounds

It is hard to imagine how exciting the step from monaural to stereo must have been when stereo appeared on the market. Today's market offers various forms of multichannel listening, although it has not caught on as much as it might, as "the standard" is not yet established.

Many readers will not have access to multichannel sound systems and are then confronted with a choice: working with two loudspeakers in mind or with headphones. What might the differences be? Just to name two, when a particular sound moves from left to right or vice-versa on loudspeakers, that usually occurs in front of the listener; with headphones, the sound moves intimately through your head. At a more sophisticated level, it is not really possible to offer a 2D or even 3D listening experience by way of those two loudspeakers, but using current binaural recording technology, one can become immersed in a space using headphones whereby sounds may appear to be above, behind, in front of and at either side of the listener or any place in between. The sound can move in circles or any other geometric shape as is the case when sophisticated multichannel systems are used, although not too many of these are strong in terms of height. Alternatively one can try to simulate the 3D experience through the use of reverberation, filtering and other effects to attempt to place your sounds spatially in a more artificial manner.

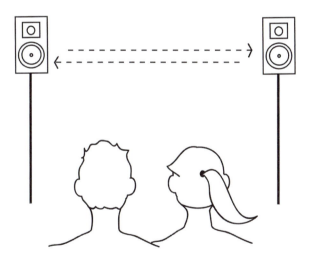

FIGURE 5.5 Sounds moving in a loudspeaker listening environment

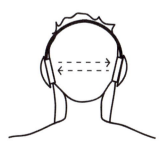

FIGURE 5.6 Sounds moving in a headphone listening environment

Many of today's software systems for sound-based music allow you to work in more than two channels, thus anticipating increased spatial opportunities. Having made several compositions using various numbers of loudspeakers, to me stereo is a compromise once a work has been devised beyond the single dimension. Hopefully, that standard for multichannel systems is not too far away and the resulting system will become increasingly affordable in the coming years.

Spatialising sound may appear to be a luxurious add-on to sound-based music, but is in fact one of its fundamental components. One of the very first things we did in Chapter 2 was to pay close attention to sound in space and how both sound and space are highly interrelated in terms of the listening experience. They are no less relevant to the creative experience.

Creating a storyboard or an evocative score introduces the maker of a sound-based work to the sonic universe that a work might involve. Similarly, collecting sound materials can lead to a similar level of development. The creation of gestures and sequences takes us a step closer to having important building blocks and structuring them takes us to the level of the entire work. At one point sounds need to be placed within the sonic space however that is configured. Some sounds will be stationary; some will move; some will appear to be far away and others close by. Placing your sounds in space helps to make your work become alive and is no less important than any other aspect of construction. The following activity is intended to help you discover spatialisation opportunities taking both the number of channels of sounds you can work with and the agility of the software that you are using or, alternatively, the means of sending sounds into space by way of, for example, a mixer, into account.

Spatialisation activity This activity focuses on different types of techniques related to spatialisation. The approach allows for a stereo loudspeaker set-up, the use of headphones and a multichannel loudspeaker set-up. In the latter case, one can either prepare a stereo recording and diffuse it in the multichannel environment or, if this is possible, create a multichannel recording from the start that takes the loudspeaker placement and the performance space into account. The idea is to use much of the same sound material in both/all of the exercises below to see how the means of listening influences what you make. The material you will need includes: ambient sounds to create the general sonic spatial atmosphere; fixed sounds that do not move; sounds that can appear in more than one point in the general space; and sounds that can move about a space in a continuous fashion, such as bird flight. These sounds need not be contextual; therefore you may want to make one study that focuses on more contextual sounds, perhaps a soundscape composition, and another one that focuses more on musical sounds.

Stereo loudspeakers Create a study lasting one to two minutes that combines the three types of elements above. Are you able to make the size or type of space clear to the listener? Can you make certain sounds appear to be far away or close by? How can you describe the placement of the sounds that appear in more than one location? What is the experience of listening to sounds moving about in this space? If you have made both contextual and musical studies, which one was more effective as far as the experience of space is concerned? Why do you think this is the case? Did you find that you needed to introduce any new techniques in order to prepare this study? They should be added to your diary as you may find that these new techniques will come in handy in your future work. Before moving on to the next exercise, listen to your work on headphones. How does this other form of listening alter the experience of what you have made? Now that you are aware of this second listening experience of the study, can you imagine how you might alter it specifically for headphone listening?

Stereo headphones Very few composers make works specifically for headphone listening. Quite a few of these have done so as this ensures a 2D or even 3D listening experience based on the binaural or other spatialisation techniques used. The stereo experience with headphones is quite different from that with loudspeakers in many cases, even including note-based music. In today's world, with all of the technology on offer, it is surprising how little music is made in stereo loudspeaker and stereo headphone versions.

The first part of the headphones activities requests that you do exactly this: make a different version of your first study or studies specifically for headphone listening. All of the goals introduced above remain the same. The aim here is to discover the different listening experience and, in consequence, to attempt to identify means of creating an improved spatial listening that only works with headphones. It is not expected that you have access to binaural technologies, so you will focus on the traditional stereo image.

There are no rules for this and, to the best of my knowledge, no specific compositional tricks on offer. What is possible is a clearer experience of location, distance and movement. Due to the intimacy of headphone listening, specific details related to space will become more vivid. With this in mind, how can one optimise the spatial experience in this setting? Again, this may differ based on the use of more contextual or more musical sound material. You might try to create distance with some reverberation or echo or proximity using careful settings with digital filters. How would you try to create a headphone stereo space?

As above, if you have added any new techniques to achieve your results here, please add them to your diary. The number of techniques that you

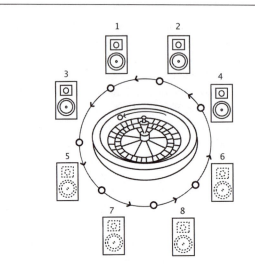

FIGURE 5.7 A sound moving in a circular manner in an eight-channel surround sound listening environment

have acquired by now is such that the risk of forgetting one might now be tangible. The diary will assist in terms of your ability to retrieve information related to all aspects of your work including the evaluation of the results that you are achieving in this activity.

For those who have access to a binaural microphone and, ideally, software that can deal with the resulting recordings, the next step is the attempt to create a spatial recording of at least the ambient sounds (or simulation when using musical ones) and then place all other sounds in that space creating a surround environment that one cannot hear using loudspeakers but is very clear using headphones. One complaint heard about such spatial listening is that the space turns when the listener turns her or his head around. Perhaps one day we shall have the technology to take that into account; still, this is a means of creating spatialisation that goes well beyond left and right using a stereo output medium.

How you achieve this will be quite dependent on the software used. In some cases, four or more channels are used to "fill the space" that is subsequently translated back to stereo for listening. In other cases, the space is automatically encoded into stereo although defined spatially. This is the most sophisticated spatialisation assignment thus far and many readers will unfortunately not have access to the opportunities proposed here.

How "real" is the product of your labour? Do you feel you are in what is known today as an immersive aural environment? If not, what seems to be missing or unsuccessful? Are all or some of those goals regarding location distance and movement achievable? If the answer is negative, are you able to optimise the aspect of spatialisation regardless of the system's imperfections? What would you like to be able to achieve that was not possible in this case?

For those reading this book a few years after it has been written, it is assumed that what is on offer is easier to use, cheaper and more accessible than the tools available whilst the book was being prepared. The success of those technological developments will determine how common and how valuable spatial headphone listening will become in the future.

Multichannel loudspeaker environment For those who have access to a multichannel listening situation, this activity offers two exercises: one uses a stereo recording that is spatialised by way of sound diffusion*; the other involves the creation of a multichannel recording thus assuming that software is available for more than two channels of output. It is by no means assumed that readers will have instant access to this type of equipment.

FIGURE 5.8   A mixer with a "loudspeaker orchestra"

In the case of the *stereo recording*, perhaps one made for the stereo loudspeaker exercise or adapted for this situation, the goal is to perform the stereo recording on more than two loudspeakers. This will take some practice if you have never tried it before. In some cases, you may want the sounds all to be heard on stage, some perhaps behind or to the side of the public and some with a "bathtub effect", all around the audience. In the early history of this kind of music, most spatialisation took place in this manner.

Having tried to send sounds around the space, perhaps even moving them about using the faders of a mixer, did you feel that you needed to adapt your recording further towards this goal or was the original sufficient? How is the

piece enhanced in this environment? What did you find limiting in this situation? Were you better able to achieve aspects such as distance here?

For the final part of this spatialisation activity, you are to make a *multichan-nel recording* where each channel will be sent to a separate loudspeaker. (It is
also possible to diffuse a multichannel work around more loudspeakers than
there are channels, of course, but that is not being asked for in this case.) For
example, you can make a four-channel study to be sent to the four corners
of a space or use one of the current Dolby combinations such as 5.1 or 7.1
including the bass bin (subwoofer) that sends out low frequencies around
the space or eventually an eight-channel (or more) recording depending on
the equipment at hand.

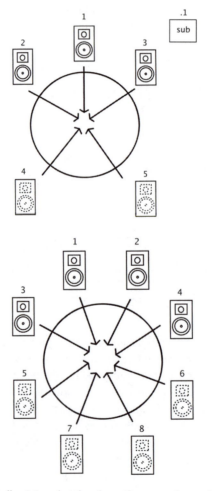

FIGURE 5.9–5.10 Dolby 5.1 and eight–channel surround sound systems

Ideally, in this case your software will allow you to specify how you send particular sounds around the space whether in the form of an arrow going from point A to point B or in some geometric shape such as a helicopter's often-encountered circular flight path. This is no simple task but is perhaps the most rewarding of our exercises thus far as it allows you virtually total control of the placement and movement of all of your sound material. For example, a gesture may be a spatial gesture more than one involving any other parameter. As suggested before, this is a means of making your sounds come alive, as they exist in a space that is bigger than the line between the left and right stereo loudspeakers.

How do the results of this exercise compare with those in all of the other spatialisation exercises? What did you find most challenging and how do you think you might be able to improve upon your results in the future? Were there any limitations encountered such as the lack of a sense of higher and lower sounds due to the placement of your loudspeakers? Which one of the various approaches best serves the music that you intended to make?

There is one major challenge related to the most recent spatialisation exercises that deserves to be discussed at this point. Currently almost all radio and Internet audio is presented in stereo. In other words, when you make a multichannel recording, it is often expected that you also make a stereo version. I have terrible difficulty with this as the stereo versions of my own work are always disappointing compromises. I simply prefer them to be as they were conceived. This is not a healthy point of view in terms of getting one's music heard. We all need to see where flexibility ends and compromise begins. It might be worthwhile conceiving spatialised pieces in two forms: the multichannel version and a differently composed stereo version that may actually end up having another duration so that it functions well as a stereo piece. It adds up to more work, but it will better support the work's dissemination. Some people may be perfectly happy making a stereo reduction of a multichannel work; others may need to think along the lines of the two versions as suggested. When multichannel output from our radios or their future equivalent as well as our computers and other audio systems become more common, perhaps this particular issue will disappear, but for now it is absolutely essential that every sound-based musician who works with this type of spatialisation must keep the issue related to stereo/spatialised versions in mind. I always find it rewarding when a piece of sound-based music is heard as it was conceived and therefore choose for the multiple version option whenever possible.

One aspect that can be extremely rewarding in terms of this subject is an element of surprise, such as a sound suddenly appearing from an unexpected place or appearing in two places at once where they perhaps could not appear in nature. In other words you can be as creative or as faithful with spatialisation as you like.

That is one of the greatest challenges it poses and a means towards achieving very gratifying artistic results.

To Have a Beat or Not to Have a Beat, That is an Important Question

There are those in sound-based music who avoid a beat or rhythm in general like the plague. As sound-based music is inherently innovative, why do something traditional such as producing a beat?

I do not believe in this type of either/or nature related to the arts. Art is an open field and that is what is so attractive about it. Some people have found a need to be dogmatic to demonstrate that music can exist without a beat. In fact, beatless music has already existed for centuries in Arabic and Far Eastern countries, for example. Gregorian chant need not be sung with a strong beat either. Fortunately, we also have plenty of proof that it can work with one, too. What about our sound-based music?

One of the venues for innovation with sound can be found in today's experimental club culture. Although most music heard at clubs involves sound-based approaches, what is made is largely note-based. The music we are making moves that focus to the sounds, as we are well aware, but then what happens to the beat, so inherently associated with note-based music?

The answer is that we have also identified many other aspects of sound that are also present in note-based music, such as pitch, as being relevant to our work. We are now addressing the subject of duration under another guise. The means of construction and the sounding result will finally be different from, but may also demonstrate associations with note-based music. This nuance is at the heart of the present special subject: is a beat allowed? Clearly the answer is yes. In this section it is proposed that you create a study that contains at least one section that possesses no audible beat and at least one section that does—a study with contrasting elements.

Activity focusing on the presence and absence of a beat The activity is not intended to prove that sound-based music can possess a beat; that is simply assumed. The interesting challenge here is to move from a sequence without a beat to one with one (or vice-versa) or keep moving back and forth. The music may demonstrate an affinity with some sort of note-based music, whether one with popular, folk or art music roots, but should not focus on note-based traditions beyond that general influence. It is also possible to achieve a result with little to no connection with note-based musical traditions.

One thing that may be considered is a gradual move towards or away from the passage with a beat analogous with our order-to-disorder activity (although there is no implication here that beat needs to represent order). Furthermore, the tempo need not remain stable. It is all up to your imagination. The simple goal is to illustrate that aspects that are also related to note-based music can be used whilst organising sounds. Some of you may end up with something that "goes both ways", that is, incorporates elements from both sound-based and note-based music. Please note that any techniques introduced thus far related to sound sources, manipulation, spatialisation and so on are all at your disposal here.

Is this a relatively easy or difficult activity given the ability to work with something that you are perhaps more acquainted with than some of the other techniques that have been introduced? For those who were at least partially influenced by music related to club culture or any other form of dance music, was the step from the note to the sound an obvious one? Why was this so? Do you believe that the presence of a beat alters the listening experience and, if so, how? For example, did the piece you made make you want to move with the beat and, if that was the case, what happened when the beat disappeared? Did the fact that the beat was present mean that you also used other techniques borrowed from note-based traditions and, if so, which one(s)?

Ideally this first experience of including a beat, if it was the first one, will demonstrate how aspects related to note-based music may also serve sound-based music effectively. Similar to what we have experienced with parameters that have two clear extreme points, the presence or lack of presence of a rhythm forms a continuity of possibilities. Similarly, working within the note-based and sound-based traditions forms another continuity. Therefore, a piece may find itself located at one of the extremes, fully note-based or sound-based, or anywhere between the two extremes at any given moment. Thus working with combinations of aspects related to the two types of music with their multiplicity of traditions is an option, as we already discovered whilst discussing music-based music.

Allowing Music "to Breathe"—an Old Trick: Tension and Release

When talking about similarities or shared aspects between note-based and sound-based traditions, one need not be restricted to items such as pitch and rhythm. There are other aspects that are fundamental to many types of note-based music that can be applied equally successfully in sound-based music. Of these one has been selected for these final Chapter 5 activities, namely the notion of music's being able to breathe.

If this word comes across as a bit odd, there are more traditional terms associated with the idea, namely tension and release, that are similar to the movement between inhaling and exhaling. If this concept appears novel to you think of a piece of music that you really enjoy that is not static most of the time. (Many of you may never have listened to a static piece of music; in that case don't worry.) Do you hear where the energy or emotion or other aspect builds up and then recedes? This can take several seconds or even minutes. It can also happen very rapidly. This sense of a tide of energy or suspense rising and then receding, whether rapidly or slowly, is exactly what musical breathing is all about. Personally, I often find music that does not breathe enough boring or simply difficult to listen to.

So how might this work in terms of sound-based music? As suggested, tension and release can take place in any number of manners. In a song it may be as simple as working up to a lengthy high note or through a loud crescendo before things descend, or eventually the reverse: tension can be generated through things becoming too quiet or low. Music may become tense through the unexpected or unresolved and then released leading towards something more predictable or closed. Then there is the shift in moods that can take place and eventually return to a more stable state.

All of these types of developments can take place in sound-based music. Interestingly, this can happen within a single sound, within a gesture of any length or pair of gestures, within or amongst sequences and theoretically within an entire piece.

The activity below is in two parts. The first is related to listening and the second, as all other activities in this chapter, is concerned with the creative process of making.

Tension and release activity It has been a while since we had an activity that focused on listening. The first part of the tension and release activity requests that we go back to listening in order to identify how this manifests itself in nature and in sound-based music.

Listening Our final soundscape activity has had to wait for quite some time. The goal here is to listen to sounds at a given location to try to identify where tension is built up sonically and how it is subsequently released. The results will vary enormously depending not only on where you are, but what the local circumstances are at the time that you are there. It is conceivable that you will not hear anything that fits at all, but fear not—just move to another location. Tension and release in nature, whether urban or rural, is virtually omnipresent.

How would you define such tension/release events? How long do they and their constituent parts last? Do you ever hear more than one such sequence at once? Does this consist of all sounds that you hear or only a subset of them?

Now go back to some of the music that you have been making, including some of the shorter studies. Can you identify passages of tension and release in them? What kinds of durations are involved and were these changes working at sound, gesture or sequence levels? Can you describe in detail how they actually work? Try to find different ones and see whether they are working at different levels of duration. As above, were all sounds involved in this build up and relaxation, or only selected sounds? Did any of the pieces consist of a long passage leading towards tension and the subsequent part completing the release?

Another option is to listen to someone else's sound-based piece and attempt to answer the questions above. Perhaps you might discover some techniques that you have not yet employed yourself. How would you define them?

As we have been discussing archiving information and evaluating/analysing our own work, the time has come to do the same, be it perhaps in less detail, with others' work. If you know the other people, you can discuss your findings with them. If not, there is still a great deal one can learn by finding out more about others' work, in particular when it is sound-based music, that you find particularly attractive or regarding a particular interest of yours. Ironically, this activity's focal point, breathing, might be something the maker has not been dealing with consciously and therefore s(he) might not be able to clarify how it plays a role in a given piece. That illustrates how naturally it occurs.

Making It is a logical step to take what you have discovered in the listening half of this activity and apply it musically. We shall commence with small-scale items that are to be made in isolation. You need not try to create a single sound that involves tension and release, although that is in fact not that difficult, in particular if synthesis and/or sound manipulation is involved. Remember our discussion of the envelope of sounds that often involves some sort of attack at the beginning and release at the end.

Everyone will find the creation of a tension/release gesture possible—you might consider drawing it first in the form of a score—or, alternatively, a pair of gestures whereby the first one creates the tension and moves on to the release gesture.

Subsequently, it is important to try to achieve similar sorts of tension and release progressions at the sequence level and at the level of a short study. The former should not cause any difficulties. When it succeeds at the piece level, the progression is most likely the study's something to hold on to. In other words, a major or even the focus of such a study, regardless of content, is the process that leads to and develops away from tension. In this case, the tension need not peak at a specific point; instead it may all be a gradual two-way process.

It is important in all cases above that you are very clear about what you are trying to achieve and how you plan to achieve it, as you will find it worthwhile to have verified by other listeners whether you have indeed succeeded in achieving what you have envisioned.

The next step, as far as this activity is concerned, is to integrate the tension/release sounds, gestures and sequences into a larger context. The reason for this is simple: it is important to see whether these segments need to be embedded into other sounds to work most efficiently or are better off on their own. As these were all made separately, there is no need to combine them in a new study, but instead find ideal longer sequences or studies in which to use them.

Finally, it is worthwhile making a mid-size study that includes different types of tension/release elements. As some need time to be "digested", they should not necessarily occur one immediately after the other, but be highlighted or at least play this type of bridging role within the study.

The word "role" was just used. The object of breathing is important to music, but we have already discovered that it can manifest itself differently and play different roles. In your study, can you define these? How did the various movements from tension to release enhance the piece?

Please ensure that you have noted in your diary what you have done creatively, in terms of preparation, and of evaluation. Feedback from peers will also be worthwhile notating. Having done this, you should continue to be conscious of this important tool in the future and are likely to discover similar tools common to both note-based and sound-based music that are not usually presented as part of a musical study. Ironically, performers seem to be more aware of it as part of their study of interpretation. When we speak in our native tongue, we often ignore grammar, as it just comes naturally. If one speaks a second language, normally the awareness of the grammar is greater. What is being signalled here is that our being conscious of tension and release is very useful in any type of music making as well as in terms of listening. The more aware you are of such important tools, the more tools you will possess that will inform your sonic signature. This knowledge should now be developing as a source of pride.

Another Way of Working—Formalised Approaches

Top-down approaches have not played a significant role in this chapter nor have most approaches that are not led by the ear; however, it would be a major mistake to continue this line of thought. This section may appear as a subject jump. I would prefer to call it a very important missing puzzle piece thus far.

Formalised approaches to note-based music, although they existed to a greater or lesser extent throughout music history, came to the fore in the previous century.

Our parameter discussions would have been impossible were it not for the developments of the early twentieth century, for example those related to particular ways in which to order pitch into sequences as Arnold Schönberg and others proposed in twelve-tone music, where every note within the twelve-note chromatic scale appears once before any of the twelve are allowed to appear once again. In this way pitch was singled out for formal treatment whilst other parameters were approached differently.

To launch this discussion we shall introduce a scale, yet another parameter, ranging from determinate processes to indeterminate ones. In plain English this means processes in which predetermined ordering principles are applied to those that are largely left open to chance. Where Schönberg is associated with a major step towards determinism, the later composer John Cage was famous for his "letting go" as a composer and thus using various forms of chance operations to determine the content and/or performance of a given work. In general, the word indeterminate when used in a musical context means the creation of a work, the outcome of which cannot be predicted.

Determinacy and indeterminacy can be applied to one or more or even all aspects of a piece of music. When discussing sound-based music, one might think of: the choice or generation of sounds; the manipulation of sounds; any parametric aspect of sounds; the ordering of sounds; the creation of and filling in of structures; spatialisation; and formalised or indeterminate aspects at the work level.

For example, one could make up a series of rules that would determine which types of sounds are to be used, how long each sound is to last, when and where sounds are to be heard simultaneously, how they are to be ordered, and so on. A term borrowed from mathematics that describes such an approach is algorithmic music★, music based on a set of rules. Another example is known as generative music; that is, music in which a process is set in motion and that determines (aspects of) the final composition. Many generative works sound different from performance to performance. Processes can range from simple forms of repetition and variation related to any element of sound to more sophisticated ones whereby the sounds and their sound qualities, durations, dynamics and others are being determined as the work is being created. The nuance between rule-based and process-based determinism is relatively small for our purposes.

For those, like Cage, interested in the indeterminate end of the scale, you might imagine choices of potential material, manipulation and so on that are made by chance, be it by using something like dice to make choices, to a spontaneous decision during a performance, to automating things whereby a computer makes random choices on your behalf. To state the obvious, musicians do tend to take the credit for the product of an algorithm or random process, so you should have a general idea of what you are doing and why you are doing it if you wander to either end of this scale.

Like all of our parameters, there is a huge "grey area" in the middle whereby determinate or indeterminate processes are involved, but the musician makes

FIGURE 5.11 One way to allow chance to play a role while composing

the final decision of which outcomes are useful or not. Personally I find people working at either end most interested in the experimental or philosophical consequences of allowing order or chance to take over the creative process. Those working in the middle, on the other hand, are combining an experimental approach with the more traditional give and take of the empirical process of putting together a piece of music. In fact, for some, this type of approach may aid the efficiency in terms of getting a work completed.

Formalist and indeterminate approaches can be quite sophisticated and even extremely complex. For those interested in this type of musical adventure, you can find a wealth of written work on the subject pertaining to sound-based music on the EARS site and this is complemented by literature related to contemporary note-based art music that is largely easily accessible. These discoveries will most likely lead you to sound examples that represent different types of methods, some of which will be available for listening online. For now a simple introductory activity is proposed just to allow you to get your toes wet and see whether this type of approach might be of interest to you.

Formalism activity In this activity you will be asked to approach one aspect of a study formally and one aspect of a second study involving chance operations. If either or both leads to a promising result, you should come back to it and try things out in a (slightly) different manner or extend the experiment to other musical aspects.

Using determinism It is perhaps easiest to approach this study by choosing one parameter and creating a modest system that you will be able to use regarding that parameter. You might select a set of durations or a list of potential sound qualities or types to be used and then set up one or more rules that will determine how these are placed in a sequence or even throughout the study. If the result of this initial attempt sounds random, and that is the object of the chance study more than this one, you might tighten up the rule to make the results appear more coherent, perhaps by focusing on certain types of outcomes. Once you have succeeded regarding the single parameter, you will probably be able to think of ways of applying these sorts of rules or something quite different to other ones at the same time.

Have you ended up with a study that sounds like you might have made it this way in the first place without the use of a formalist approach? If so, try to find out why this might be the case. If not, what is your reaction to the result? Does it broaden your options or simply sound like it wasn't you who made it? In the latter case, would you be able to come up with some rules that are more compatible with your own evolving style?

Applying chance As above, we should start by influencing one parameter and to do this we need to create a list of possibilities related to that parameter. It is at this point that chance, as opposed to strict rules, will take over. You can choose from a host of means of applying chance: use some dice, a list of random numbers, pick your solution out of a hat, have all possibilities written on a large sheet of paper then close your eyes and where your finger points is the next outcome, and so on.

If the things that you are choosing from range broadly, you may end up with something that sounds random and may or may not be satisfied with the result. If you restrict the possibilities slightly, whereby the outcome by definition will be somewhat less indeterminate, your results may sound more familiar.

Once you have achieved a reasonable result, how about applying chance to more than one parameter of your sonic study? Following this, all of the questions posed at the end of the determinate study can be applied here in the form of an evaluation.

Please note that the way you set up a determinate or chance-based system will largely influence the result. The old expression "rubbish in, rubbish out" is often relevant when dealing with determinate and indeterminate approaches. The more you have some idea of the range of possibilities, a contradiction in terms in complete indeterminate situations, the more likely the result will offer potential in terms of that sonic signature to which we inevitably return.

It is easy to work progressively with these approaches. For example, one might make a study in which the composition of the sounds themselves is deterministically generated. These sounds can subsequently be further treated, sequenced and layered based on deterministic outcomes. The creation of those sounds is not top down, but another form of bottom-up composition. The deterministic decisions regarding structure and the like may very well be from the top down and therefore both approaches will meet in this multi-faceted deterministic approach.

This has been an advanced topic, as is the next one, but it is one that may very well play a role in the music of many of this book's readers. The intention here was to plant a seed in what may become a very large garden. Having said that, many sound-based musicians are completely happy with their bottom-up approaches and will tell you that for them this is a puzzle piece that they can live without. From my point of view, knowing that the approaches introduced above have been extremely successful for a number of musicians simply leads to the fact that the track record of certain formal and chance-based techniques speaks for itself and may prove very useful in terms of that rapidly growing toolbox you are creating.

A Word about Performance

This book has offered limited scope regarding the subject of performance. Although it is a fact that the borders separating the compositional act and that of performance and, to an increasing extent, that of the listener who is being called upon in certain circumstances to participate in sound-based performance are becoming fuzzy, the topic of performance and presentation is a second stage of a two-stage process. If ever a follow-up book to this one were written, one of its most important subjects would be the real-time performance of sound-based music. Our studies have almost always involved the creation of a recording that can be listened to again and again. The performance side of this is how it is presented—in which space, on what type of system and so on. Performance discussions have not focused on anything beyond hitting a start button since the end of Chapter 2, other than the discussion related to sound diffusion.

Today's technology involves unbelievable processing speeds. It is for this reason that digital music performance has increased so rapidly over recent years. What could only be achieved in the studio in the past can be performed live today, including real-time sound manipulation, spatialisation and even sound generation and retrieval. Laptop performers, DJs and digital instrument designers offer the widest variety of performances in concert halls, galleries, clubs as well as alternative venues, specific sites unique to the pieces being performed, online in networked performance or networked between two or more sites (also known as telematic performance). Our following subject, sound installations, can also involve performance, in this case by the spectator/listener. Furthermore, we should not forget that activity in Chapter 2 where one performance involved no technology at all in the sense of electricity or alternative power source. Remember, acoustic performance also forms part of sound-based music.

There is no specific activity that will be included regarding this subject as your ability to execute it will be highly dependent upon the facilities available. It is perhaps most important at this point to imagine what might be involved if you were to perform a work of your sound-based music. What would you need to prepare beforehand? What would you be able to do on the spot? What types of equipment would you need and where would your work ideally be performed?

Another very important question would be: if you were to perform with someone else or even with a group of other musicians, how might this work? Would someone need to take the lead and be the sole composer or could we all create this piece together? To what extent would you have to alter your sonic signature to be able to participate efficiently in this collaboration or would you be able to retain it fully?

If you work online, what type or types of sound-based music would you like to make? Would the system need to be largely predefined or would you prefer a model that allows you to perform in the same manner in which you would live in a venue? If you work online, how would you deal with the latency involved? (Data moves along the Internet at the speed of light; this is extremely fast, but not immediate.) Regardless of your background or experience, how might improvisation possibly fit into such types of performance?

How would you make a piece for performance at a specific site? What types of equipment would you use there? Might performance circumstances such as the weather influence what might be performed? Would you need to indicate contextual options in that case?

Sound-based music works well when there is nothing to see, as has been the case during most of our activities. It also works well in a performance situation. Most people living in this age of the image culture do prefer something to see, whether it is moving image on a screen, dance or theatre or someone performing a digital instrument. Others are very happy listening to sound without any visual information. I propose that both scenarios can be very effective and that live performance indeed can be extremely rewarding as long as what is offered to the eyes is meaningful and interesting. Anyone would agree about the same regarding the aural experience of the music.

If you possess the equipment and the means to apply the techniques that you have acquired in this book in the area of live performance, go ahead and take on the challenge. We all are interested in people's feedback on our efforts when it comes to pre-recorded sound-based music. Receiving feedback whilst you are in the act of performing will be at least as exciting. It is all down to the combination of the aural and visual aspects of performance, that is, what works best for the eyes. In other words, we are talking about the difference between the audio only and any audio–visual musical experience.

Making Sound Installations

The subject of sound installations has cropped up from time to time. It is, as has been said already, something that by definition implies input from at least two art forms. This book has focused on one art form, be it one that relies heavily on input from many others as well as non-artistic fields of study.

The fact that these are interdisciplinary art forms implies that an installation's public will have an interest in at least one of the two thus merging a fine art with a music audience. Having said that, many sound installations are placed in non-specialist spaces, such as public places, and are offered as a form of public art. In this way, an innovative art form can reach a public that has little to no experience with such things and offer the opportunity for a new audience to develop and consequently new artists to evolve.

One very special aspect of some sound installations is their ability to be "performed", that is, anyone is able to "play" them. The installation artist is not needed for the installation to produce sound, nor a specialist performer.

Some installations simply produce sound as long as they are turned on or are in an environment that acts as a trigger, for example wind influencing kinetic objects. Others can be triggered in one way or another. Sticking with weather conditions, perhaps one makes sound based on the brilliance of the sun, the amount of rain or the speed of the wind. Another trigger can be the intervention by human beings moving around a space as cameras or other sensors that have been installed track their movement. A person can literally trigger an installation's sound by touching it, thus interacting with it, which in turn sends a "play" signal. Then there are highly sophisticated forms of what has just been described. In all cases where the sounds produced by the installation can be influenced in one way or other, one speaks of interactivity. In simple cases, the installation simply responds to its input. In more sophisticated cases, it might learn how a participant is playing it and prepare its response based on the evolving "dialogue" with the player, thus choosing carefully from the variety of responses it can offer.

Few sound installations offer an experience that has a fixed beginning and a fixed end. This differentiates them from most musical works. People who are shy or simply not very interested may interact with or simply listen to them for seconds and move on; others may interact with them for hours. Obviously this is a combination of the interests of those present and the amount of engagement offered by the installation.

It is not assumed that you will be able to construct a sound installation beyond that of a sonorous acoustic sound installation. Therefore, again, no specific activity is being proposed. The door is simply being opened to those who might like to pursue this very gratifying avenue of sound-based music, perhaps the most

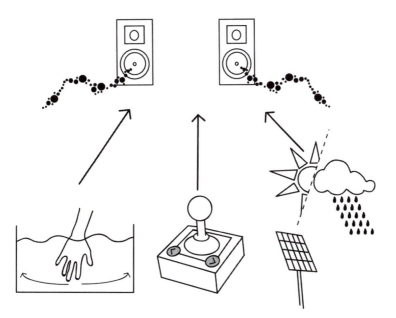

FIGURE 5.12   Three different ways of triggering sounds

accessible of all to the general public. I must admit with some embarrassment that I have attended festivals where hundreds of people engaged with installations but only dozens of people attended the associated concerts. The reason for this had to do with the lack of knowledge and possibly lack of curiosity related to unknown music versus the immediacy of the installations. I would suggest that anyone who can enjoy an installation could enjoy the music too (and vice-versa). It is for this reason that I find sound installations so important. They can create instant magic for people of all ages and backgrounds and offer some magnificent forms of sound organisation. They can equally act as a bridge leading people towards sound-based music works of all types. They are one of the most dynamic areas of sound organisation today and will remain so for the foreseeable future.

Analysing and Evaluating Composed Work

This final section of Chapter 5 is a very important postscript. Throughout this chapter and, in fact, throughout the entire book, an attempt has been made to treat all aspects of sound-based music holistically. Although we, for example, started to listen to soundscapes in isolation, links to other issues—sound types, space, pitch, layers, contextual and musical listening and so on—were presented as often as possible. For those who have called upon resources beyond the book, such as online resources related to specific aspects of content or repertoire, two things might have been noted: first, that much information is often treated in isolation, which is far from ideal; second, that bringing in information related to the book's content should reinforce this holistic approach and deepen your understanding and abilities.

The three key aspects of this holism are listening, understanding and making. The former relates not only to awareness as set out in Chapter 2, but also to the expansion of repertoire knowledge. Understanding is hardly limited to the musical or technological concepts presented progressively here, but also to aspects related to every activity that was presented. In other words, the listening activities in Chapter 2 were not solely about the increase of aural awareness, but also the greater understanding of its underlying concepts. In Chapter 3 the activities related to finding, generating and manipulating sounds all had very specific goals. Alongside those goals links could be made to issues related to Chapter 2's awareness and listening strategy aims. Beyond this, simple theoretical and technical concepts were introduced that were brought in connection with those related to listening and making. These last two chapters dealt with similar synergies at a progressively larger scale. As the scale increased, your making tools increased as well and your sonic signature evolved. This signature is not just simply something in your reflexes, but instead, it is something based on your aesthetic values, your techniques and, last but by no means least, your understanding of what you are doing.

An integral part of this understanding is your documentation and analysis of your undertakings. Another integral part of this understanding involves feedback coming from your peers as to whether your intentions have been received and, when this is not the case, it involves the search for new means to make the intention/reception loop more successful. The more successful this is, the greater the understandings involved.

Let us now return to the remark concerning sound-based music's ability to offer new forms of shared experience. That which has just been described concerning your own understandings of your work in tandem with the intention–reception loop is the best formula to follow to succeed in sound-based musical creativity. Although the creative act is the final goal, the creative experience of listening, making and understanding is the ultimate level enabling this final goal to be achieved.

Therefore, the ability to articulate intention combined with the understandings that are of fundamental importance related to every act of construction, the knowledge of the broad and specific contexts related to the music that you are making and a willingness to take reception-based feedback into account form the holistic basis of understanding. Your own evaluation and analytical comprehension of your work contribute immeasurably to this understanding

Many musicians are taught history, theory, where relevant technology, composition and performance separately. Many are never exposed to the cultural aspects of their work and the subject of intention is often carefully ignored. In this relatively young and rapidly evolving area, it is proposed that all of these ingredients are naturally interdependent, just as my own artistic work and my scholarly work support one another.

It is for all of these reasons that analysis and evaluation have been proposed to play an integral role throughout this book and ideally should continue to do so in your future sound-based music work. Without evaluation there will be no value system related to anyone's work. Without analysis and, contained within that, knowledge of the intention/reception experience, our art can be placed somewhere between arrogance and superficiality. It is for this reason that the notion of the thinking practitioner is at the basis of everything you have experienced above.

Documentation, evaluation and analysis may have appeared to be a chore, in particular during the substantial number of studies and pieces produced in this chapter. Please rest assured that your time was not wasted. You will better understand what you have done, what you have succeeded in and who you are becoming as a sound-based musician because of this work. You will also understand and appreciate other people's initiatives in this field much better. As has been said many times already, art is about communication—by way of the art itself and by way of our communicating about our experience of that art, whether you made it or someone else did. You are now equipped to make many types of sound-based music. You are also equipped to understand how it is put together, what the listening experience is like, how it relates to other works and, not least, what you value in it. If this last sentence comes as no surprise, then this book has fulfilled its purpose and you can graduate to higher-level publications concerning any subject related to sound-based creativity. If you share my excitement about this music, then spread the word. The more people making and enjoying this wonderful world of organised sound, the better.

6

NEXT STEPS

Many of our senses have been involved throughout this journey. It has mostly been about the ears, but the eyes have also been involved: in our soundwalks; with our scores and storyboards; learning how to use our software and the various bits and pieces of equipment that we have needed; with our sound installations and performances; and, naturally, watching other people react to the music, in particular your own. Touch was relevant when working with the tools of our trade and, again, with some sound installations and performances. Even smell may have enhanced the total awareness experience. Can any readers remember whether your taste buds were involved at some point?

This journey has taken us from completely contextual sound-based activities to more abstract musical ones; from the first monaural recording to discussions of multichannel spatialisation; from sample-based to the world of generated synthetic sounds; from bottom-up organisation starting with sound hunting continuing with sound sculpting and ending with sound organising to more formalised means of making sound-based music; from the concert hall to any space to virtual environments; and from the miniature gesture to the longer composition. You should also have had a chance to listen to sound-based music representing the breadth of the genres and categories presented in Chapter 1 and will have tried out a few different genres yourself. Finally, the journey allowed you to bring together information related to listening, making and understanding, thus involving you in every aspect of the sound-based musical experience.

You may now ask: where do I go from here? Frankly the challenges posed throughout this book could keep you going for years, as they have for me. Nonetheless, Chapter 5 concluded with a remark about your graduation. Chapter 6 proposes what might be discovered at the next level following this book's incremental model.

In terms of *further reading* the book's bibliography includes three supplementary lists: further reading for this book's readership; further reading related to books published for university-level readers; and further recommended websites. These lists are intended to complement the cited references, in particular the modest number of sources related to education. The university-level texts—many of the cited texts were written for that level as well—are included simply to help people to make the next step.

The better, more dynamic bibliographic source supporting this book is the EARS site. To use it, readers simply need to familiarise themselves with the EARS index. As the index is based in general on a tree structure, it is useful to look at both lower, more specific levels when searching as well as the higher levels, just to be certain, as texts have been allocated keywords based on their specificity.

What has not been included in the bibliography is a list of "how to" books as most of these are geared towards note-based music. Some of these might none-theless be worth pursuing as they may include such items as field recording, mixing and the like as well as offering information regarding sound manipulation. The EARS II site offers sufficient information for the purposes of this book, so you may only need to look at higher-level more specific technical readings whenever needed.

Beyond supplementary reading, the rest of Chapter 6 will investigate the following areas: study opportunities, repertoire, creative opportunities, collaborative opportunities, Internet music and installations. This will be followed by the book's conclusion.

The first discussion concerns further *study opportunities*. Obviously your continuing reading on the subject is one of the most effective ways of furthering your knowledge of this area. Expanding your knowledge of repertoire (see below) is also essential. Until schools at secondary level acknowledge the importance and value of this kind of music and the creative as well as generic skills that evolve after working in the field, one needs to pursue other avenues of action. Beyond the reading and listening there is also online information in these and other relevant media. As time goes on, even more sound-based music repertoire will be online, more creative opportunities and more pedagogical information will be on offer as well. In the meanwhile it is hoped that the combination of the original EARS site as glossary and bibliography as well as the EARS II pedagogical site will prove useful for your immediate study plans. Literature will range from history books to articles on theoretical and compositional concerns to more philosophical questions as well as cultural issues. It is important to keep an eye on both theoretical and technology-based concerns in order for you to be able to take on challenges that you may discover during these studies.

In terms of formal education, the prospects are quite positive. It will take time to get sound-based music and related music technology education to become part of many nations' secondary school curricula, but the fact of the matter is that as long as the music increases in importance, the greater the need will be for education to reflect those interests, as will be the case in the so-called cultural industries. As sound-based music moves out of the margins and into various communities of interest, one can only assume that there will be a greater willingness to teach the subject as part of creative arts development.

Let's look at an example to support this optimism. In the United Kingdom, where I work, there are dozens of higher education institutions, including universities, which offer music to their students. For a number of years now there have been more students studying popular music, music technology and sound-based music than there have been studying "traditional" music studies including Western art music performance and musicology. This demography reflects the music world as it evolves. Ideally, schools at pre-tertiary level will be provided with the time and the means to reflect today's musical spectrum in a more realistic manner as well.

In any event, more and more universities offer modules in sound-based music under the guise of music technology, sonic art, electroacoustic music or another name. Around the globe the number of PhDs in the field seems to be growing rapidly as well, reflecting the rapid developments in all aspects of the field. I have always wondered as an educator what life would be like when younger people had an early start in making this kind of music. I would suppose that the numbers of participants would soar and the knowledge base of incoming university students would rise enormously as well.

One thing that has prevented sound-based music's introduction in schools has been the lack of availability of sources and resources for teachers, many of whom hardly know about the music, as it is not what they have been taught. Hopefully, books like this one and resources like EARS and EARS II will fill the gap. In this way future music teachers will be provided with a solid basis as part of their teacher training studies.

The pursuit of *repertoire* can be one of the most gratifying aspects of sound-based musical discovery. It can also, especially in the early stages, be one of the most frustrating. What you choose to listen to is crucial and many understandably have difficulty in choosing.

The reason for this is simple. Many people, in particular young people, are not used to listening to longer pieces. Similarly, many people, especially children, are unused to listening to pieces actively as opposed to hearing them in the background. Therefore active listening is one challenge and listening to "heavy" pieces, ones that are serious, complex, a bit cold emotionally, represents an even greater challenge. Therefore, pieces should be presented or chosen on an incremental basis, thus enabling connections to be made in a way that is similar to the incremental structure of this book.

Some readers, in particular teachers, may have wondered why I have not been prescriptive with repertoire. Repertoire is reflective of age, experience, cultural circumstances, taste and other aspects. What can be said is that if one is treated to an alienating experience early on, it will be quite difficult to recapture interest afterwards. On EARS II we present options and are making certain that accessible and, in general, shorter works or segments are provided to listeners with little experience. Listeners are guided through some works in order to make them aware of the things to hold on to. Potentially alienating works are avoided, at least at this level. Some works are embedded in the introductions to ensure that users will not be confronted with difficult examples at an early stage. Works that are more appropriate for intermediate users offer that level of information in their descriptions.

As one progresses, one might imagine expanding the breadth of repertoire, the number of techniques that are audible in such works, and the sophistication and duration of the works as well. Some people who have worked their way through Chapters 1 to 5 may still need to listen to the most accessible works to aid their understanding; others may have moved on to more complex or different types of works. In a sense, what is being attempted here is the avoidance of a "one size fits all" approach to repertoire. If ever sound-based music forms part of an agreed curriculum, perhaps this luxury of individualising education will most likely give way to standard lists. I hope that this can be avoided.

As the Internet develops, it is expected that repertoire will be tagged in different ways, thus making a search for particular types of sounds or approaches to sound-based music easier than it is currently. Furthermore, it is my expectation that terminology will become more defined, again supporting searches for repertoire and associated information.

As stated earlier in this book, composers or pieces are not singled out here. If I had done so, I would have to ask the publisher to be allowed to update the book every year or so, and that is not feasible. As holism has been the goal throughout, repertoire should be gained before, during or after any aspect of study that leads you there. In other words, you might be led to a certain piece due to its relationship to a genre, to a technique that was used in its creation, to sound materials that have been used, to aspects related to its performance and so on.

Many composers have relinquished the protection of the rights to some or all of their compositions. These works belong to a new world of sharing; therefore, the search for appropriate works by way of EARS II, which has chosen some works without copyright and works that belong to archives that have allowed us to use them for pedagogical purposes, or other means should not be too taxing. Suggestions are always welcome regarding new works to be included as well as new ways of searching for or accessing them.

In a sense your future *creative opportunities* should be a natural extension of where you are having completed this book and what you would most like to do next or, alternatively, what you have been asked to do for a particular occasion, event, production or something like that. This short discussion will be presented in two parts, the first focused on making music and the second on performing sound-based music. After this, two special cases, Internet music and installations, will be briefly presented.

As far as *making sound-based music* is concerned, the remark about extending our activities is by far the most obvious one. You have been offered the possibility to investigate many points on the map of this music thus far and can easily determine which areas to return to or attempt to discover in the near future. Beyond this there is the issue as to whether the equipment that you have been using thus far will be able to satisfy your future needs. Some readers will have had access to professional-level software, robust computers, good microphones for studio and field recording, digital recording equipment and even mixers sending sound within a multichannel listening environment. However, understandably, most readers will not have had that luxury. So the next step up would be to find means of accessing higher-level systems. Nowadays, it is not only the most sophisticated studios or education organisations that possess such equipment. Some schools have been able to invest in things like digital recorders, high-end audio software including multichannel sound systems, microphones and a variety of types of music technology equipment relevant to sound-based music. Some professional software systems exist in different forms, often including a free low-end (LE) system so that people can become accustomed to what the software can achieve and ideally find places to use the higher-end systems afterwards.

There is always a careful balance to be made as one climbs this particular ladder, as it is possible to start using new sorts of software, hardware and peripheral equipment every couple of years, thus leading to one spending most time learning how to use something and too little time mastering it. This is in dire contrast to the mastery that one can achieve with modest, yet limited systems. In other words, the ideal of every child and most people involved with sound-based music of obtaining more "toys" is not always a good thing. I have always found it useful to look for specific sounds for pieces and, similarly, I have found it useful to seek specific equipment so that my possibilities are directly related to the combination of my expertise and the particular needs of a given artistic endeavour.

For example, a typical audio software package might be ideal for bottom-up composition; however, if one were to be asked to do some work based on a determinist or formalised system, perhaps it would be better to use something that is more suited to that type of approach. In this case, one leaves one's comfort zone of the software most usually used, but instead gains expertise, as that is part of the specific piece's goal. In this way one's palette of options increases on the basis of logical progressive steps.

The moral to this part of the story is that many of you reading this book will have access individually to a certain collection of software and hardware to be used when creating sound-based music. Leaving the individual environment should take place when: a given work involves demands that your personal possessions cannot handle; you are working collaboratively; you become attached to an environment that offers higher-level tools than you possess and you have regular access to them; or you are able to afford to expand what you are able to use personally.

Many of those extras that individuals tend not to possess are related to *performing sound-based music*. This might include sophisticated software that is primarily applied in real-time performance contexts. There are also all sorts of performance devices, not to mention digital instruments or adopted traditional (note-based) instruments, that will be relevant to many readers. Sound-based music does not possess a basic set of devices and instruments as note-based music does. As alluded to above, this has led to a situation where, on the positive side, our opportunities for creating a sophisticated performance in real time have increased, but the means of delivery remain somewhat underdeveloped, thus making the visual aspect of live performance often disappointing if not downright dull. Readers who have experienced people performing on their laptops on stage will know what I mean.

I believe that if I were to write a second edition of this book in about five years' time, there would be a need for a new chapter dedicated to newly established performance opportunities whereby specific incremental activities could be included, as found in Chapters 2 to 5. In the meantime readers internationally will be able to see what types of opportunities are evolving, as this music has found its home in many alternative venues, such as clubs specifically focused on today's electronica practices. The number of performances has been steadily rising and the music has achieved remarkable success internationally.

Of course performance need not restrict itself to work between like-minded sound-based musicians. There are many collaborative opportunities available with other art forms. For example, about half of all of my creative work has involved at least one other art form. Such collaborations indeed involve some give and take, not to mention getting used to other approaches to creativity. Interdisciplinary collaborations can lead to some of the most gratifying results imaginable.

Let's take an obvious example. Dance normally needs sound or music as an audio-visual art form. Open-minded choreographers or devising dance companies are often interested in experimenting with unusual materials such as sound-based music. With today's technology, we are increasingly able to have the dancers actually conduct the sounds by way of their movements so that they are not following live musicians or a recording. The same holds true for work with theatre, the experimental medium called performance art, with film and video and other related art forms.

Working in the theatre, it is the person who works with sound who has command of the three dimensions of the performance space. The actors are usually only on stage, so this is a very exciting and potentially powerful position to be in. Whether it is called sound design or simply music or, with live musicians, performance, collaborative interdisciplinary sound-based music is an area within the theatre world that is due to expand rapidly in the future.

Some interdisciplinary or even music-only forms of collaboration are not intended for live performance involving physical presence. This leads us to the following subject: the Internet and other immersive environments.

The case of *Internet music and sound-based music for immersive environments* deserves special attention. I have already suggested that music on the Internet will form part of tomorrow's folk music for a large number of people in many countries. This does not infer the consumption, as is the case today, of commercial MP3 recordings, but instead the fact that one can make music and, increasingly, make music with others collaboratively online. Parallel to these developments the success of the games industry should not be ignored. Whether speaking of games or tomorrow's various forms of immersive environments, the opportunities to make sound-based music for specific applications or environments should become quite substantial. In the games world it is quite developed already and pioneers in sound-based Internet music have been developing ideas for well over a decade now.

Finding, or more challenging still, creating, an Internet sound-based performance environment that suits you is probably not easy. With time more and more environments will be introduced and, in my view, two types are most likely to suit this book's readers: those that have a similar stylistic ethos to what you have been developing and those that are most open, thus allowing individuals to work in their own ways combining their sonic signatures with those of people of other backgrounds and interests. If you think of how often you are looking at a screen from day to day, it seems logical that a good deal of music making in the future will happen within such environments.

An interesting thing about computer games is that their music often follows the course of your own play. That means that what you hear, whether note-based or sound-based, is determined by your own actions and thus fits within our formalised music discussion. If you asked many people playing computer games whether they would ever care to listen to a piece of formalised music, you can imagine what their response might be.

Many games involve sound effects and some specifically include sound-based music and I would expect this to increase in the future. Therefore one area that you might find yourself developing sound-based music for could be the games industry.

Similarly, our current futuristic immersive environments are due to become a fact of life in the future as we move towards 3D viewing and a more realistic audio-visual experience. Surround sound is an integral part of this. The potential roles of sound-based music in immersive environments are yet to be determined. As sound-based music is one of what is known as the new-media arts and immersive environments are amongst the trendiest sorts of new-media development areas, the link is an obvious one.

It is hard to predict how all of this will evolve and what sorts of new types of sound-based music will be developed for games, immersive environments and the Internet. Frankly, I am optimistic that we only have our toes wet at the moment and many exciting developments are not that far away.

Perhaps *installations* involving sound-based music will not enjoy the same fate as what has just been described above. Nonetheless, they are of particular importance as they represent, as introduced in the previous chapter, one of the immediate means of connecting with new listeners as well as experienced ones of all ages and interests. Where a collaboration such as those discussed above often will involve representatives of each art form, installations tend to be made by a multi-artist, that is, someone who is at home with the construction aspects of the installation, its physical presence as well as its sonic aspects. There are, of course, musician–dancers and even more who make both dimensions of audio-visual video works, but this is currently more or less the norm with installations. Although I understand such artists' views that sound is an integrated aspect of their work, I do not see why more sculptors or installation artists who are interested in sound do not work more often with music specialists who might share their vision but offer more experience as far as sound organisation is concerned.

Regardless, sound installations have helped to redefine performance, particularly in the sense previously discussed of the spectator/listener becoming the installation's performer when the installation is interactive. This hybrid art form and others that have roots in the fine arts, mostly associated with sound art, are amongst the most accessible forms of sound-based music today and there is no reason for this to change in the future. Part of the reason for this is the fact that these artists like to have their work connect with the contexts in which their work is found. By making such a connection, these artists are offering at least one thing for their (participating) audience to hold on to. Much sound art is about life and much art that is about life makes strong connections with its public.

Many of our activities are also applicable within these hybrid art forms as the aspects related to aural awareness, the things to hold on to and the intention/reception loop are all highly pertinent. Sound-based music has a very comfortable home in the world of installations and other forms of interdisciplinary creativity involving the fine arts. The success of so many manifestations of sound art has been so striking that it is inevitable that new forms will come into being using new technologies. For example, just think of what will be happening with your mobile phone in a few years, integrating sound with image and space in innovative and exciting ways.

We finally reach our *conclusion* and it is a pleasure to inform you (and your students) that you are now a leader, no longer the curious beginner, who can and hopefully will further define the field of sound-based music. We have come a long way from identifying sounds, recording or downloading them and thinking about what we might do with them. You have hopefully found many of the activities rewarding and have discovered many aspects of your sonic signature, and therefore been able to define your taste in sound-based music along the way. As you continue to develop, listen to work of your peers in the field and discover new knowledge and technical as well as artistic potential, you will come to enjoy the challenges and delights of this music as I do. As our numbers grow, sound-based music will have to become part of our schools' diet; it will be heard more often on the radio, in concerts, in specific sites and online; and at last many more people will develop a pride for and participate in one of the most accessible and fascinating art forms that has become virtually universally accessible due to our digital age. Good luck!

GLOSSARY[1]

Acousmatic Music The term acousmatic is said to come from Pythagoras who, according to tale, offered lectures to his disciples from behind a curtain, whereby the disciples were unable to see that which they heard and were left imagining the unseen visual elements of what they were hearing. Today acousmatic, which evolved from musique concrète, is founded upon this "reduced listening" situation.

Acoustic Ecology Ecology is the study of the relationship between individuals and communities and their environment. Acoustic or soundscape ecology is thus the study of the effects of the acoustic environment, or soundscape, on the physical responses or behavioural characteristics of those living within it. Its particular aim is to draw attention to imbalances which may have unhealthy or inimical effects (EARS; Truax 1999).

Additive Synthesis Additive synthesis describes the building up of a complex tone or waveform from simpler elements such as sine waves according to the law of superposition (which is also known as fourier synthesis) (EARS; Truax 1999).

Algorithmic Music An algorithm is a procedure or formula, e.g., for solving a problem. This term is one of the most employed words for formalised approaches to composition. Algorithmic music involves the application of algorithms as part of the composition process (EARS).

---

1   This glossary leans heavily on my previous work. Where the definitions have been borrowed from my or others' previous publications or the EARS site, this will be included at the end of the entry.

Amplitude Modulation or AM AM can be used as an effect whereby one input signal modulates the amplitude of another sound. When done in the sub-audio range by, for example, a sine wave, the result is a tremolo. When executed at higher frequencies, more complex sounds will result.

Analysis/Resynthesis Resynthesis techniques concern the re-creation and eventual modification of existing recorded or synthesised sounds, generally through the analysis and eventual modification of some form of computer representation of the sound. Frequently, resynthesis techniques will involve the creation of a new sound based on the desired signal processing applied to the original input sound (EARS).

Binaural A binaural recording is one where the microphones are placed in the position of the outer ears, or in a simulation of this. This is in order to give the listener the sense of 3D space when listening. Binaural recordings are generally intended for audition over headphones (EARS).

Chorusing Through the use of multi-layering one or more sounds, often with the use of very small-scale delays, the chorusing effect leads to the impression of a chorus consisting of an ensemble of the input sound(s).

Collage Derived from the French word, collage concerns artwork in which fragments of any sort are literally or figuratively cut and pasted together. In sound-based music this may concern extremely brief elements of sound material up to musical fragments (EARS).

Composite Gesture A composite gesture is, similarly to a multiple gesture, a complex gesture consisting of a number of gestures within it. In this case an accumulation of gestures together form a single gesture. Where multiple gestures are generated sequentially, composite gestures involve simultaneity.

Computer Music This term covers a broad range of music created through the use of one or more computers. The computer may work as (assistant) composer. In this case one speaks of algorithmic composition. Alternatively the computer can be used as an instrument; that is, the computer is the place where the sounds are to be generated. Here one speaks of sound synthesis. The computer is sometimes brought on stage to create and manipulate sounds made during performance. Finally, the computer may analyse incoming performance information and "reply" in what is known as interactive composition. The former two possibilities sometimes necessitate a good deal of compilation time; the latter two belong to the category of real time. More recently, music making has witnessed the extensive use of networked computers (Landy 1994a, 127–128; EARS). The International Computer Music Association's annual conference, ICMC, extends this definition to include things ranging from computer-aided cognition, analysis, information retrieval and much more, thus going well beyond the act of music making. Much computer music therefore has little to do with sound-based music.

Contextual Listening This is a listening strategy in which attention is being given to the relationships between specific sounds and the real or imagined contexts in which they are taking place. Contextual listening sits at the opposite end of a spectrum to musical listening. Some authors (e.g., Norman 1996) have split contextual listening into two: referential listening (focused on the identification of specific sources) and contextual listening (placing those sources in an aural context).

Cross-Synthesis Cross-synthesis concerns sound production whereby one parameter (e.g., amplitude, frequency) of a sound is applied to influence a parameter, not necessarily the same one, of another sound (EARS).

Delay The notion of delay pertains to the use of a device (or digital equivalent) allowing for the introduction of one or more precisely timed delays to a given input signal. This can be used for a variety of effects including, for example, the creation of the sensation of spatial depth (EARS). Where echo implies sound reflection in a given space, delay can be applied to a single sound channel.

Diffusion Electroacoustic diffusion refers to the practice of distributing sound throughout a space using multiple loudspeakers, usually with real-time control over the sound levels, equalisation (filtering) and the placement of the sound. The source material may be live performers, synthesisers and/or stereo or multichannel recordings (EARS; Truax 1999).

Electroacoustic Music Music in which electronic technology, now primarily computer-based, is used to access, generate, explore and configure sound materials, and in which loudspeakers are the prime medium of transmission. There are two main genres. Acousmatic music is intended for loudspeaker listening and exists only in recorded tape form (tape, compact disc, computer storage). In live electronic music the technology is used to generate, transform or trigger sounds (or a combination of these) in the act of performance; this may include generating sound with voices and traditional instruments, electroacoustic instruments, or other devices and controls linked to computer-based systems. Both genres depend on loudspeaker transmission, and an electroacoustic work can combine acousmatic and live elements (Emmerson and Smalley 2001).

Electronic Music Originally, music in which the sound material is not prerecorded, but instead uniquely generated electronically, historically through oscillators and noise generators, currently digitally. There are some, particularly in the United States, who use this term today as a synonym for electroacoustic music. The German equivalent, elektronische Musik, has more precise historical connotations, referring to electronically generated post-serial composition that commenced in the early 1950s in the broadcast studios in Cologne. In French, electronic music is also currently used as a synonym for genres of popular electronic music such as techno (EARS).

Electronica This term is used in two different ways. It is synonymous with certain innovative electronic forms of pop music including so-called Intelligent Dance Music (IDM). Most of this music is primarily note-based whilst using sound-based elements and techniques. It is also used as a term for a type of sound-based music that has been created as a reaction to more elitist forms of sound-based music. Here the reaction can be found in the type of materials used, such as unwanted sounds including noise or the glitch sound created in CDs that are not working properly and other sorts of digital or analogue detritus, thus creating a lo-fi effect that exists independently of most pop and art music developments. (See also the electronica discussion in Chapter 1.)

Elektronische Musik This term is not only the German equivalent of electronic music; it was the initial term used from 1949 (originally by Werner Meyer-Eppler) throughout the 1950s for music that was made at the German radio broadcast facilities originally at the NWDR in Cologne. All sounds were electronically generated, thus not involving any acoustic recordings or acoustic or electronic instruments. This term when used outside of the German language refers to these early years and the type of formalised music based on the ordering of musical parameters that was made by early pioneers including Herbert Eimert. Elektronische Musik was the polar opposite of musique concrète.

Envelope The profile of the evolution of the intensity and/or spectrum of a sound during its duration (EARS). Those who use synthesisers or software-based systems will be acquainted with the terms that are often related to an envelope's design: attack, decay, sustain, release or ADSR.

Filter A device used to affect certain parts of the spectrum of a sound, by causing the attenuation of certain frequency bands, while allowing other bands to pass unattenuated. Some common types of filters are: high-pass, low-pass, band-pass, band-reject (or stopband), octave, half-octave, third-octave and tenth-octave filters (EARS). The comb filter represents one case of a specialised filter used for the creation of resonant sounds.

Flanging Flanging is an effect associated with chorusing when the use of multiple very short delays (in ms) leads to a sound's multiplying itself.

Frequency The rate of repetition of the cycles of a periodic quantity, such as a sound wave (EARS; Truax 1999). The musical notion of pitch is normally related to the fundamental frequency of a sound.

Frequency Modulation or FM FM involves the modulation of one frequency by another. FM can be applied as an effect or used as a form of synthesis (see below). When the modulating frequency is low and the waveform is simple, such as a sine wave, the result is a vibrato. When the modulating frequency is higher, a more complex sound quality is generated.

Frequency Modulation (FM) Synthesis This is a form of sound synthesis where the input or carrier sound frequency is modulated by the frequency of a modulator sound within the audio range. FM synthesis is able to easily create complex sound qualities.

Gesture Gesture is concerned with action directed away from a previous goal or towards a new goal; it is concerned with the application of energy and its consequences; it is synonymous with intervention, growth and progress, and is married to causality (EARS; Smalley 1986).

Glitch A term denoting musics based on the structuring and manipulation of small audio artefacts traditionally considered as defects, such as clicks. The term implies a celebratory lo-fi aesthetic, and inherently is closely related to the concepts of grain and granularity (EARS).

Granular Synthesis Granular Synthesis is a method by which sounds are broken into tiny grains that are then redistributed and reorganised to form other sounds (granularsynthesis.com).

Harmonising Through the use of relevant digital techniques, several versions of an input sound of identical duration are created at specifically chosen pitches.

Limiter The notion of limiting concerns the prevention of an audio signal's exceeding a chosen dynamic level. This can be achieved by the use of a digital or analogue device or by way of its software equivalent (EARS).

Listening Walks The term says it all: a walk where the participant (or participants) concentrates on listening (paraphrase of Schafer 1994, 212–213). When one consciously listens, the normal level of aural awareness increases, which is the primary goal of this activity. When more than one person is involved, silence is expected throughout, and an exchange related to the aural experience is expected at the end.

Live Electronics A term dating from the analogue age of electroacoustic music that describes performance involving electronic devices or instruments which can be performed in real time. The term is more commonly expressed today as music involving interactive instruments (EARS).

Loop Originally this word was used specifically for a tape loop; that is a fragment of tape of which the beginning and end have been cut and spliced together and therefore create a type of (continuous) ostinato, which could be of any length. Today this term is also used for samplers, computers and other real-time digital instruments: sounds of a specific length have been recorded but these might be shorter than a length needed during performance. An internal loop within the sound created by the user allows the sound to be sustained indefinitely (EARS; Landy 1994a).

lowercase sound Also known as lowercase music, lowercase audio or simply lowercase, lowercase sound is an area of aesthetic and creative activity that can loosely be termed a genre/category. Most who associate themselves with the term, however, value a sense of fluidity in the area's boundaries. Lowercase artists privilege listening as a creative act, and tend towards focused and attentive listening contexts, frequently to quiet, small, or commonly "overlooked" sounds (EARS). This term is normally written in lower case.

Microsound Broadly, the term refers to conceiving of and representing sound in terms of particles. These sounds fall within the domain that Curtis Roads calls the "micro-time scale". He defines this scale as one that embraces . . . a broad class of sounds that extends from the threshold of timbre perception (several hundred microseconds) up to the duration of short sound objects (ca. 100 milliseconds) (EARS).

Multiple Gesture A multiple gesture is, similar to a composite gesture, a complex gesture consisting of a number of gestures within it. In this case a gesture's termination normally serves as the following component's onset, thus creating a gesture of gestures.

Musical Listening This term is used as an antonym of contextual listening. Musical listening focuses on the nature of sounds to their musical relationships without reference to their source or cause. This term is often used in conjunction with reduced listening.

Musique Concrète A term created by Pierre Schaeffer in 1948, this new music started from the concrete sound material, from heard sound, and then sought to abstract musical values from it. Schaeffer is also the person who coined the term reduced listening, thus suggesting we ignore the source and cause of the concrete sounds. Many early works, due to the unsophisticated tools on offer, could be listened to both in terms of their sources as well as their musical qualities. This approach is quite common today as well.

Noise Music This term is associated with various forms of music that have focused on noise as their key sound quality. In the early twentieth century, noise was a focus of some works by the Futurists and Dadaists. More recently it became a key ingredient of the music of many punk musicians. Today we use the term noise music as a category describing their work. Many of these artists are associated with electronica and use noise as their main source material. Note: not all noise music has to be loud.

Organised Sound This is the term adopted by the composer Edgard Varèse (in the 1920s) to describe his music. His use of this term reflects in particular his insistence on the musical potential of an expanding "palette" of possible sounds for use in the concert hall, in particular, new kinds of percussion, electronically generated sounds and recorded sounds. The term is often cited in attempts to define music and anticipates the notion of music as a "plastic" art form (Landy 2007a, 10).

Physical Modelling This area includes any means of synthesising sound from scratch through a mathematical acoustical model, generally of an existing musical instrument. Normally physical modelling is based on models of the manner in which a resonator responds to some form of excitation (for example a guitar string being plucked) (EARS).

Pitch Shifting This refers to the changing of the pitch in either direction. Traditionally, pitch shifting went hand in hand with the change of speed of a tape recorder. With today's digital technology, pitch shifting can take place alongside time stretching and compression whereby the duration need not be altered, only the pitch.

Plunderphonics Plunderphonic composition is a specific, radical form of collage in which all materials have been appropriated from existent music. It is a politically motivated genre that is focused on the notion of free samples and challenging perceived hypocrisy of musical copyright law. The term is derived from the seminal CD by John Oswald called *Plunderphonics* (EARS).

Radiophonic Art/Radio Art Radio art is the use of radio as a medium of art. Sound quality here is secondary to conceptual originality (EARS; Landy 2007a, 11).

Real Time In early computer music, this term was used to signify sound generation systems that took no longer to compute than the length of what it was computing. More recently, this term is used as in most disciplines to signify a user's perception of the result of digital processing as sufficiently immediate (EARS).

Real-World Music This umbrella term has been applied in this book to describe sound-based music in which the source and cause (e.g., striking, rubbing, tapping) of the sound material is largely audible. Even when new sounds are made intentionally to re-present real-world sounds, one can speak of real-world music.

Reduced Listening (originally Écoute Réduite) In Schaefferian theory, reduced listening is the attitude which consists in listening to the sound for its own sake, as a sound object by removing its real or supposed source and the meaning it may convey. More precisely, it is the inversion of this twofold curiosity about causes and meaning (which treats sound as an intermediary allowing us to pursue other objects) in order to turn it back on to the sound itself. In reduced listening our listening intention targets the event, which the sound object is itself (and not to which it refers) and the values which it carries in itself (and not the ones it suggests) (Chion 1883; EARS).

Reverberation Reverberation is the result of multiple reflections of a sound. The application of artificial reverberation in terms of sound sculpting has to do with the creation or simulation of a given real or synthetic space sonically.

Sampling The reuse of existing sounds (including those found in note-based music) and musics with attendant notions of "borrowing", "stealing", "recycling" and "recontextualising" (EARS).

Sine Wave The purest of sounds, looking like a sequence of hills and troughs, the sine wave (or sinusoid) creates the sound of a single frequency with no harmonics or interference. Other basic types of wave with a simple formulaic harmonic structure, yet more complex quality, include the triangle, sawtooth and square waves.

Sonic Art This term generally designates the art form in which the sound is its basic unit. A liberal view of sonic art would take it to be a subset of music. It is also used in its plural form (EARS; Landy 2007a, 10).

Sound Art This term has been used inconsistently throughout the years. Currently it is typically used to designate sound installations (associated with art galleries, museums and public spaces), sound sculptures, public sonic artefacts and site-specific sonic art events. It is often used to include radiophonic works as well (Landy 2007a, 11). One important aspect of sound art is that it is normally not intended for concert performance, often does not have a beginning or an end (and thus does not demand full-time presence or attention) and normally takes its site/context into account.

Sound Installation Within the realm of public art, the sound installation can be a musical equivalent of a sculpture, an aural experience designed for a space generally used for the exhibition of visual art of a site-specific work. Many installations have profited by applying a variety of sound-based techniques and technology in their creation and spatial presentation. Sound installations are normally experienced from any random starting point to any ending point as opposed to the traditional work with a beginning and an end (EARS). Some installations involve interactivity with people present or other factors such as noise levels, the weather, etc.; others simply create their sounds in time.

Sound Quality This is used as an umbrella term in this book referring to a single or composite sound's aural characteristics. Instead of discussing source and cause, in this case one describes the sound's colour or timbre, aspects related to its texture and any other description related to its sonic as opposed to contextual value.

Sound Synthesis Synthesis techniques concern means of producing sound, electronically or digitally, in which no physical acoustic source is used (except perhaps as a model) (EARS).

Sound-Based Music The term sound-based music typically designates the art form in which the sound, that is, not the musical note, is its basic unit. A liberal view of sound-based artworks would indicate it to be a subset of music (Landy 2007a, 17).

Soundscape Composition Environmental sound recordings both form the source material and inform a work at all its structural levels in the sense that the original context and associations of the material play a significant role in its creation and reception. Soundscape composition is context embedded, and even though it may incorporate seemingly abstract material from time to time, a piece never loses sight of what it is "about" (EARS; Truax 2000).

Soundscapes A soundscape is an environment of sound (or sonic environment) with emphasis on the way it is perceived and understood by the individual, or by a society. It thus depends on the relationship between the individual and any such environment. The term may refer to actual environments, or to abstract constructions such as musical compositions and tape montages, particularly when considered as an artificial environment (EARS; Truax 1999).

Soundwalks The soundwalk is an exploration of the soundscape of a given area using a score as a guide (Schafer 1986, 212–213). The score includes a map. Soundwalks are sometimes seen to support ear training in the sense of aural awareness of our environments.

Spectralism This is a term applied to composers whose musical concerns include the use of instrumental, vocal and environmental sound as models from which any number of attributes of a musical composition may be extrapolated. The term is derived from "spectrum" and work associated with the term has been facilitated through the use of the computer to spectrally analyse, model and visually represent sound (EARS). Spectralism is a form of instrumental and vocal composition that in many ways has been influenced by electroacoustic or sound-based music.

Speech Synthesis The synthesis of human speech sounds. Speech synthesis has been used for industrial applications as well as a means of generating sounds for musical use. Musical uses include the synthesised spoken/singing voice to the creation of "impossible" vocal sounds such as a voice gliding a note upwards and downwards at the same time.

Subtractive Synthesis Based on complex waveforms or noise coupled to one or more filters, subtractive synthesis concerns the reduction of these complex spectra. The most extreme case would be the reduction to a pure sine wave (Dictionnaire des arts médiatiques; EARS).

Synthesisers Any grouping of electronic modules intended for sound processing. Such equipment usually incorporates a combination of oscillators (tone generators), filters, mixers, envelope generators, noise generators, reverberation units, etc. The term is now generally applied to digital sound synthesisers as well as their analogue antecedents. All analogue synthesisers use the principle of voltage control to determine the values of the various sound parameters. Sequences of control voltages may be produced by a keyboard or by a sequencer where the voltages are preset and then generated in a fixed sequence. Digital synthesisers utilise techniques of digital sound synthesis using one of a variety of digital sound processing (DSP) techniques. Increasingly non-keyboard based synthesisers are being replaced by software-based systems on personal computers (EARS; Truax 1999).

Text–Sound Composition This is an "in-between art form" that involves the sounds of the spoken voice and eventually other vocal utterances as the primary source material for composition. Some text–sound works are solely performed live. Most, however involve technology. Another term for text–sound composition is text–sound poetry (or simply sound poetry), identifying that it has to do with poetry/literature as well as music.

Timbral Composition A composition in which the sound quality forms the focus in terms of the listening experience.

Time Stretching and Time Compression In digital music, time stretching and compression involve the elongation or reduction of a recording without changing its pitch. Whilst using tapes, the pitch rose or descended according to the amount of increased or decreased speed. Large-scale stretching can lead to granular textures; large-scale compression can lead to the source becoming masked.

Turntablism This expression is strongly associated with hip hop and DJ culture. A turntablist is a musician who conceives the scratching and mixing of records on a twin-deck turntable as an artistic and expressive medium. Turntablism is the process of creating music this way, by employing techniques such as scratching, backspinning, cutting and crossfading.

BIBLIOGRAPHY AND RECOMMENDED READING

Cited Texts

Blackburn, M. 2009a. Composing from Spectromorphological Vocabulary: Proposed Application, Pedagogy and Metadata. Available at: www.ems-network.org/ems09/proceedings.html (accessed 10th April 2010).

Blackburn, M. 2009b. Unpublished images used when presenting Blackburn 2009a.

Blackburn, M. 2010.Portfolio of Electroacoustic Music Compositions. PhD Dissertation (Compositions and Commentary). University of Manchester.

Chion, M. 1983. *Guide des Objets Sonores: Pierre Schaeffer et la recherche musicale.* Paris: Buchet/Chastel.

Emmerson, S. 1986. The Relation of Language to Materials. In Simon Emmerson, ed. *The Language of Electroacoustic Music,* 17–39. Basingstoke: Macmillan.

Emmerson, S. and Smalley, D. 2001. Electroacoustic Music. In S. Sadie, ed. *The New Grove Dictionary of Music and Musicians,* 2nd edition. Basingstoke: Macmillan

Landy, L. 1987. Comp(exp. $\int$) = $f_t \sum$'parameters'($\sim$). *Avant Garde* (Presentation). 27–40.

Landy, L. 1994a. *Experimental Music Notebooks.* Chur: Harwood Academic Publishers.

Landy, L. 1994b. The "Something to Hold on to Factor" in Timbral Composition. *Contemporary Music Review* 10(2): 49–60.

Landy, L. 2006. The Intention/Reception Project. In Mary Simoni, ed. *Analytical Methods of Electroacoustic Music,* 29–53 (+ appendix on DVD). New York: Routledge.

Landy, L. 2007a. *Understanding the Art of Sound Organization.* Cambridge, MA: MIT Press.

Landy, L. 2007b. *La musique des sons/The Music of Sounds.* Paris: Sorbonne MINT/OMF (distributed by www.zurfluh.com).

Norman, K. 1996. Real-World Music as Composed Listening. *Contemporary Music Review* 15(1): 1–27.

Puckette, M. 2007. *The Theory and Technique of Electronic Music.* Hackensack, World Scientific Publishing Company. Available at: http://crca.ucsd.edu/~msp/techniques/latest/book-html (accessed 10th April 2010).

Rudi, J. 2007. Computer Music Composition for Children. *IEEE Signal Processing Magazine* 24(2): 140–143.

Schaeffer, P. 1977. *Traité des objets musicaux: essai interdisciplines*, 2nd edition. Paris: Seuil.

Schafer, R. M. 1994. *The Soundscape: Our Sonic Environment and the Tuning of the World.* Rochester, VT: Destiny Books.

Smalley, D. 1986. Spectro-morphology and Structuring Processes. In Simon Emmerson, ed. *The Language of Electroacoustic Music*, 61–93. Basingstoke: Macmillan.

Smalley, D. 1992. Listening Imagination: Listening in the Electroacoustic Era. In John Paynter, Tim Howell, Richard Orton and Peter Seymour, eds. *Companion to Contemporary Musical Thought*, vol. 1, 514–554. London: Routledge.

Smalley, D. 1997. Spectromorphology: Explaining Sound Shapes. *Organised Sound* 2(2): 107–126.

Stockhausen, K. 1974. Mikrophonie I. (Score, composed in 1964) Vienna: Universal Edition.

Truax, B. 1999. *Handbook for Acoustic Ecology* CD-ROM Edition. Burnaby, BC: Cambridge Street Publishing, CSR-CDR 9901.

Truax, B. 2000. The Aesthetics of Computer Music: A Questionable Concept Reconsidered. *Organised Sound* 5(3): 119–126.

Weale, R. 2006. Discovering How Accessible Electroacoustic Music Can Be: The Intention/Reception Project. *Organised Sound* 11(2): 189–200.

Cited Websites

Audiomulch
    www.audiomulch.com (accessed 10th April 2010)
Creative Commons
    creativecommons.org (accessed 10th April 2010)
Csound
    soundforge.net/projects/csound (accessed 10th April 2010)
Dictionnaire des arts médiatiques
    www.dictionnairegram.org (accessed 10th April 2010)
DSP for Children (in English)
    archive.notam02.no/DSP02/en (accessed 10th April 2010)
Granular Synthesis
    www.granularsynthesis.com (accessed 10th April 2010)
Metasynth
    www.uisoftware.com/MetaSynth/index.php (accessed 10th April 2010)
Reason
    www.propellerheads.se/products/reason (accessed 10th April 2010)
Sound Organiser (creative software that is used on EARS II)
    www.soundorganiser.dmu.ac.uk (in development at the time of writing)
The ElectroAcoustic Resource Site (EARS)
    www.ears.dmu.ac.uk (accessed 10th April 2010)
The ElectroAcoustic Resource Site Pedagogical Project (EARS II)
    www.ears2.dmu.ac.uk (in development at the time of writing)
The Freesound Project
    www.freesound.org (accessed 10th April 2010)

Related to Chapter 6: Further Recommended Texts Slightly Annotated for this Book's Target Audience

Brown, A. 2007. *Computers in Music Education: Amplifying Musicality*. New York: Routledge.
The title says it all—this book is not solely about sound-based music, but about any use of IT in the music classroom. The book is not intended to be used as a textbook, but instead covers a very wide range of potential IT applications in music with up-to-date references related to software, literature and online resources.

Cain, T. 2004. Theory, Technology and the Music Curriculum. *British Journal of Music Education* 21(2): 215–221.
A position paper concerning the potential use of technology in music education at all levels. This is the education-based side of the debate supporting the ideals of this book.

Dennis, B. 1970. *Experimental Music in Schools: Towards A New World of Sound*. Oxford: Oxford University Press.
Although a significant number of the approaches to experimental music that are presented here, as was the case in my own 1994 book, are note-based, Dennis's ideals are not far from those presented here. They key difference is the fact that technology has moved on so far in the interim, making experimentation, particularly in schools, so much more accessible. This book contains several imaginative activities. His *Projects in Sound*. London: Universal Edition, 1975 is also quite useful but is focused on presented compositions.

Dwyer. T. 1971. *Composing with Tape Recorders: Musique Concrète for Beginners* and 1975. *Making Electronic Music*. Oxford: Oxford University Press.
These books demonstrate how complicated it was to execute activities like ours three decades ago.

Gibbs, T. 2007. *Sonic Art & Sound Design*. Lausanne: AVA.
This book does not fit neatly as an educational resource or as a book for university use. What it offers is a user-friendly overview of the subject, including interdisciplinary areas involving the fine arts, with brief sections on historical aspects, artist portraits, means of construction and means of realisation and it spans a very broad spectrum of work.

Hugill, A. 2008. *The Digital Musician*. New York: Routledge.
As we have learned, sound-based music need not be plugged in. Similarly, digital music need not be sound-based. This wonderful book is a soulmate of the present volume (and its author is a colleague of mine, working at the same university). It is not intended for any particular age group, as some content is as relevant to beginners as it is to those who have already gained experience in the field. Like this book, it deals with listening, understanding and working with sound, sound organisation, creating and performing digitally. Unlike this book, it also covers socio-cultural aspects and includes some individual portraits. Its final section consists of "projects and performance repertoire" analogous with this book's exercises, most of which demand a somewhat higher level of experience than is the case here and are more focused, similar to Vella and Arthurs' book. In a sense, *The Digital Musician* is a nice follow-up or companion volume to this one.

Orton, R., ed. 1981. *Electronic Music for Schools.* Cambridge: Cambridge University Press. Like the Dwyer volumes, Orton's excellent collection demonstrates that in the 1980s it was still very difficult, complicated, not to mention fairly expensive, to participate in most types of creative activities presented here. This book attempts to demonstrate how far one could go at the time with a restricted budget.

Paynter, J. and Aston, P. 1970. *Sounds and Silence: Classroom Projects in Creative Music.* Cambridge: Cambridge University Press.
In contrast to the Dwyer and Orton volumes, most projects in this book do not necessarily involve equipment. These authors, along with the others in this list, are amongst the true pioneers of experimental music making in schools.

Schafer, R. M. 1986. *The Thinking Ear.* Toronto: Arcana.
This volume contains the author's complete writings on education. As founder of the soundscape movement, the pedagogical ideology behind acoustic ecology and many radical approaches to music including sound-based music can be discovered in this collection.

Self, G. 1976. *Make a New Sound.* London: Universal Edition.
A companion volume to the Paynter and Aston book with a variety of activities in the realm of experimental music, mainly note-based.

Storms, G. 2001. *101 More Music Games for Children.* Alameda, CA: Hunter House.
This is one of many titles from Ger Storms, who is one of few writers targeting children of (early) primary school age through a wide range of focused activities.

Vella, R. with Arthurs, A. 2003. *Sounds in Space Sounds in Time: Projects in Listening, Improvising and Composing.* London: Boosey & Hawkes.
This book, although covering a wider field than sound-based music, comes closest in terms of its open-mindedness about sounds, space and, to a lesser extent, technology. The great difference between the two is that Vella chooses a very tightly structured approach with very clear exercises for teachers based on the more traditional prescriptive model. This approach conforms to most other such books and I highly recommend it, regardless of our differences of pedagogical vision.

Related to Chapter 6: Further Recommended Texts Slightly Annotated that have Mainly been Written for University-Level Readers

Chadabe, J. 1997. *Electric Sound: The Past and Promise of Electronic Music.* Saddle River, NJ: Prentice Hall.
This book is an historical overview of this body of music including many valuable mini-portraits of practising musicians including interviews with supporting images of electronic instruments.

Chion, M. 1995. *Guide des Objets Sonores: Pierre Schaeffer et la recherche musicale,* 2nd edition. Paris: Buchet/Chastel–Ina. This book treats Schaeffer's terminology extensively. An English translation by John Dack and Christine North can be found at: http://www.ears.dmu.ac.uk/spip.php?page=articleEars&id_article=3597 (accessed 10th April 2010).

Collins, N. and J. d'Escriván, eds. 2007. *The Cambridge Companion to Electronic Music*. Cambridge: Cambridge University Press.
This volume is an overview regarding the state of play in the field.

Cox, C. and D. Warner, eds. 2004. *Audio Culture: Readings in Modern Music*. New York: Continuum.
A wide-ranging overview presented by way of primary sources across most of the previous century including several relevant to this book.

Dean, R. T. 2009. *The Oxford Handbook of Computer Music*. Oxford: Oxford University Press. This volume is an overview regarding the state of play in the field.

Emmerson, S., ed. 1986. *The Language of Electroacoustic Music*. Basingstoke: Macmillan.
This is the first book compiled, at least in English, which specifically investigates a spectrum of theoretical approaches regarding the understanding of this body of music. The authors are amongst the best-known theorists of that time.

Hegarty, P. 2007. *Noise/Music: A History*. New York: Continuum.
This volume is perhaps the most significant publication in the area of noise music and a variety of paths that led to noise music thus far.

Holmes. T. 2008. *Electronic and Experimental Music: Technology, Music, and Culture*. New York: Routledge.
This is a broad-ranging historical volume related to this book's contents.

Manning, P. 2004. *Electronic and Computer Music*, 3rd edition. Oxford: Oxford University Press.
This is a rare history book in the field as it has been twice updated (this is its third version) over the period of nineteen years.

Motte-Haber, H. de la, ed. *Klangkunst: Tönende Objekte und klingende Räume. Bd. 12, Handbuch der Musik im 20. Jahrhundert*. Laaber: Laaber Verlag.
This German-language volume provides an excellent overview of the spectrum of sound-based music related to sound art with entries by both practitioners and theorists.

Prendergast, M. 2000. *The Ambient Century: From Mahler to Trance—The Evolution of Sound in the Electronic Age*. London: Bloomsbury.
This is a very wide-ranging overview of various forms of experimentation with music with a particular interest in ambient approaches. The spectrum is more eclectic than most other authors.

Shapiro, P., ed. 2000. *Modulations: Electronic Music—Throbbing Words on Sound*. New York: Caipirinha.
An historical overview with a clear focus on electronic popular music, both mainstream and experimental, but also making connections with pioneers outside of popular music.

Supper, M. 1997. *Elektroakustische Musik & Computermusik: Geschichte Ästhetik Methoden Systeme*. Hofheim: Wolke.
This brief book offers an excellent historical and, to an extent, theoretical overview of this subject in German. A Spanish version has been published by Alianza Editorial.

Toop, D. 1997. *Ocean of Sound: Aether Talk, Ambient Sound and Imaginary Worlds*. London: Serpent's Tail.
Similar to Prendergast, this is a very eclectic volume discussing a wide variety of experimental approaches to music including sound-based music. Toop writes personally and is able to make many valuable connections.

Truax, B. 2001. *Acoustic Communication*, 2nd edition. Westport, CT: Ablex Press.
This volume introduces the theory behind acoustic ecology that is at the foundation of soundscape composition. It offers complementary information to his *Handbook* in the main bibliographic listing.

Ungeheuer, E., ed. 2002. *Elektroakustische Musik. Bd. 5, Handbuch der Musik im 20. Jahrhundert*. Laaber: Laaber Verlag.
A more recent and much less compact history of this music, in German, than Supper.

Wishart, T. 1996. *On Sonic Art*, 2nd edition. Chur: Harwood Academic.
This forms one of two valuable books combining theory and novel approaches to practice by Trevor Wishart.

Wishart, T. 1994. *Audible Design: A Plain and Easy Introduction to Practical Sound Composition*. York: Orpheus the Pantomime.
This is chronologically the second of the two Wishart volumes specifically focusing on the practical application of theoretical concepts related to sound-based music.

Related to Chapter 6: Recommended Websites

Futurelab
www.nestafuturelab.org.uk (accessed 10th April 2010)

In particular I can recommend Teresa Dillon's paper:
http://www.futurelab.org.uk/resources/documents/project_reports/innovations/Future_Music_Insight_Paper.pdf (accessed 10th April 2010) which is focused on "investigating the role of technology in enhancing public appreciation of and participation in music" (subtitle). This paper focuses largely on the use of new and recent technologies in music for usage in digital music making including sound-based music. The two key foci are new networks and interfaces and new musical practices for the twenty-first century. This was part of a series of Innovation Workshops in the mid-2000s.

INDEX